GOTTFRIED BÖHM

GOTTFRIED BÖHM

BAUTEN UND PROJEKTE
BUILDINGS AND PROJECTS

AUSZUG AUS DEN JAHREN 1985 – 2000
A SELECTION OF WORKS 1985 – 2000

AUSWAHL UND GESTALTUNG: ELISABETH BÖHM
MIT UNTERSTÜTZUNG VON JOHANNES JAEGER
SELECTION AND LAYOUT: ELISABETH BÖHM
ASSISTED BY JOHANNES JAEGER

© 2001 ERNST WASMUTH VERLAG TÜBINGEN · BERLIN
HERSTELLUNG / PRODUCTION: ROSA WAGNER
HERSTELLUNGSASSISTENZ UND LEKTORAT
PRODUCTION ASSISTANCE AND CORRECTIONS: SABINE M. VOGLER
ÜBERSETZUNG INS ENGLISCHE / TRANSLATION INTO ENGLISH: INGRID TAYLOR,
ENGLISH EXPERTS, MÜNCHEN
REPRODUKTIONEN / ARTWORK: MEDIEN ZENTRUM AICHELBERG
DRUCK UND BINDUNG / PRINTED UND BOUND BY GULDE-DRUCK, TÜBINGEN
PRINTED IN GERMANY

ISBN 3 8030 0610 4

INHALTSVERZEICHNIS / CONTENTS

EINFÜHRUNG / INTRODUCTION   7

TOKIO, OTA HALL / TOKYO, OTA HALL   8

BERLIN, REICHSTAG   16

BERLIN, HOLOCAUST MAHNMAL / BERLIN, HOLOCAUST MEMORIAL   24

LOS ANGELES, PHILHARMONIE / LOS ANGELES, CONCERT HALL   26

LUXEMBURG, PHILHARMONIE / LUXEMBOURG, CONCERT HALL   30

KÖLN, WDR HAUPTVERWALTUNG /
COLOGNE, ADMINISTRATIVE HEADQUARTERS OF WDR   38

HAMBURG, ARENA   50

SAARBRÜCKEN, SCHLOSS / SAARBRÜCKEN, CASTLE   56

STUTTGART, ZÜBLINHAUS   64

HAMBURG, MUSEUM FÜR MODERNE KUNST / HAMBURG, MUSEUM OF MODERN ART   72

STUTTGART, MUSEUM FÜR MODERNE KUNST / STUTTGART, MUSEUM OF MODERN ART   76

SEVILLA, DEUTSCHER PAVILLON FÜR DIE EXPO 1992 / SEVILLE, GERMAN PAVILION FOR EXPO 1992   80

BERLIN-TREPTOW, HOTEL AN DER SPREE / BERLIN-TREPTOW, HOTEL BY THE SPREE   82

LUXEMBURG, DEUTSCHE BANK / LUXEMBOURG, DEUTSCHE BANK   84

LUXEMBURG-ESCH, ARBED S. A. HAUPTVERWALTUNG
LUXEMBOURG-ESCH, ADMINISTRATIVE HEADQUARTERS OF ARBED S. A.   90

MANNHEIM, UNIVERSITÄTSBIBLIOTHEK UND AUDITORIUM /
MANNHEIM, UNIVERSITY LIBRARY AND AUDITORIUM   94

ULM, STADTBIBLIOTHEK / ULM, CITY LIBRARY   100

BERLIN, KAUFHAUS PEEK & CLOPPENBURG / BERLIN, PEEK & CLOPPENBURG DEPARTMENT STORE   104

ITZEHOE, STADTTHEATER / ITZEHOE, MUNICIPAL THEATRE   110

AACHEN, NEUGESTALTUNG DES BAHNHOFSPLATZES /
AACHEN, REDEVELOPMENT OF THE STATION SQUARE   116

BERNKASTEL-KUES, KAPELLE / BERNKASTEL-KUES, CHAPEL   117

ROM, UMGESTALTUNG DES DENKMALS FÜR KÖNIG VIKTOR EMANUEL II. /
ROME, REDEVELOPMENT OF THE MONUMENT TO KING VICTOR EMMANUEL II   124

POTSDAM, HANS-OTTO-THEATER   126

ELISABETH BÖHM BRINGT MIT DER GESTALTUNG DES LAYOUTS DIE ARCHITEKTUREN ZUR SPRACHE. SCHRIFTLICHE ANGABEN SIND DAHER AUF DAS WESENTLICHE BESCHRÄNKT.

THE LAYOUT OF THE BOOK, DESIGNED BY ELISABETH BÖHM, ALLOWS THE BUILDINGS TO SPEAK FOR THEMSELVES. WRITTEN COMMENT IS THEREFORE RESTRICTED TO A MINIMUM.

DR. SVETLOZAR RAÈV, KUNSTHISTORIKER UND DERZEIT BULGARISCHER BOTSCHAFTER AM VATIKAN, KOMMT MIT SEINER KNAPPEN UND PRÄGNANT FORMULIERTEN EINFÜHRUNG IN DAS WERK GOTTFRIED BÖHMS DEM PRINZIP DES BUCHES NAHE.

DR SVETLOZAR RAÈV, AN ART HISTORIAN AND CURRENTLY BULGARIAN AMBASSADOR TO THE VATICAN, HAS WRITTEN A SUCCINCT INTRODUCTION WHICH IS ITSELF A BEAUTIFUL DEMONSTRATION OF THE ETHOS BEHIND THE BOOK.

EINFÜHRUNG

Gottfried Böhm überrascht auf's Neue mit der Vielfältigkeit seiner Architekturen während der vergangenen zwei Dekaden. Auch diese zeigen keine Anlehnung an modische Stilrichtungen, es sind Kinder seines Geistes und Wesens. Bei aller Unterschiedlichkeit der Bauaufgaben spürt man sein Hauptanliegen: die Menschen, ihr Wohnen, Arbeiten, Feiern, das Leben in der Gemeinschaft. Daher versteht sich seine Sorgfalt für bauliche Strukturen und städtebauliche Zusammenhänge.
Ungewöhnliche Architekturformen findet man bei Gottfried Böhm nur als Ausdruck eines besonderen Inhalts und nur auf der Grundlage baulicher Prinzipien.
Geschichtliche Bezüge von Altbauten werden von ihm erhalten und neue Elemente unserer Zeit hinzugefügt. Beispiele dafür sind die Entwürfe für das Reichstagsgebäude und der Vorschlag für das Denkmal Viktor Emanuels in Rom.
Im Werk Gottfried Böhms läßt sich eine grundsätzliche Einstellung zum Beruf des Architekten erkennen: „Gestalterische Freiheit unter Wahrung der daraus resultierenden Verantwortlichkeiten", ein Grundsatz, der auch den Forderungen unserer heutigen demokratischen Welt entspricht.
Daß seine vielfältigen architektonischen Ausdrucksformen immer auch seine ganz eigene Handschrift erkennen lassen, war auch mit der Grund dafür, daß er 1986 als bisher einziger deutscher Architekt mit dem Pritzker Preis – dem 'Nobelpreis für Architektur' – ausgezeichnet wurde.

Svetlozar Raèv

INTRODUCTION

In the past twenty years, Gottfried Böhm has delighted us with an amazing variety of architecture. Never bound by fashion trends, all are a unique product of his intellect and spirit. Yet, for all the tremendous breadth in his work, the core themes are clearly legible: building places in which people can work, live, rejoice and live as a community. It is this which drives him to take so much care in designing architecture and urban contexts.
In Gottfried Böhm's work, unusual architectural forms only arise as a result of a specific content, and are solidly grounded in architectural principles. He preserves the historical references in old buildings, combining them with new elements from our time. Good examples of this are the designs for the Reichstag in Berlin and the proposal for the memorial to Victor Emmanuel in Rome.
Evidenced in Böhm's work are also his views on the job of an architect: "Exercising design freedom, but always in the full awareness of the responsibilities" – a principle that harmonises well with the requirements of our democratic world of today.
Shining through all Böhm's diverse architectural forms of expression is his very own unique trademark – one of the reasons for which he is the only German architect so far to have been honoured with the Pritzker Prize, the 'Nobel Prize of architecture', in 1986.

Svetlozar Raèv

TOKIO, OTA HALL
TOKYO, OTA HALL

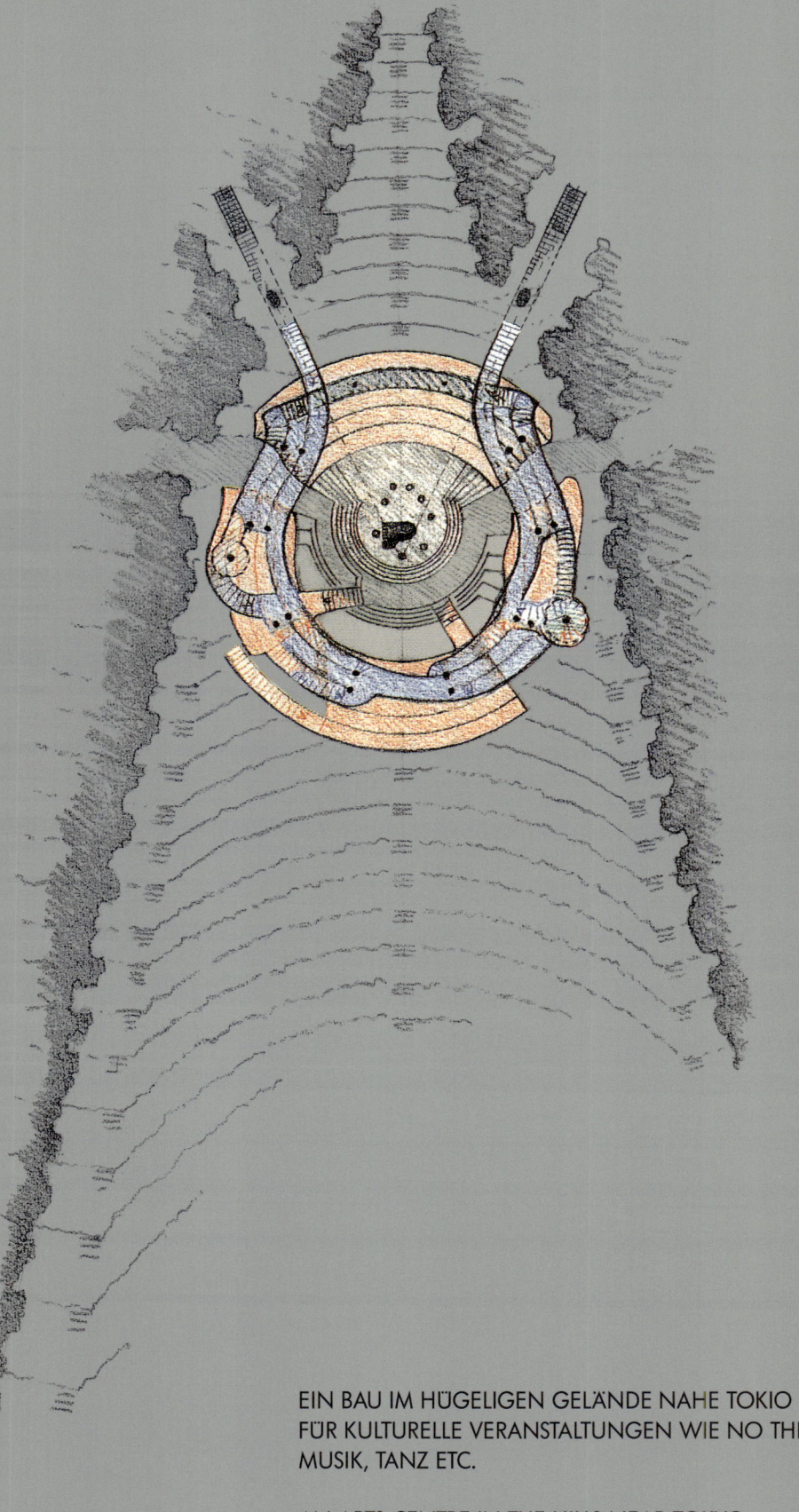

PROJEKT / PROJECT, 1991

EIN BAU IM HÜGELIGEN GELÄNDE NAHE TOKIO
FÜR KULTURELLE VERANSTALTUNGEN WIE NO THEATER,
MUSIK, TANZ ETC.

AN ARTS CENTRE IN THE HILLS NEAR TOKYO
FOR CULTURAL EVENTS SUCH AS NO THEATRE,
MUSIC, DANCE ETC.

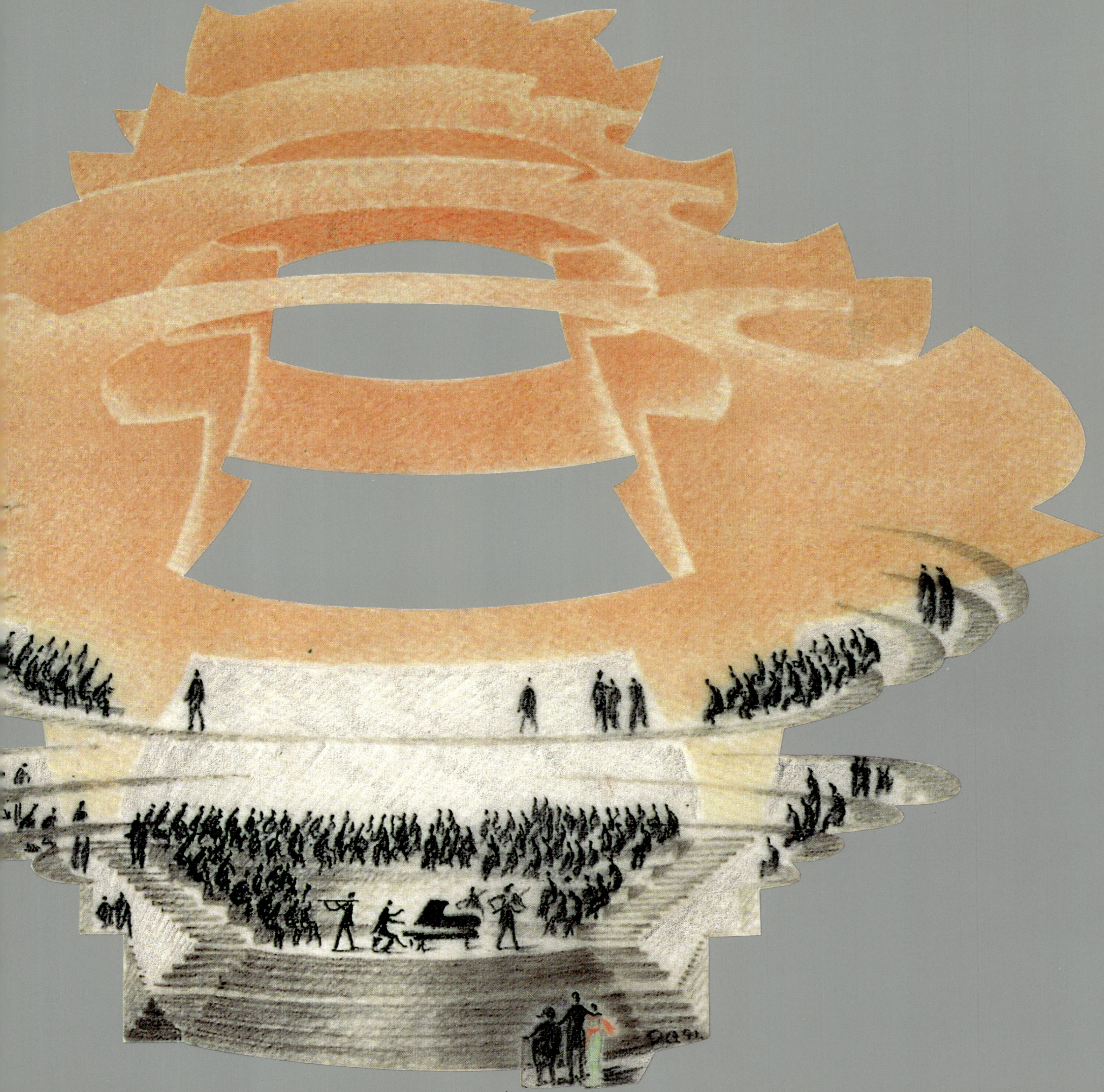

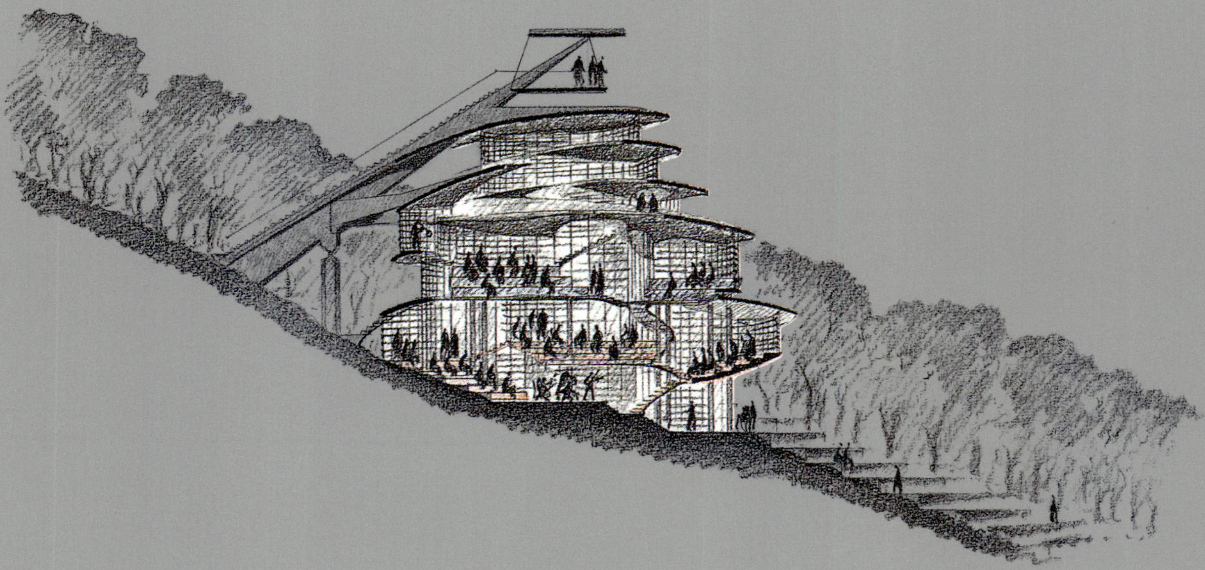

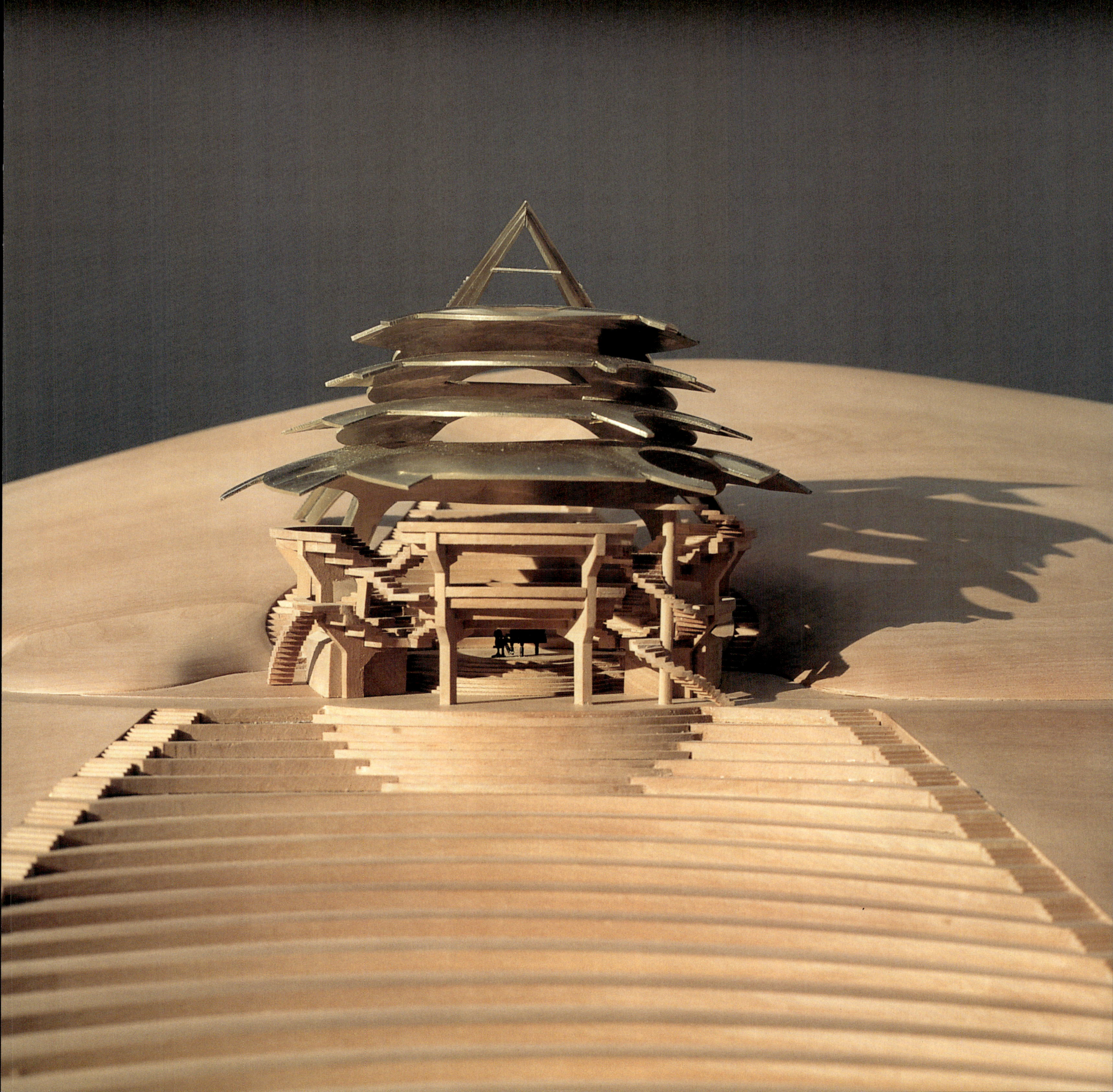

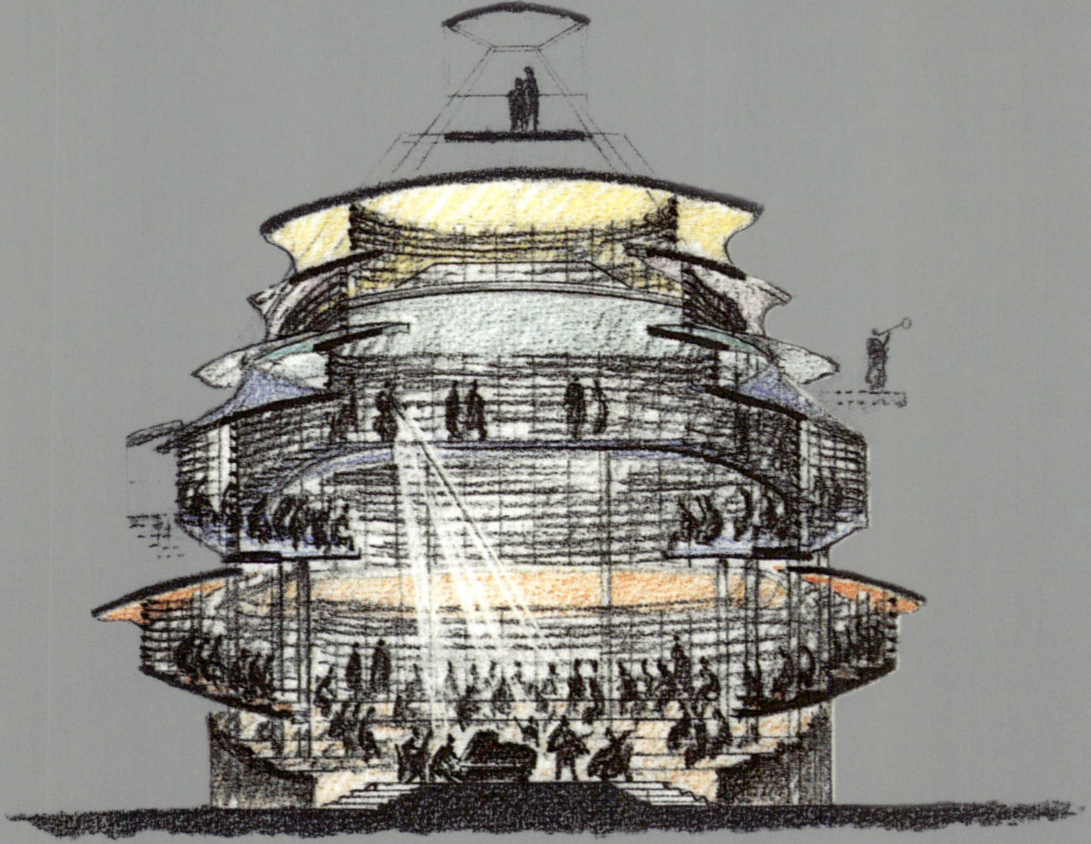

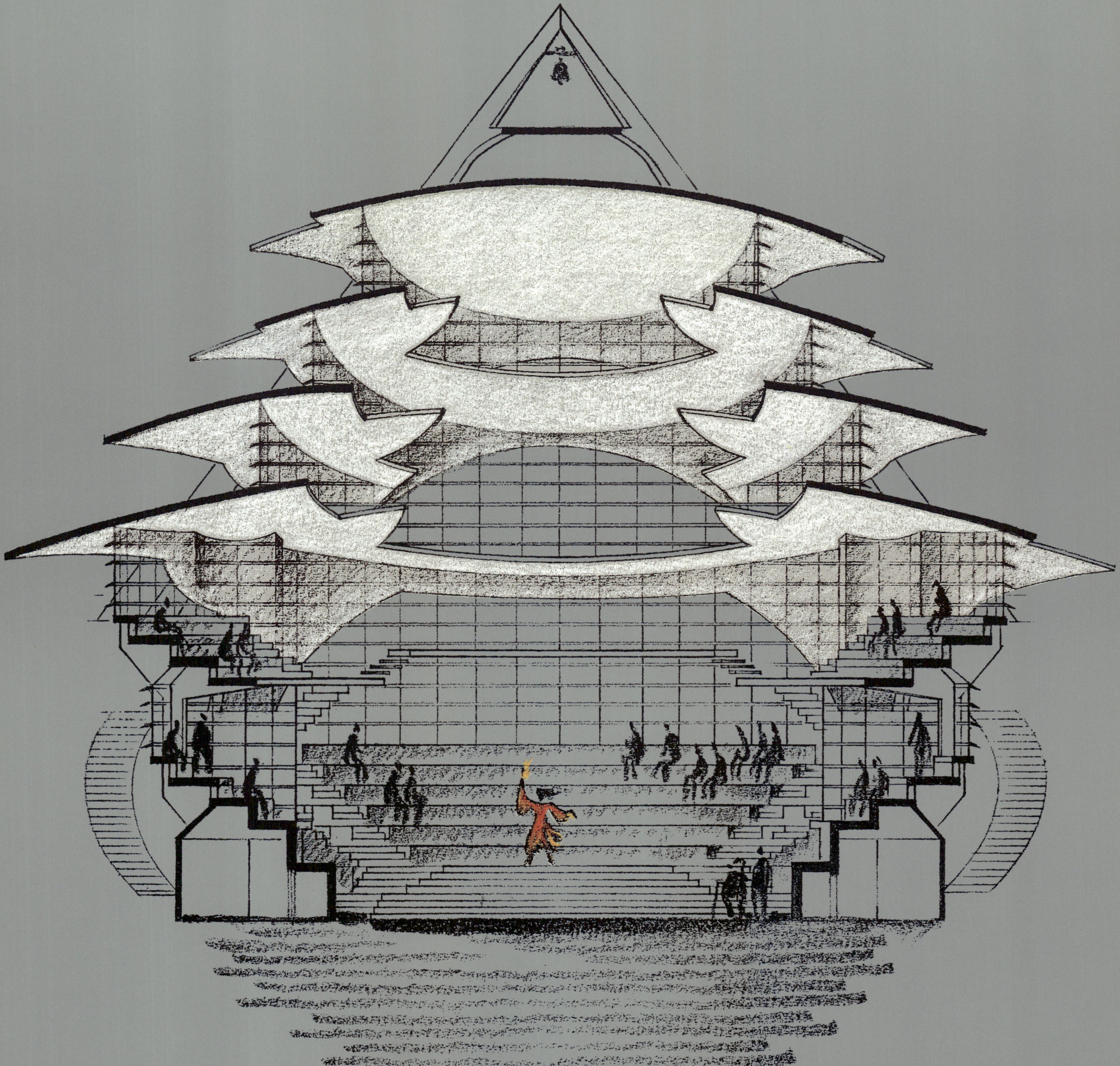

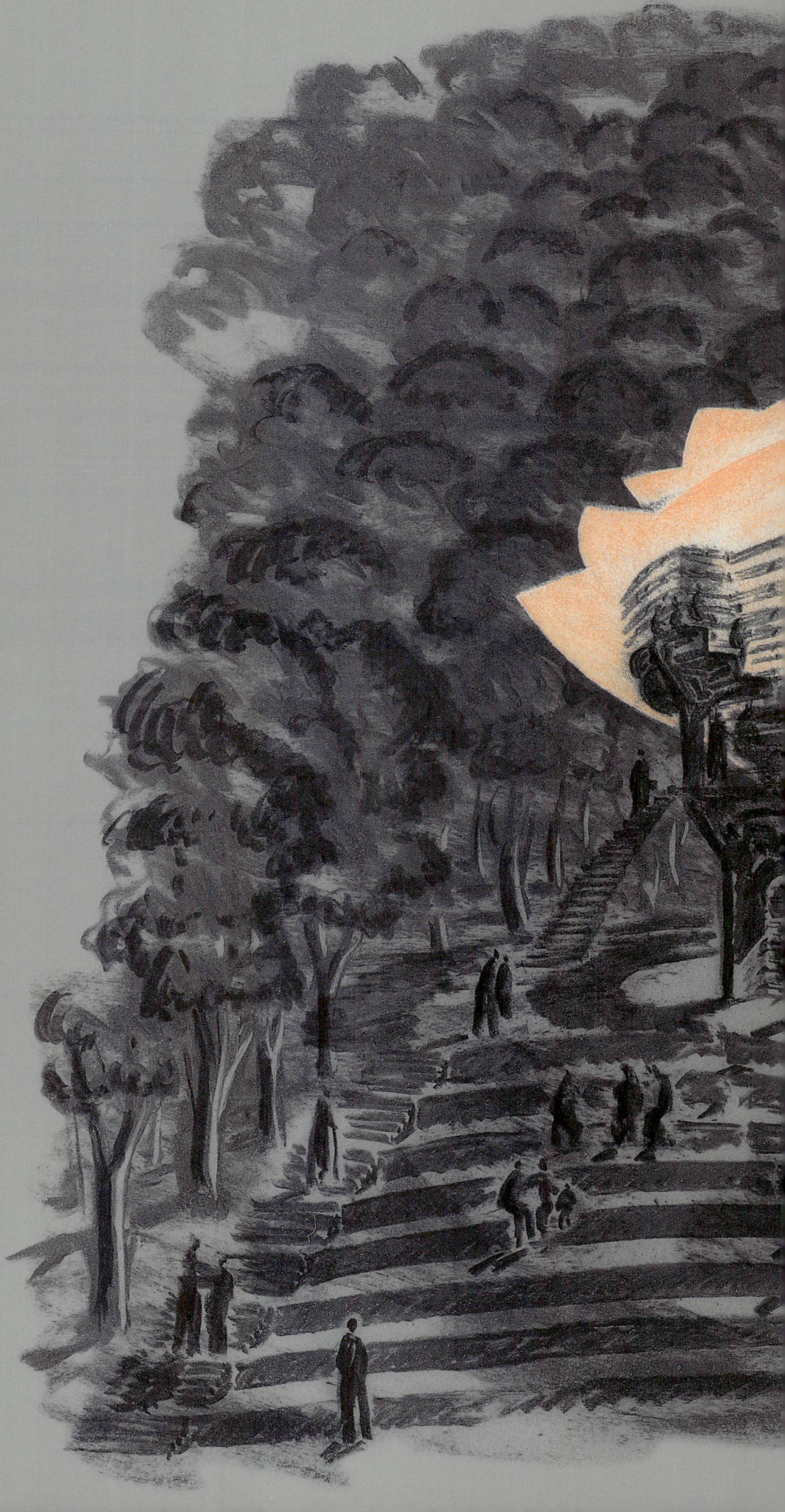

15

BERLIN, REICHSTAG
MIT / WITH PETER BÖHM, FRIEDER STEINIGEWEG
WETTBEWERB / COMPETITION, 1989 – 1993

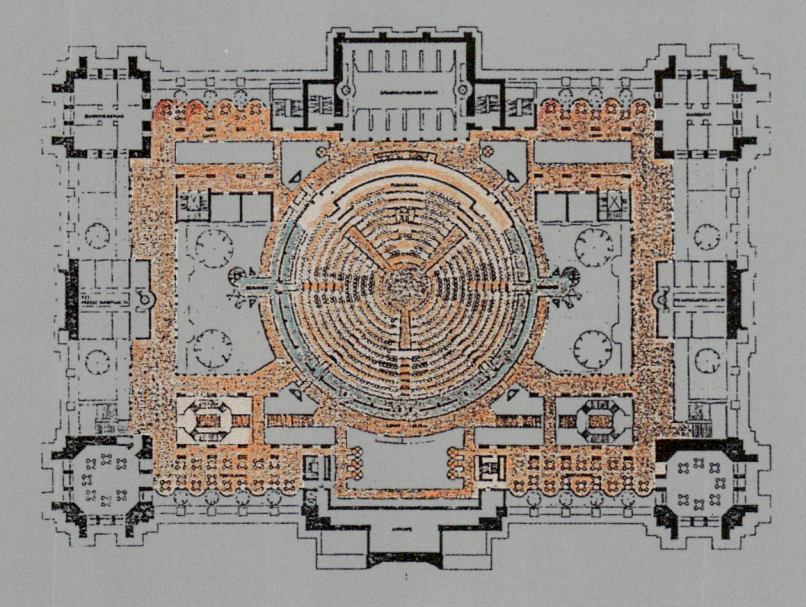

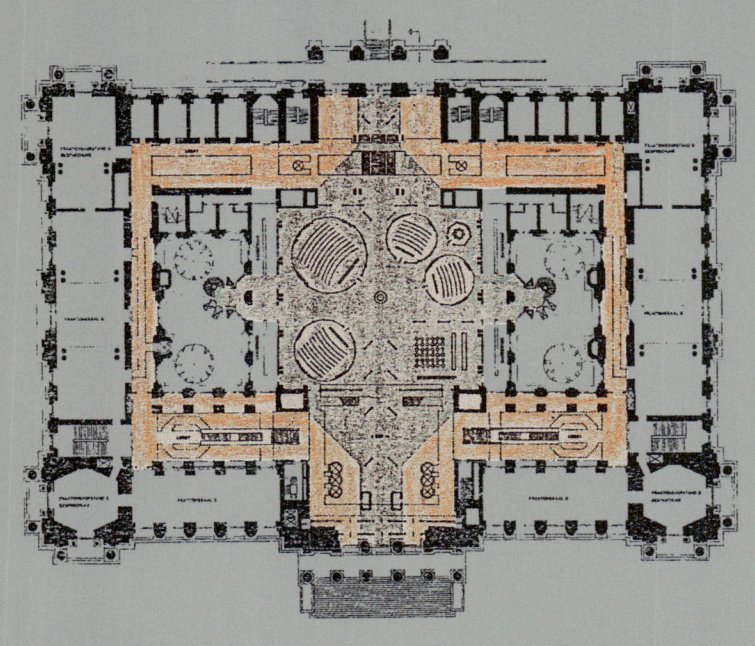

ERHALTUNG DES WERTVOLLEN ALTBAUBESTANDES
AUCH IM INNEREN DES BAUS.
DER BAUGESCHICHTLICH SEHR BEDEUTSAME
BAUMGARTENSAAL AUS DEN SECHZIGER JAHREN
WIRD ZU EINEM BÜRGERFORUM. DER KUPPELBAU
IST NEBEN SEINER REPRÄSENTATIVEN BEDEUTUNG
AUCH RAUMBILDEND FÜR DEN PLENARSAAL.

RETENTION OF VALUABLE HISTORIC STRUCTURES
BOTH INSIDE AND OUTSIDE THE BUILDING.
THE 'BAUMGARTENSAAL', AN ARCHITECTURALLY
IMPORTANT HALL DATING FROM THE 1960S, IS USED
AS A CITIZEN'S FORUM. THE DOME BOTH SERVES AS
A DISTINCTIVE URBAN MARKER AND ENHANCES
THE SPATIAL DESIGN OF THE PLENARY HALL.

17

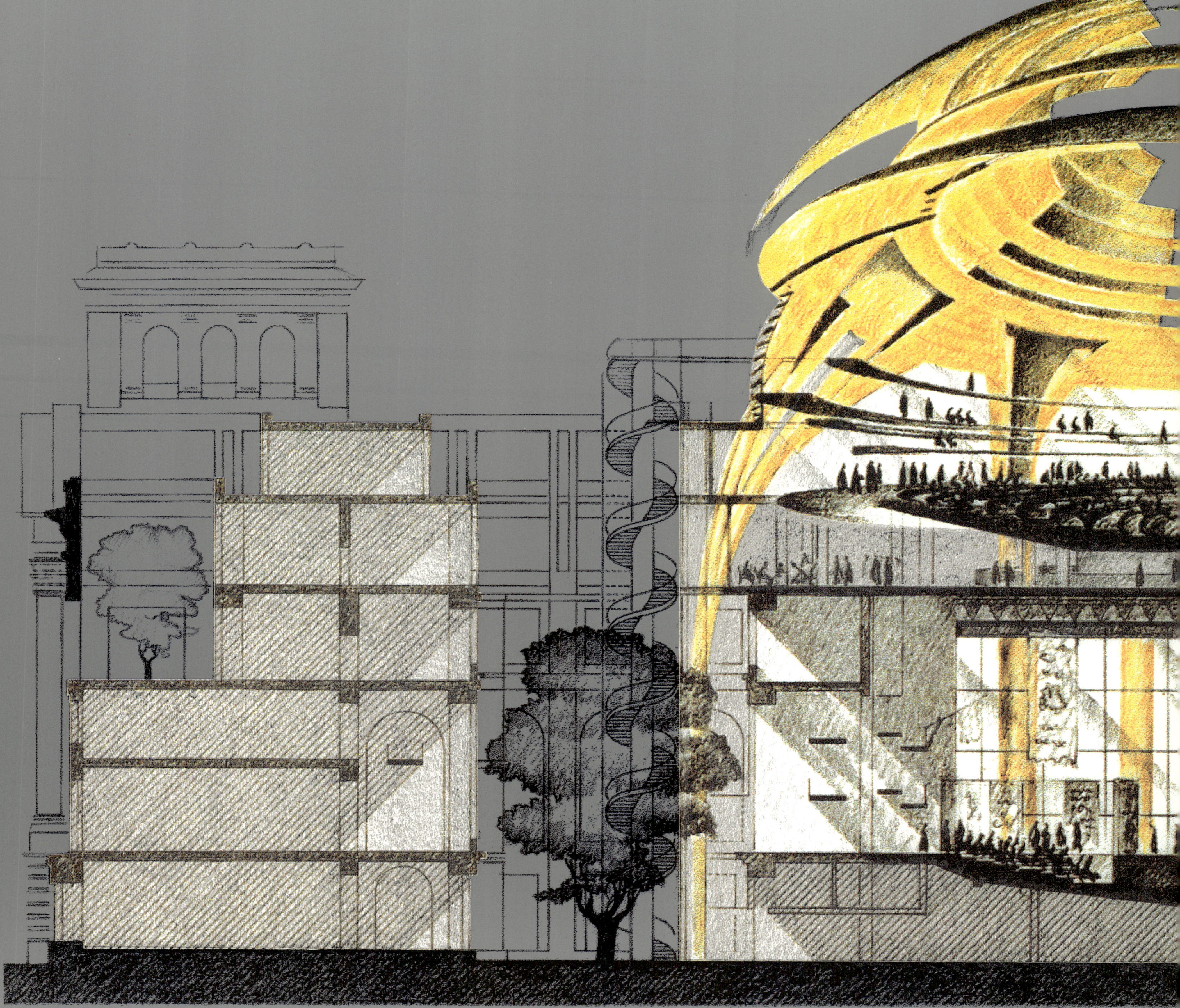

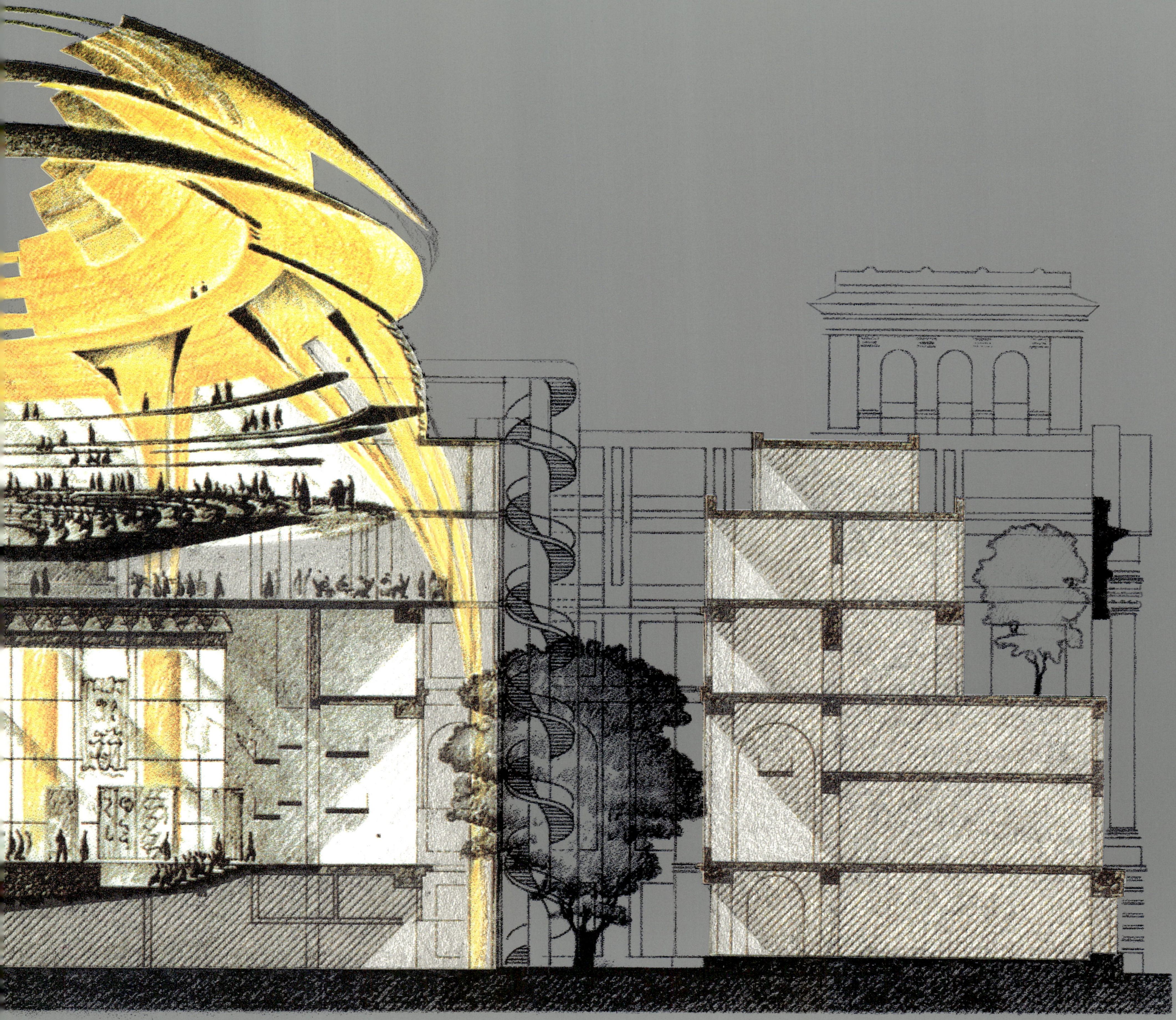

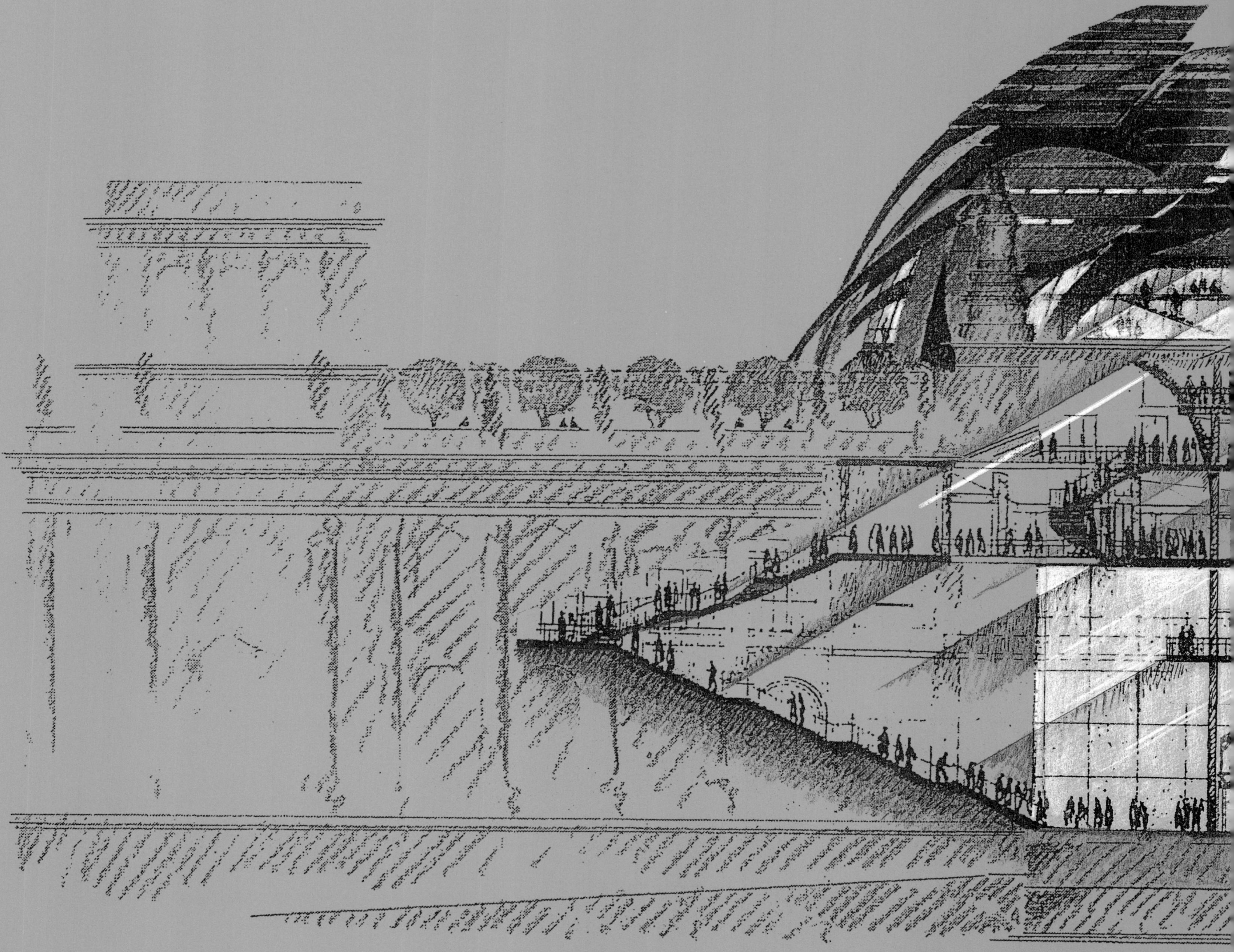

21

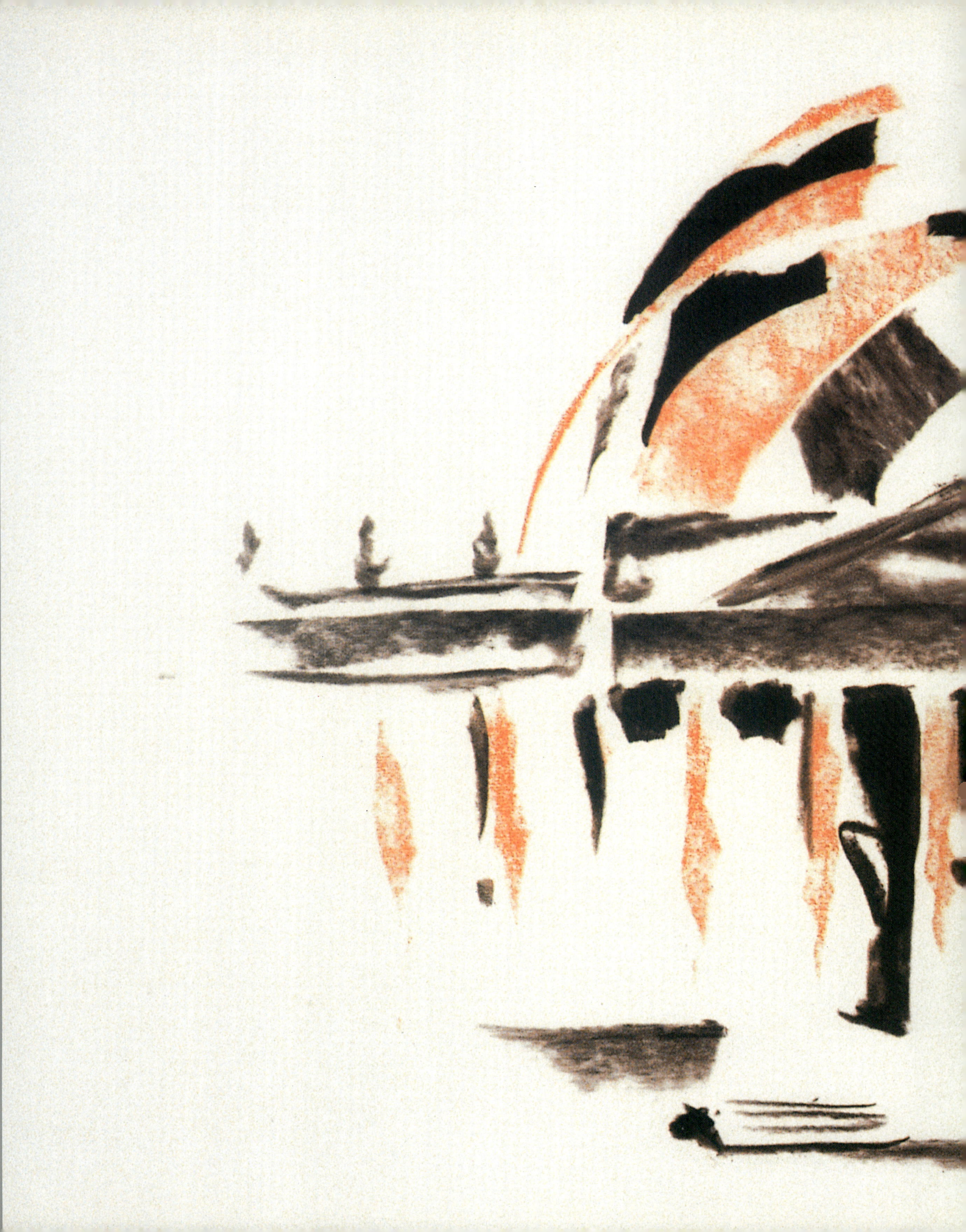

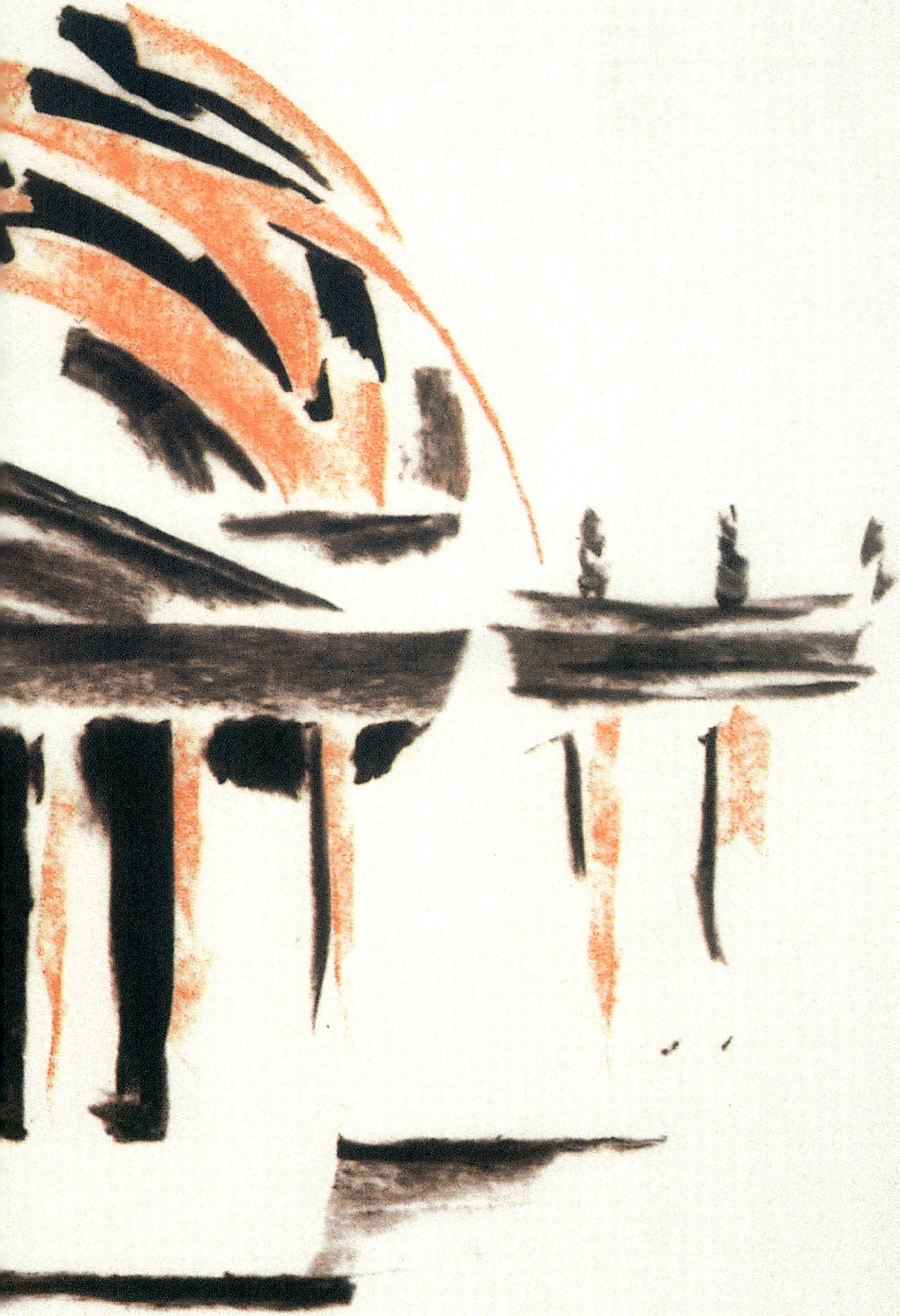

DAS HOLOCAUST-MAHNMAL BERLIN

NACH MEINER VORSTELLUNG SOLLTE DAS GELÄNDE IN GÄNZE MIT HOHEN HECKENROSEN BEPFLANZT WERDEN, EIN RIESIGES DORNIGES GESTRÜPP, GERADEZU BEDROHLICH. IN DIESEM STACHLIGEN CHAOS SIND SCHNEISEN GESCHNITTEN, DIE BERGAB TIEF UNTER DIE ERDE IN EINEN RAUM FÜHREN, DER NUR VON GANZ OBEN DURCH DAS STACHLIGE DICKICHT LICHT ERHÄLT. EIN RAUM, DER ZUR STILLE ZWINGT, ZUM NACHDENKEN UND, WEM ES GEGEBEN IST, ZUM BETEN VERANLASST. AUF DEN WÄNDEN SIND DIE NAMEN ALL DERER EINGRAPHIERT, DIE UNTER DEM N.S. JOCH ELEND UND TOD ERLITTEN HABEN

DER RAUM IST ERNST ABER NICHT BEDRÜCKEND. DIE HOFFNUNG – EIN SO WICHTIGES PRINZIP BESONDERS AUCH DER JUDEN – IST DURCH DAS DORNIGE GESTRÜPP HIER DENNOCH ERLEBBAR. ALLJÄHRLICH WIRD DIESES CHAOTISCHE DICKICHT VON UNZÄHLIGEN BLÜTEN UND FRÜCHTEN ÜBERSÄT, DIE WIE EINE ENDLOSE MENGE VON BLUTTROPFEN DIESES STACHLIGE ELEND ZU ÜBERWINDEN SCHEINEN, – FREILICH UNBEGREIFLICH – ABER DEM GEIST JÜDISCHER TRADITION ENTSPRECHEND, WO DAS „LEBENDIGE HOFFEN" IN DEN SCHWEREN ZEITEN „DAS KALTE UMSONST" IMMER WIEDER ÜBERWAND.

LOS ANGELES, PHILHARMONIE
LOS ANGELES, CONCERT HALL

MIT / WITH STEPHAN BÖHM, MARCO KARI

WETTBEWERB / COMPETITION, 1988

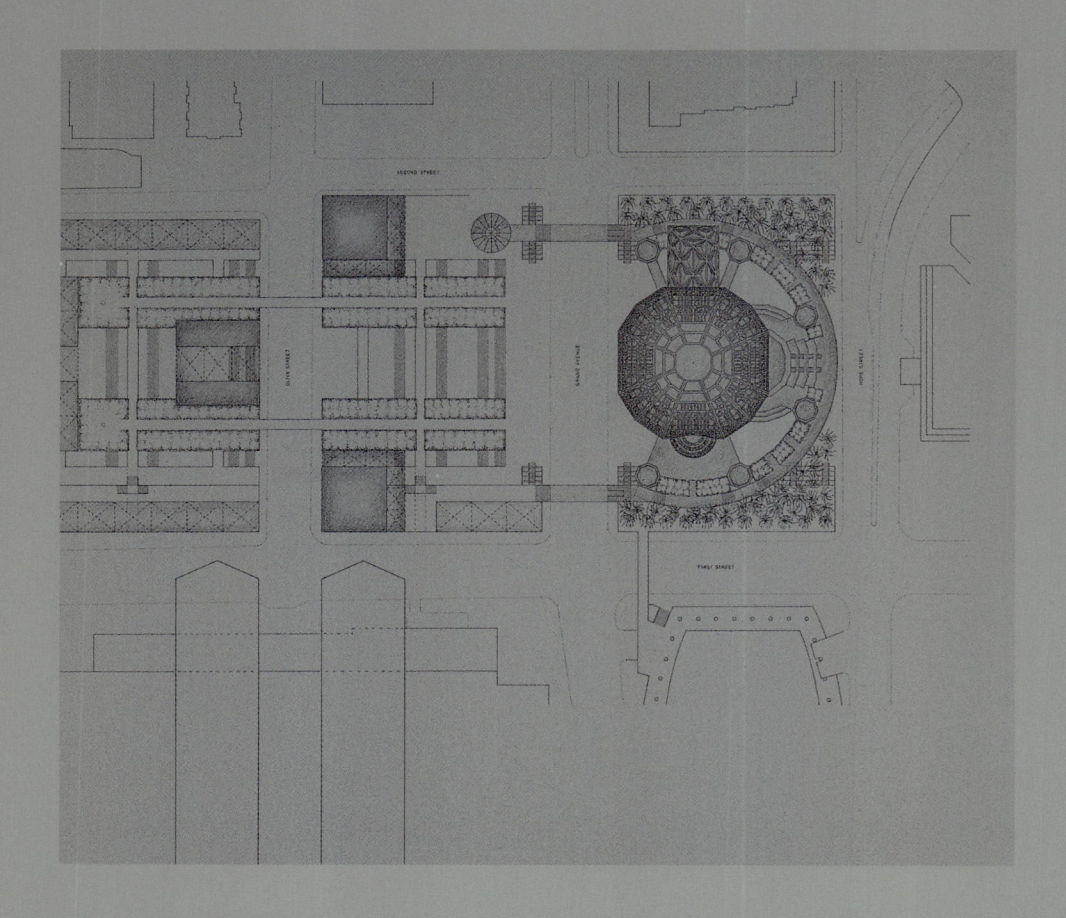

EIN KUPPELRAUM VERBINDET VERSCHIEDENE SÄLE UND BIETET MIT DIESEN ZUSAMMEN AUCH RAUM FÜR GROSSVERANSTALTUNGEN.

A DOMED SPACE LINKS THE VARIOUS HALLS, GIVING THE OPTION OF USING THEM AS A SINGLE SPACE FOR LARGER-SCALE EVENTS.

27

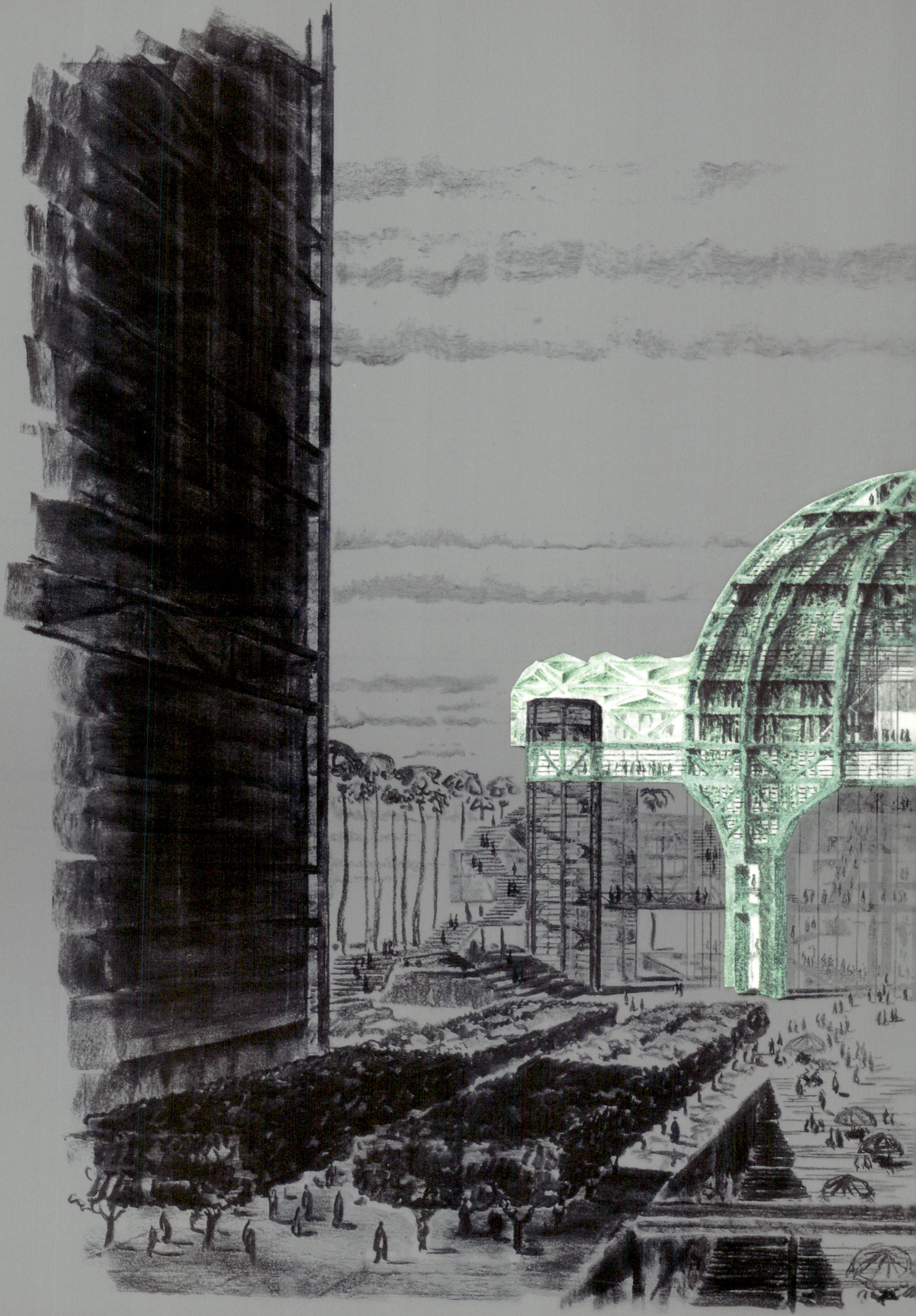

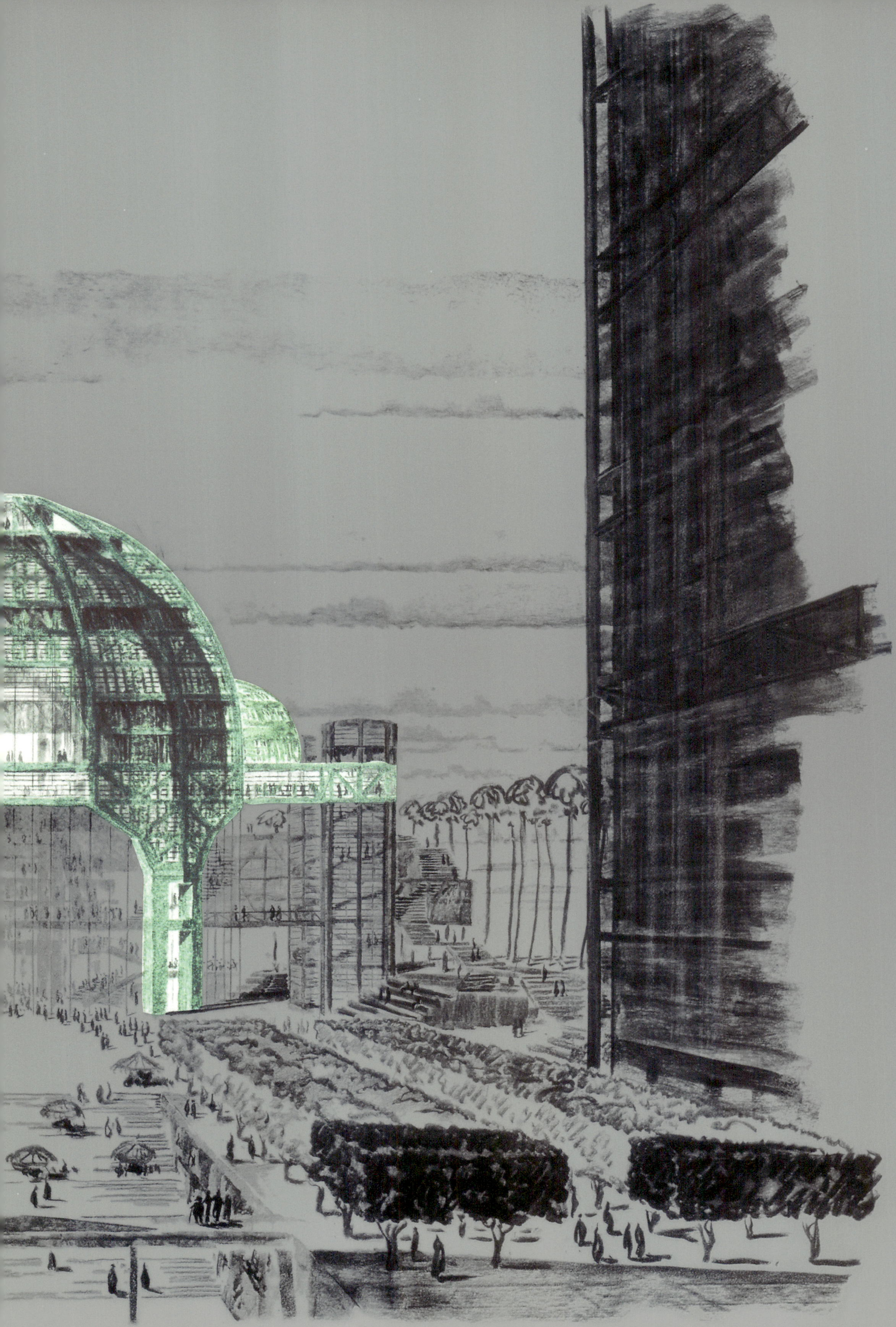

LUXEMBURG, PHILHARMONIE
LUXEMBOURG, CONCERT HALL

MIT / WITH MARIA MOCANU

WETTBEWERB / COMPETITION, 1996

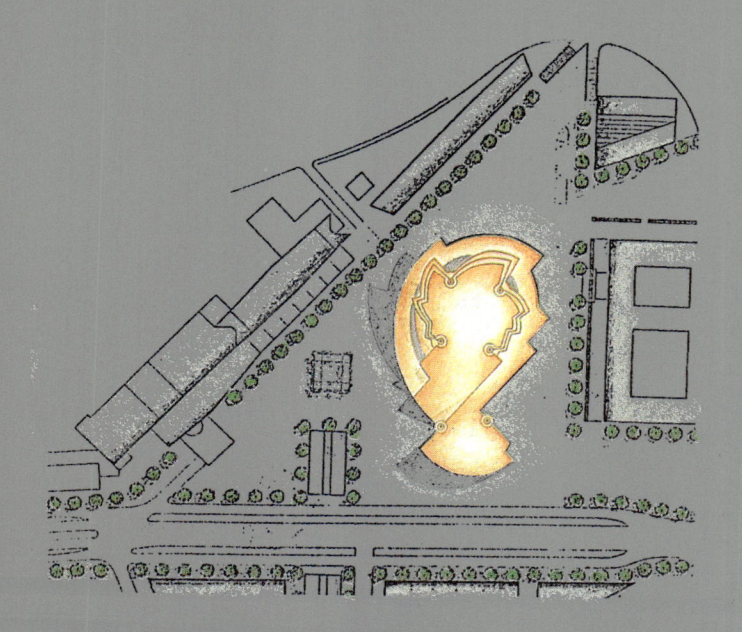

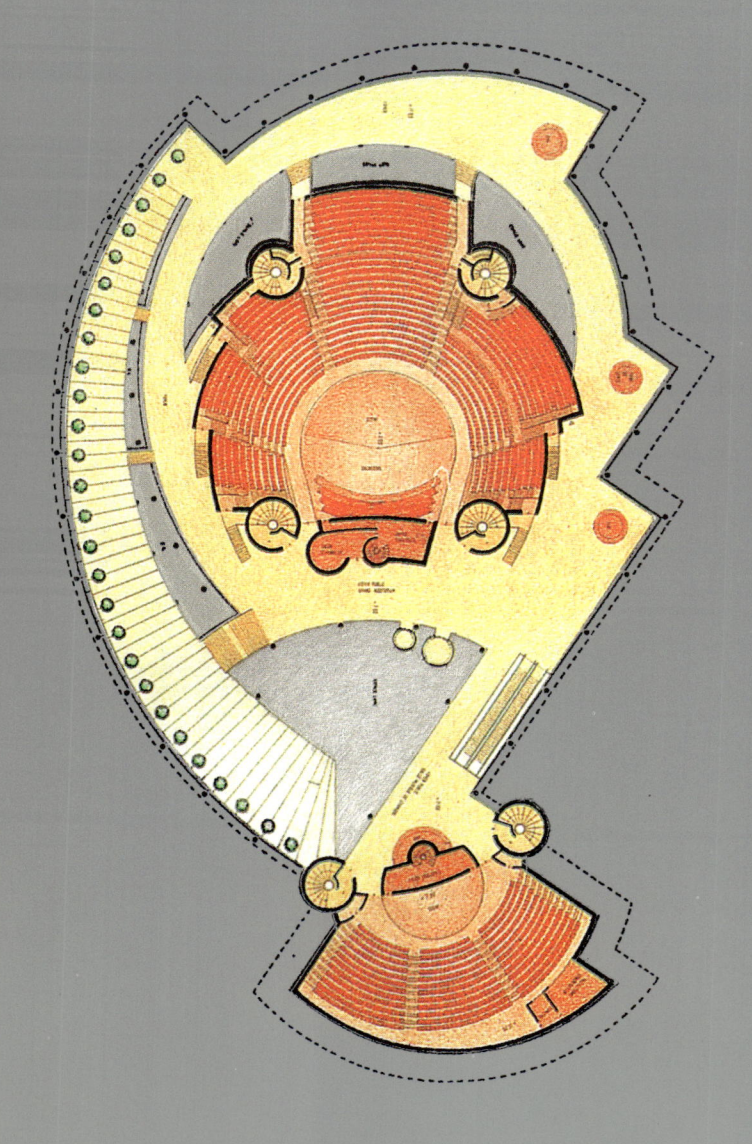

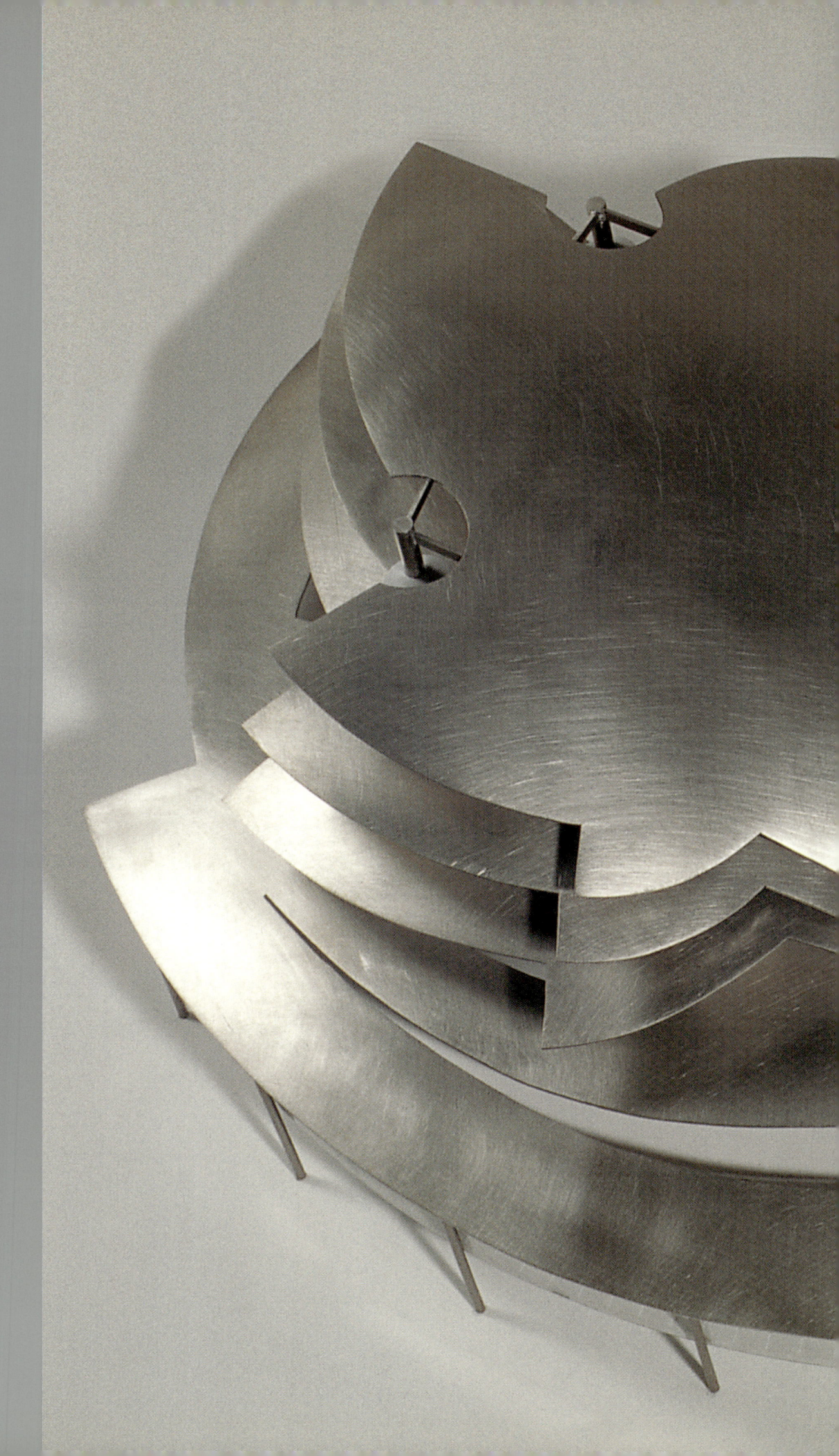

30

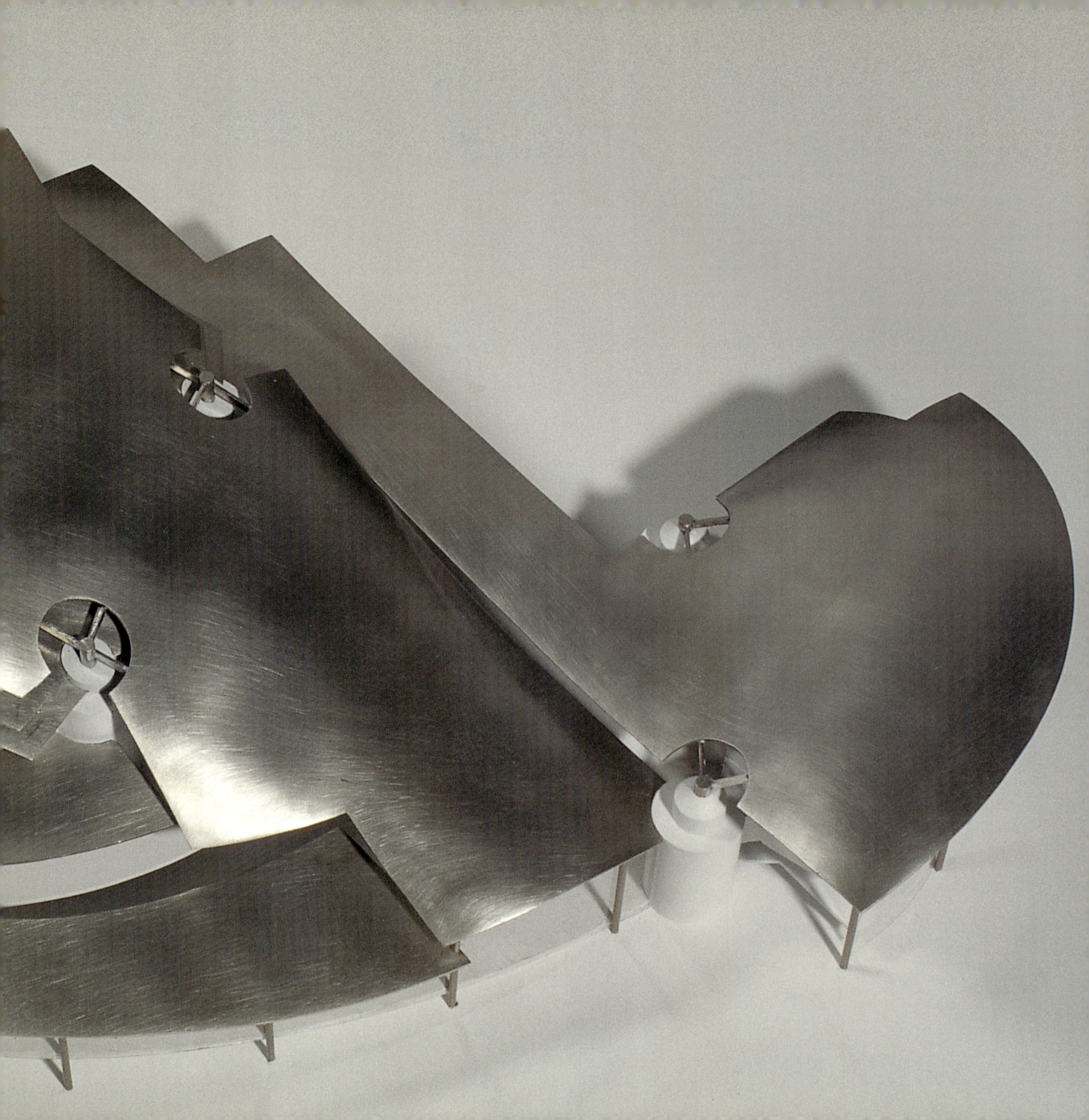

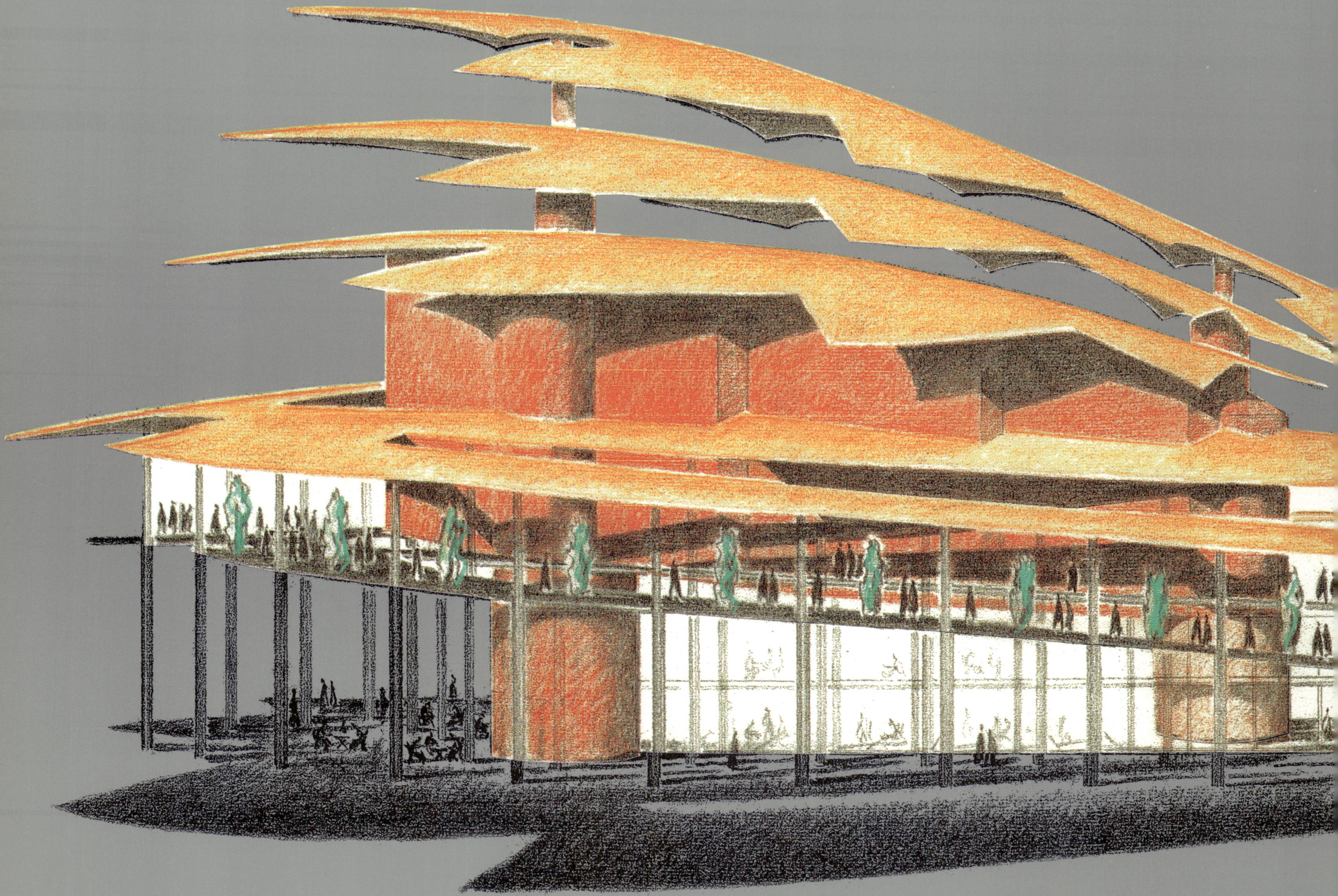

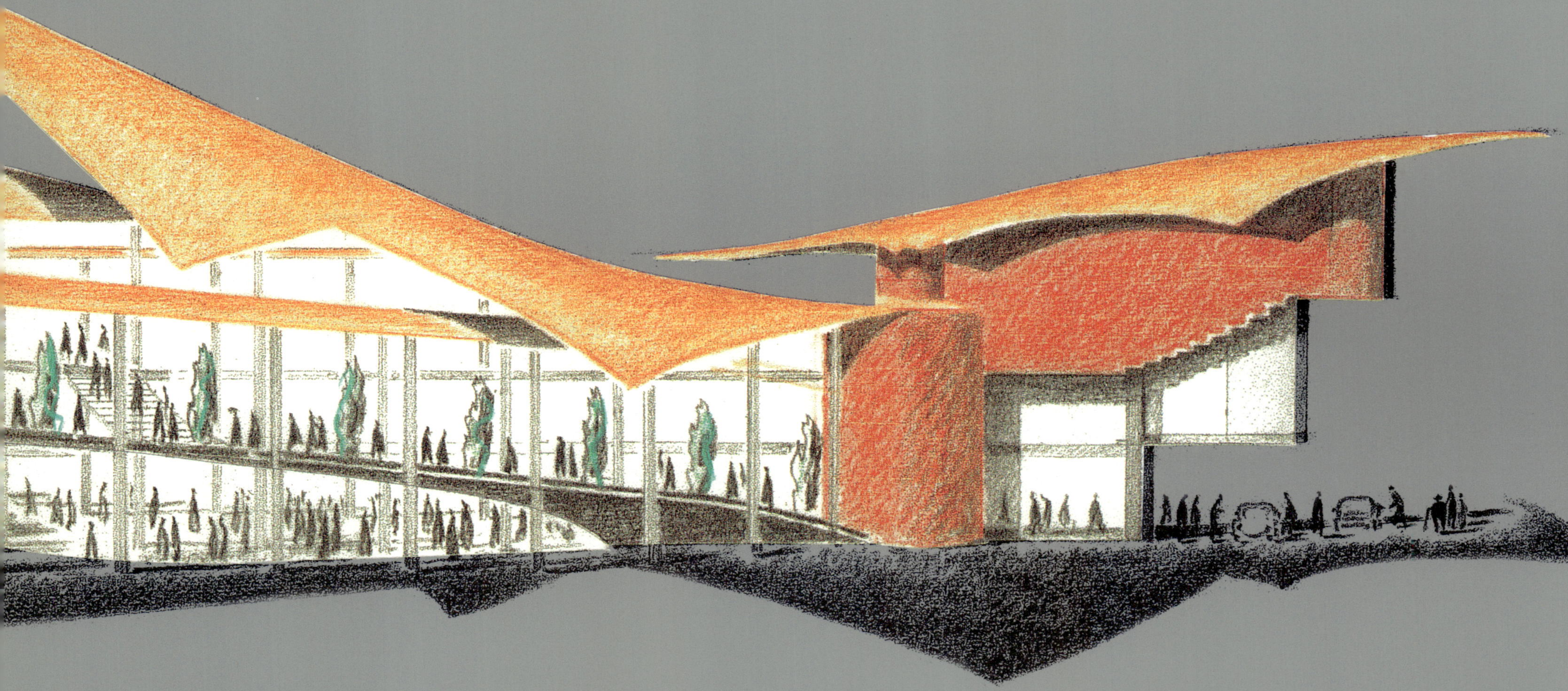

34

35

36

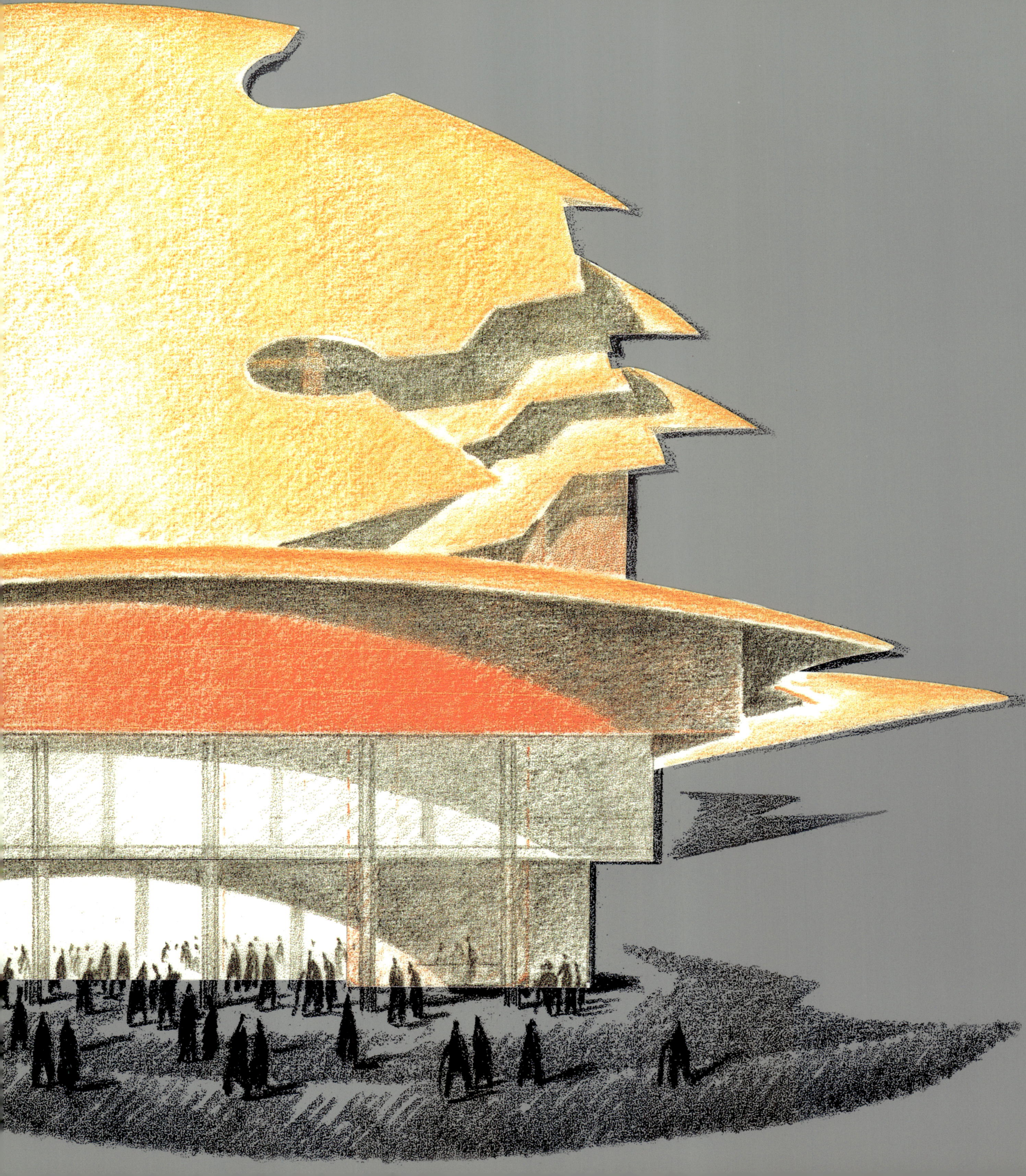

KÖLN, WDR HAUPTVERWALTUNG
COLOGNE, ADMINISTRATIVE HEADQUARTERS OF WDR
MIT / WITH PETER BÖHM, STEFAN ABELEN
1995

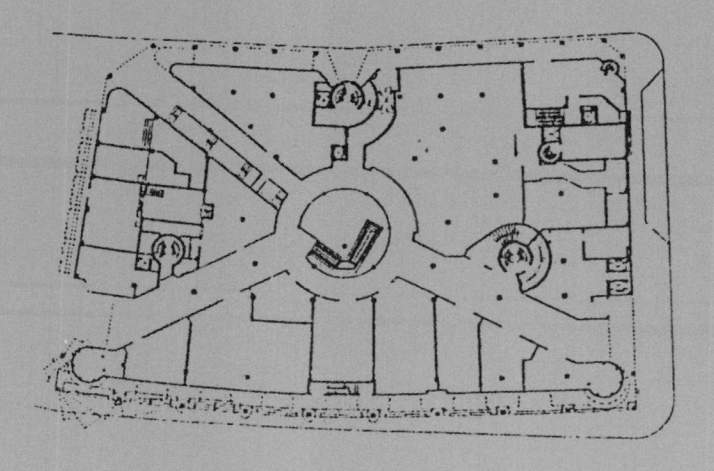

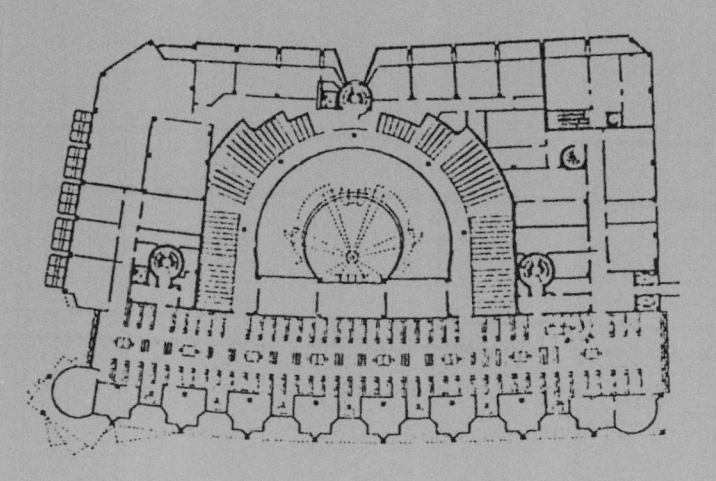

DER BAUKÖRPER IST VERBINDENDES
ELEMENT ZWISCHEN DEN VERSCHIEDENEN
BAUHÖHEN DIESES STADTGEBIETS.

THE BUILDING VOLUME ACTS AS A
MEDIATING, HARMONISING INFLUENCE
BETWEEN NEIGHBOURING STRUCTURES
OF VARYING HEIGHTS.

39

40

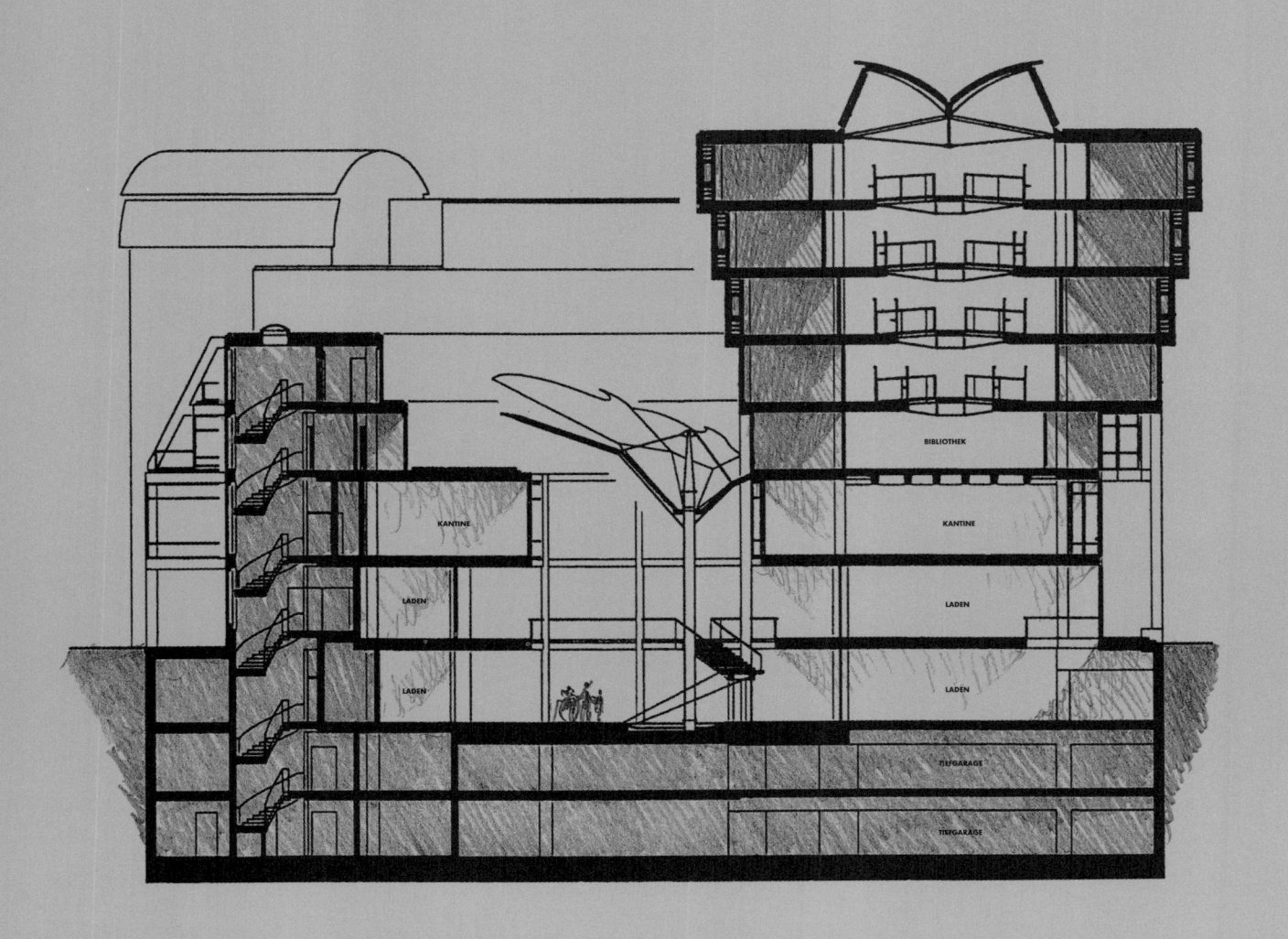

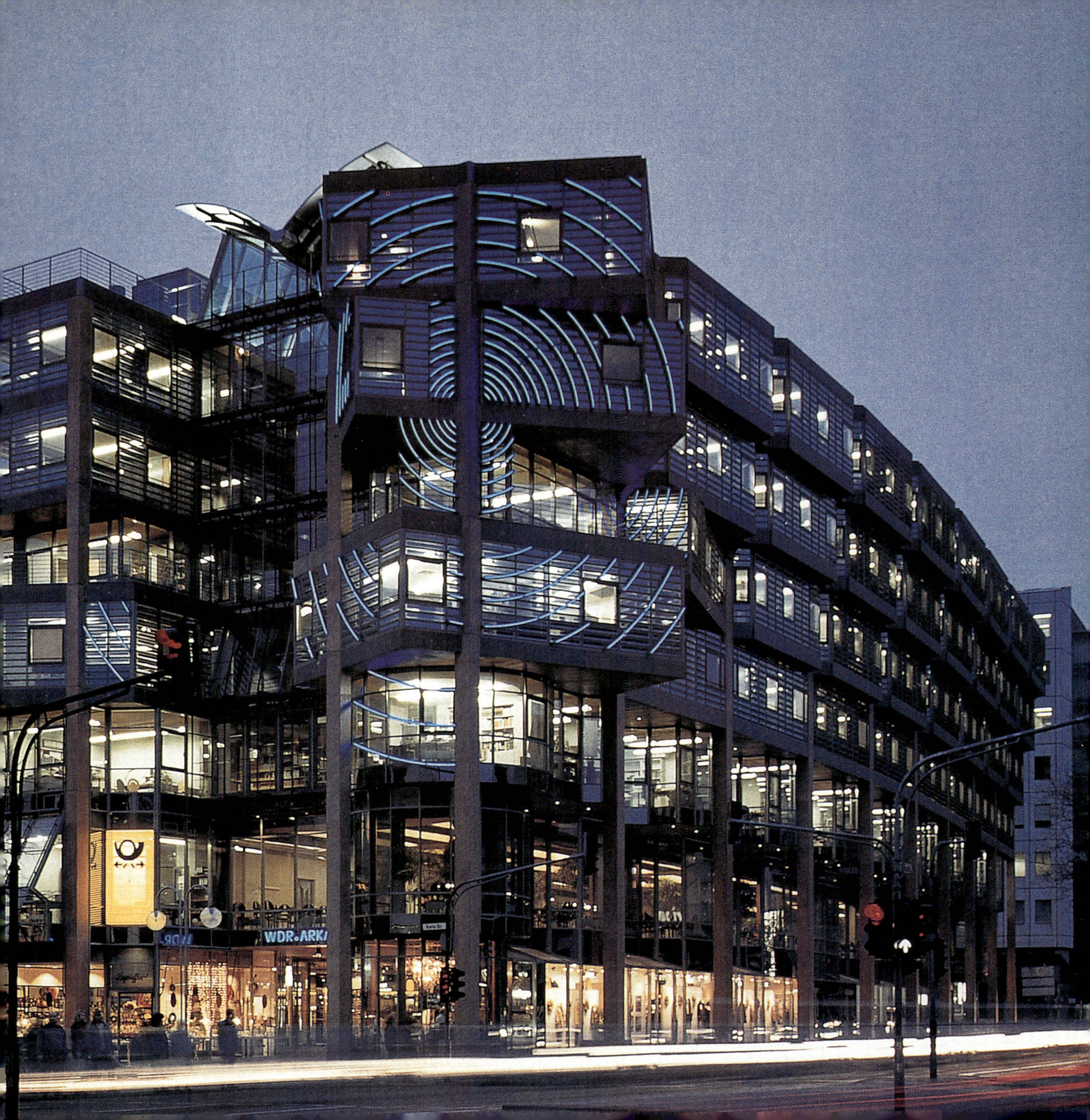

42

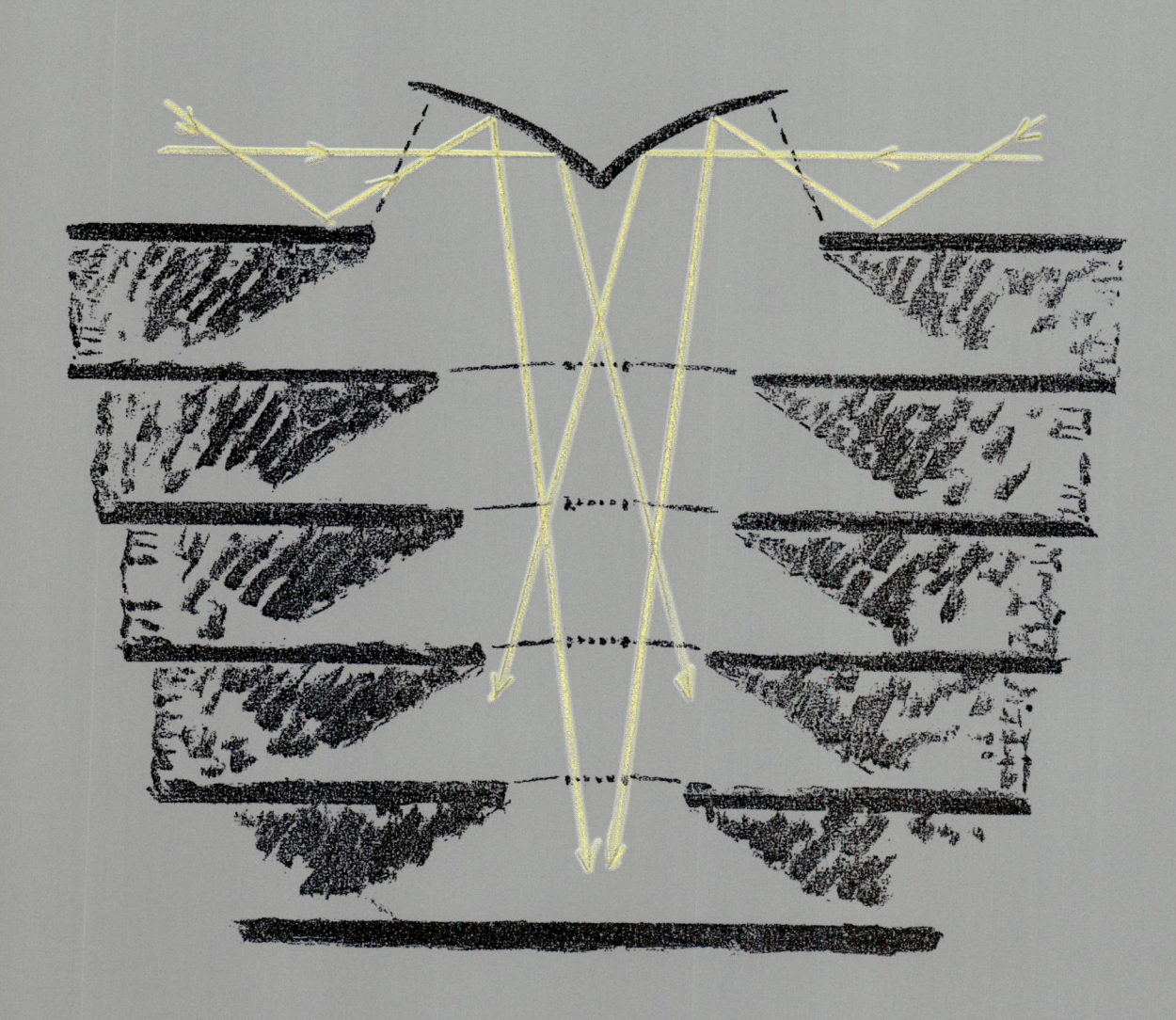

43

BIBLIOTHEK UND BÜRORÄUME
DIE BÜROLANDSCHAFT BETONT DIE GEMEINSAMKEIT
DER ARBEIT. DAS BIBLIOTHEKSGESCHOSS BILDET DIE
BASIS.

LIBRARY AND OFFICES
THE DESIGN FOR THE OFFICE SPACE SUPPORTS THE
COMMUNAL, COOPERATIVE NATURE OF THE WORK
CARRIED OUT THERE. THE LIBRARY STOREY FORMS THE
BACKBONE TO THE OVERALL DESIGN.

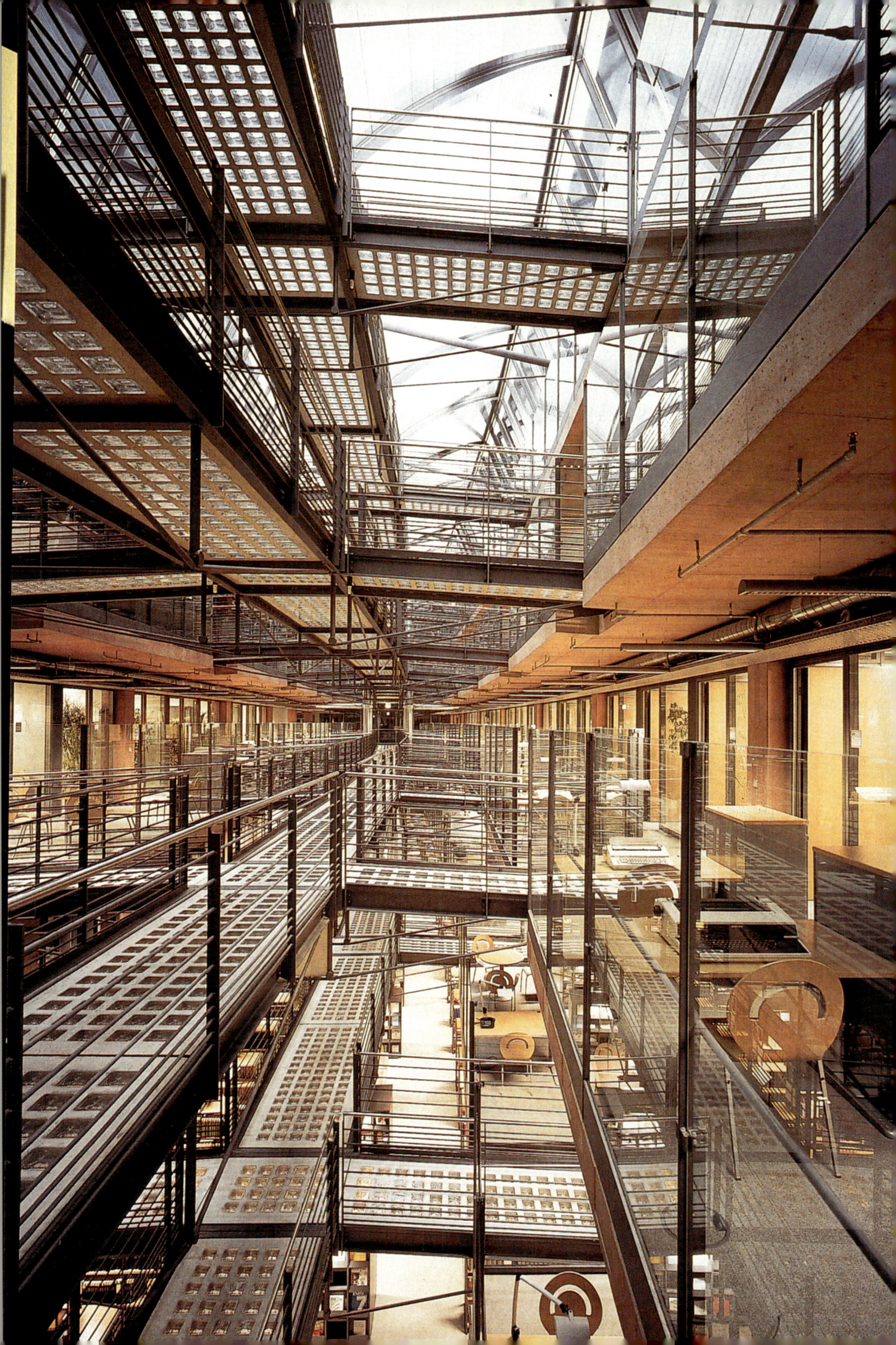

LADENGESCHOSSE MIT INNENHOF
UND BRUNNEN

SHOPPING MALL WITH COVERED COURTYARD
AND FOUNTAIN

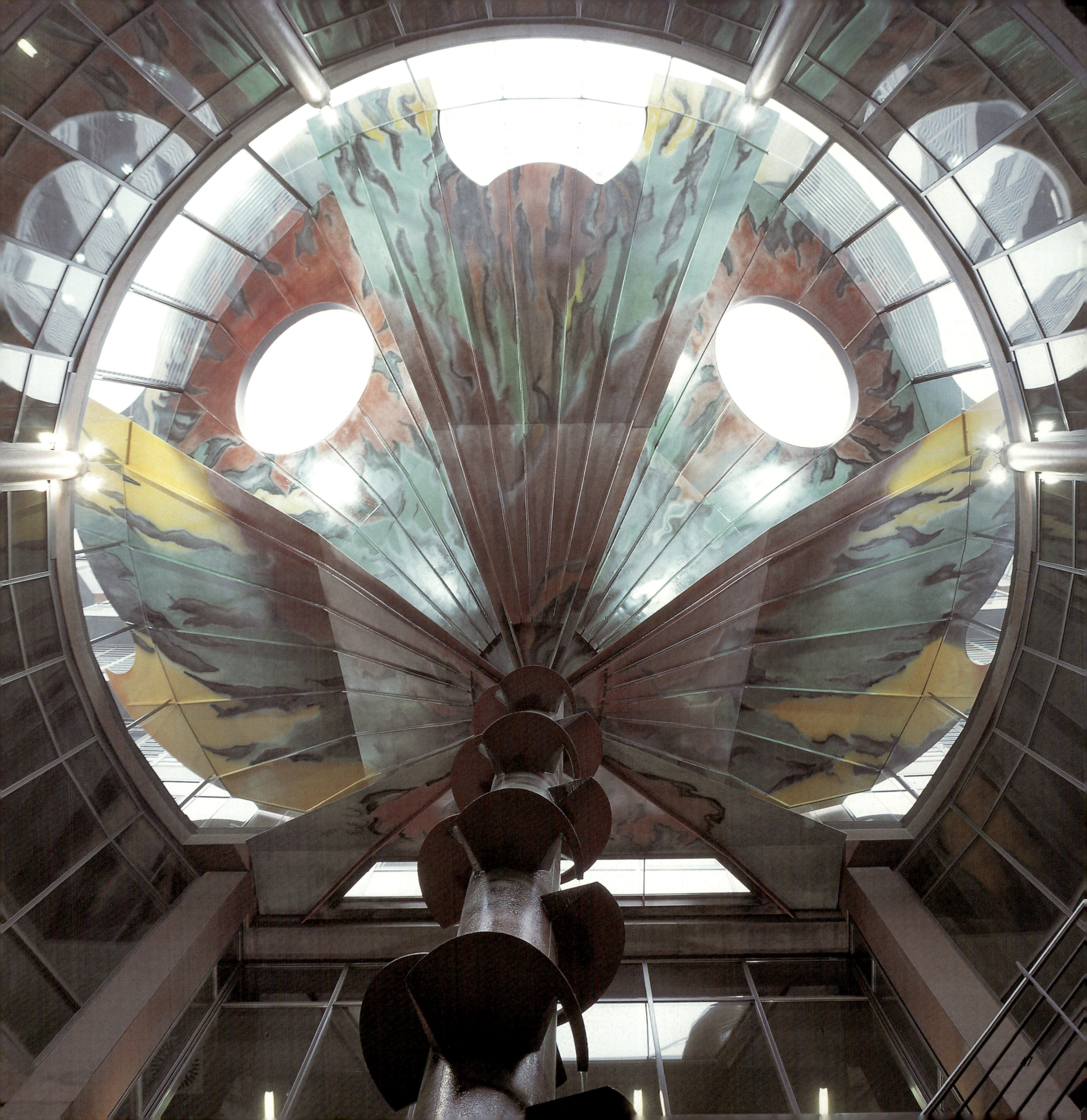

SITZUNGSSAAL
MALEREI VON MARKUS BÖHM

MEETING HALL
PAINTED DECORATION BY MARKUS BÖHM

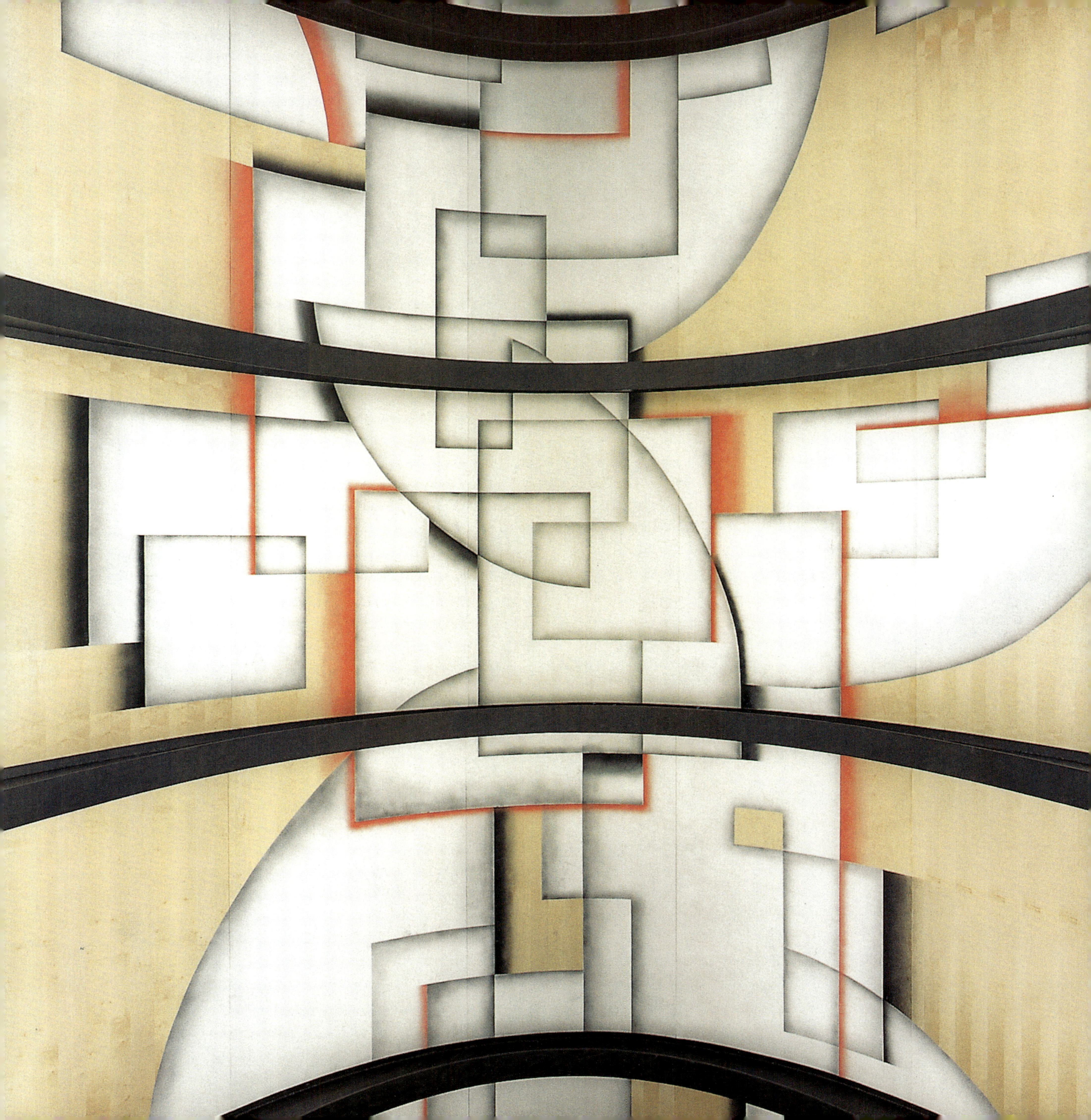

HAMBURG, ARENA
MIT / WITH PETER BÖHM
PROJEKT / PROJECT, 1991

UMGESTALTUNG DER EHEMALIGEN MARKTHALLEN –
VON HERMKES UND LODDERS IN DEN SECHZIGER
JAHREN GEBAUT – ZU EINEM SPORTZENTRUM MIT
NEUBAU EINER ARENA.

CONVERSION OF A FORMER MARKET HALL INTO A
SPORTS CENTRE WITH NEW EVENTS ARENA.
THE MARKET HALL WAS ORIGINALLY CONSTRUCTED
BY HERMKES AND LODDERS IN THE 1960S.

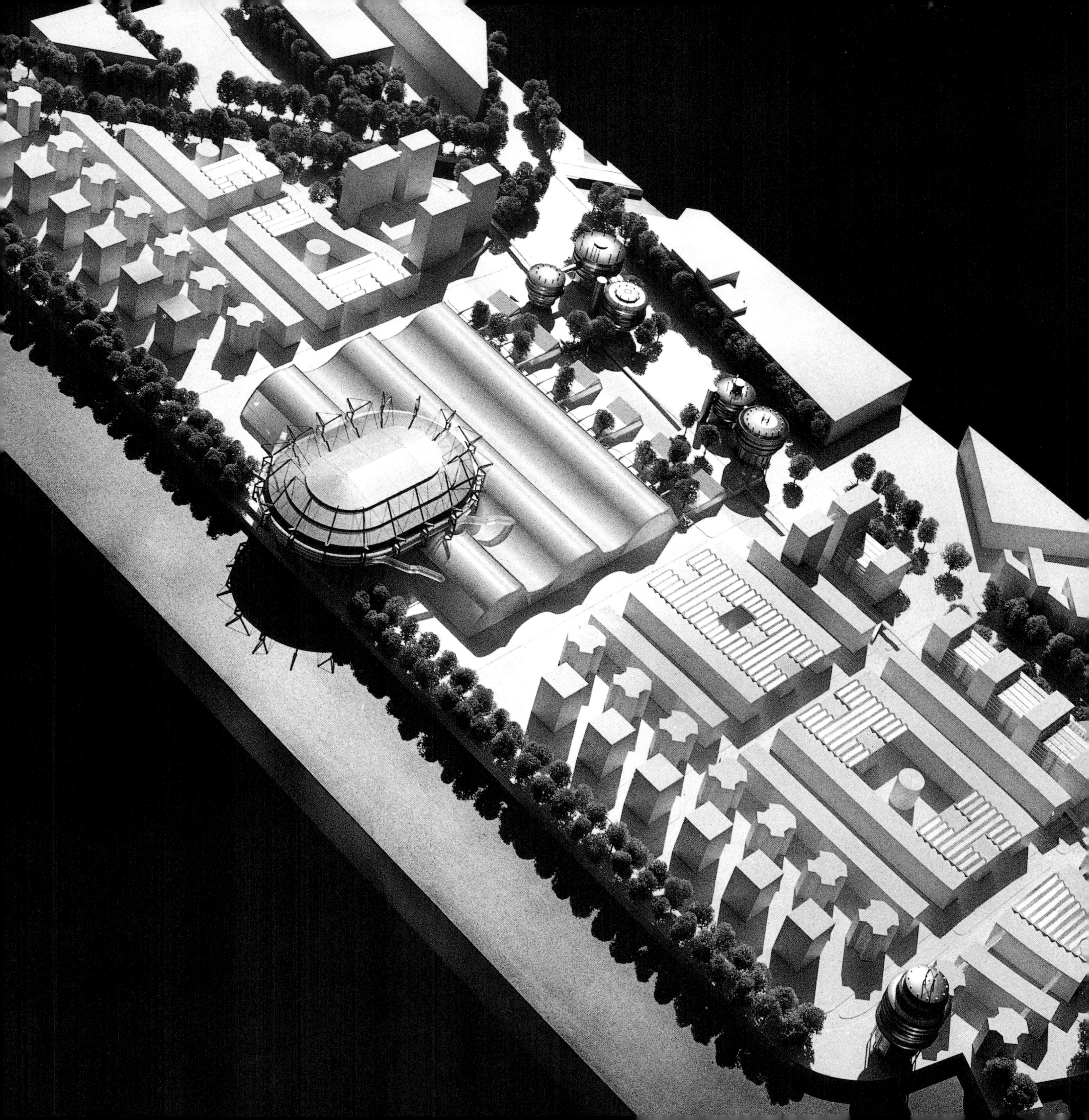

52

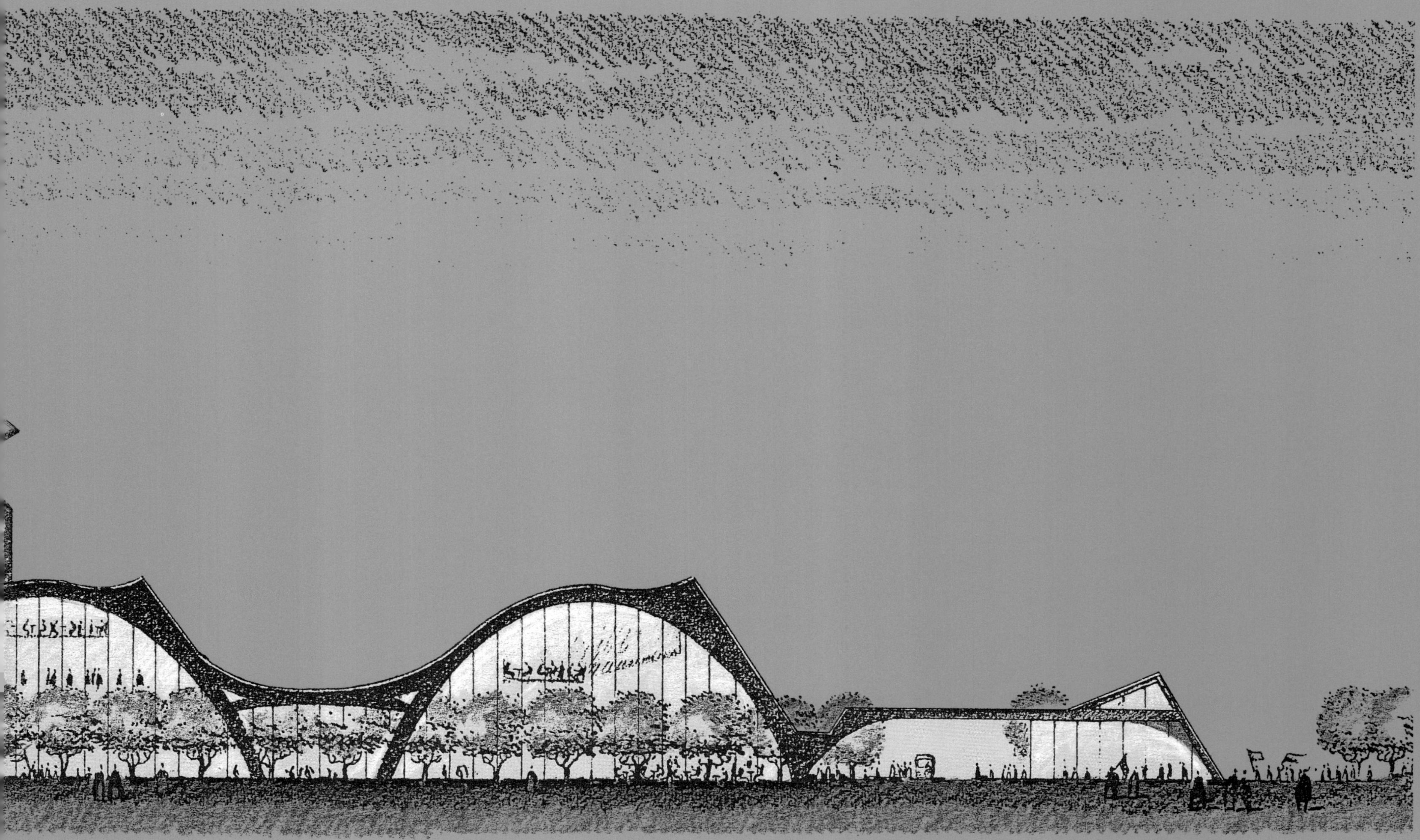

54

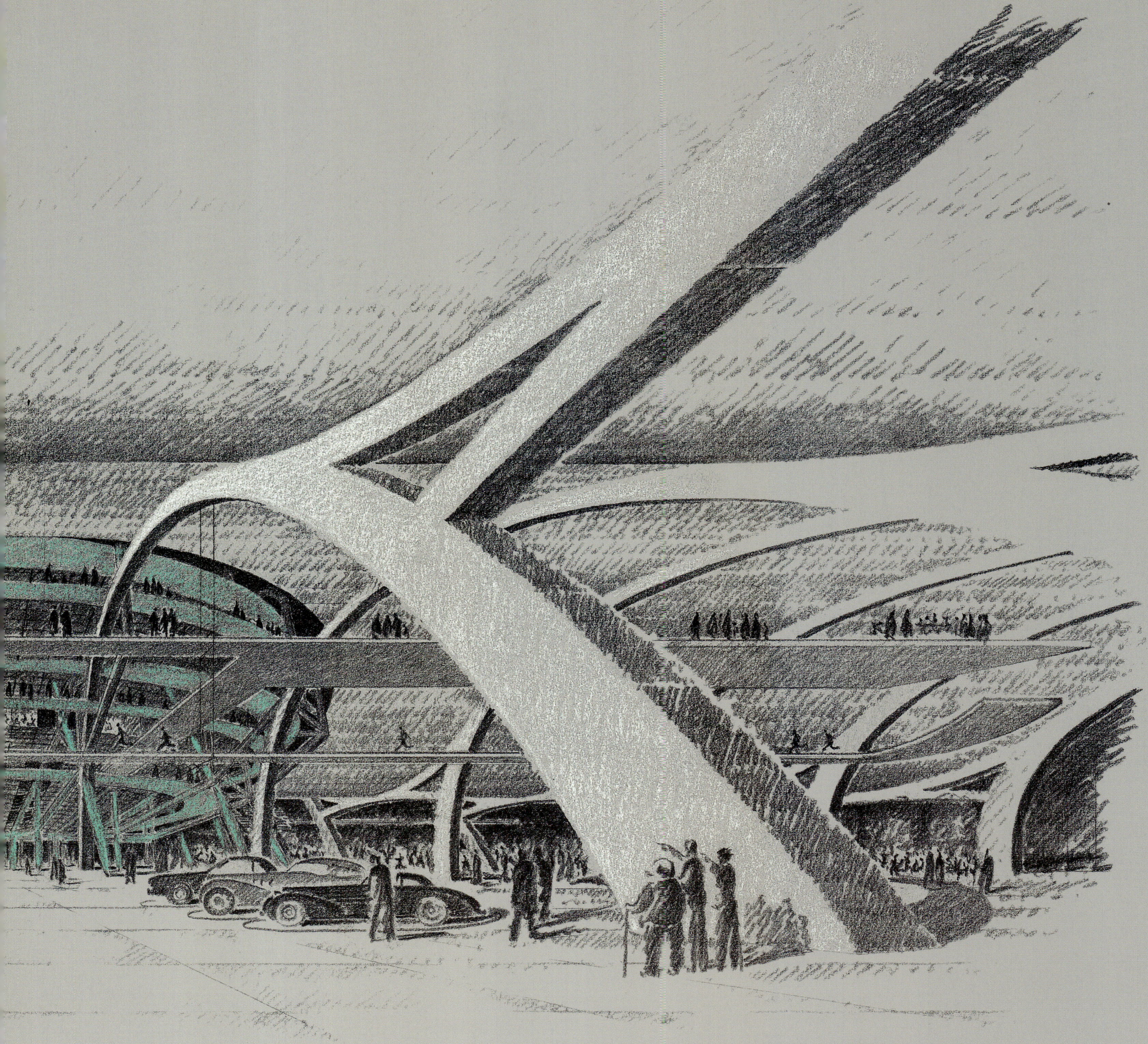

SAARBRÜCKEN, SCHLOSS
SAARBRÜCKEN, CASTLE

MIT / WITH NICOLAUS ROSINY,
HANS LINDER, BÜRO KRÜGER-RIEGER

1987

RESTAURIERUNG DES SCHLOSSES UND NEUBAU
DES MITTELRISALITS MIT PLENARSAAL

RESTORATION OF THE CASTLE AND CONSTRUCTION
OF A CENTRAL PLENARY HALL

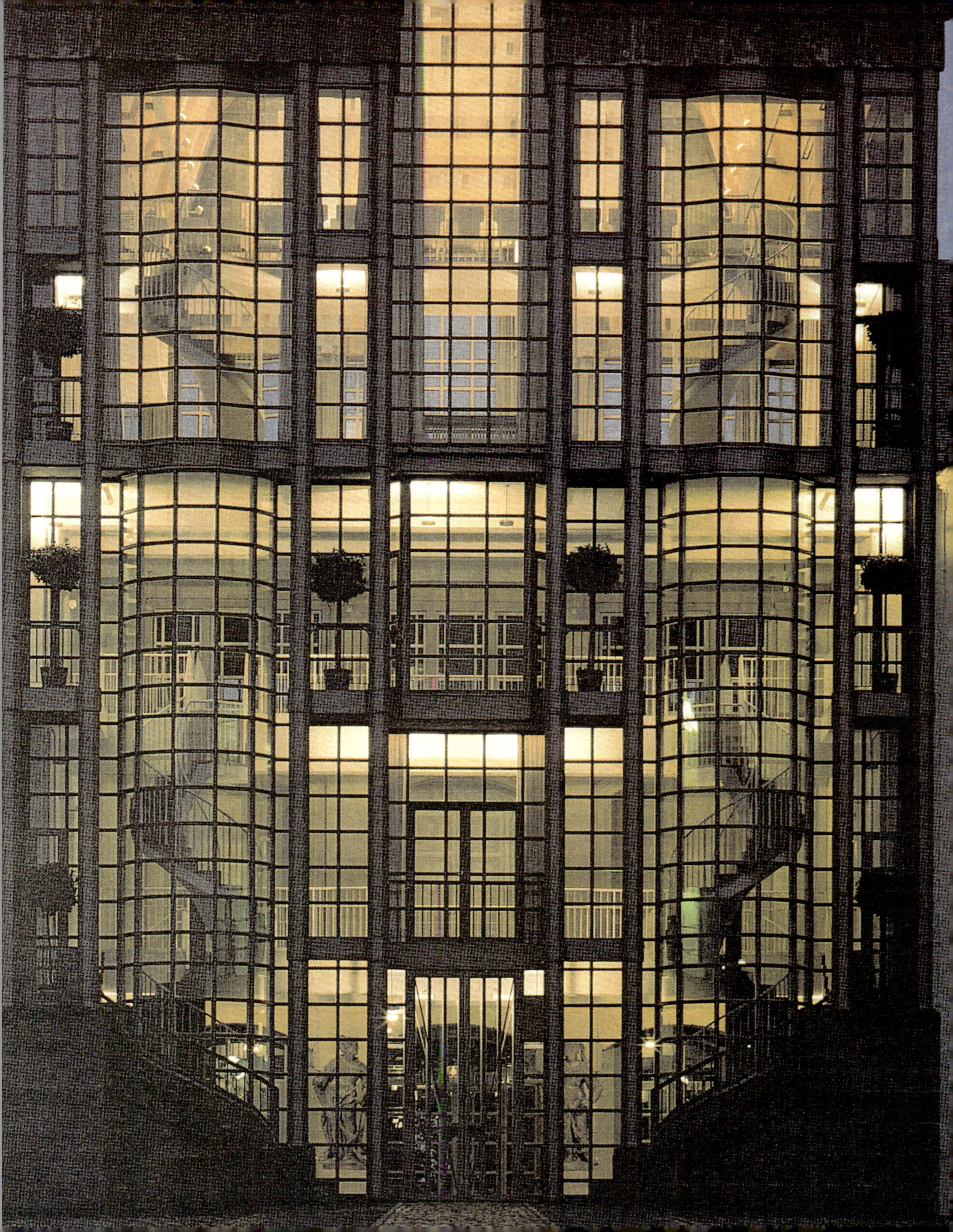

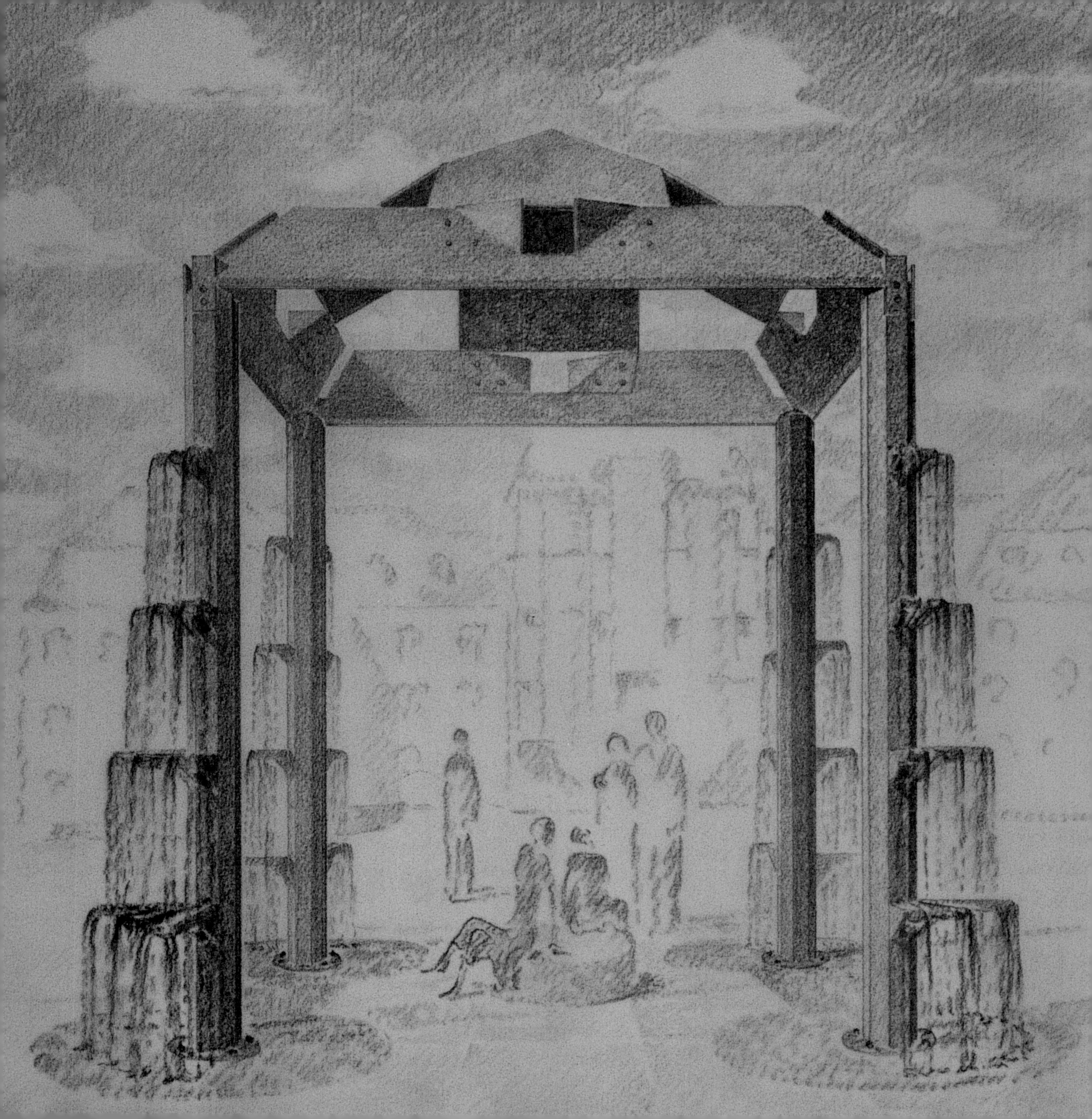

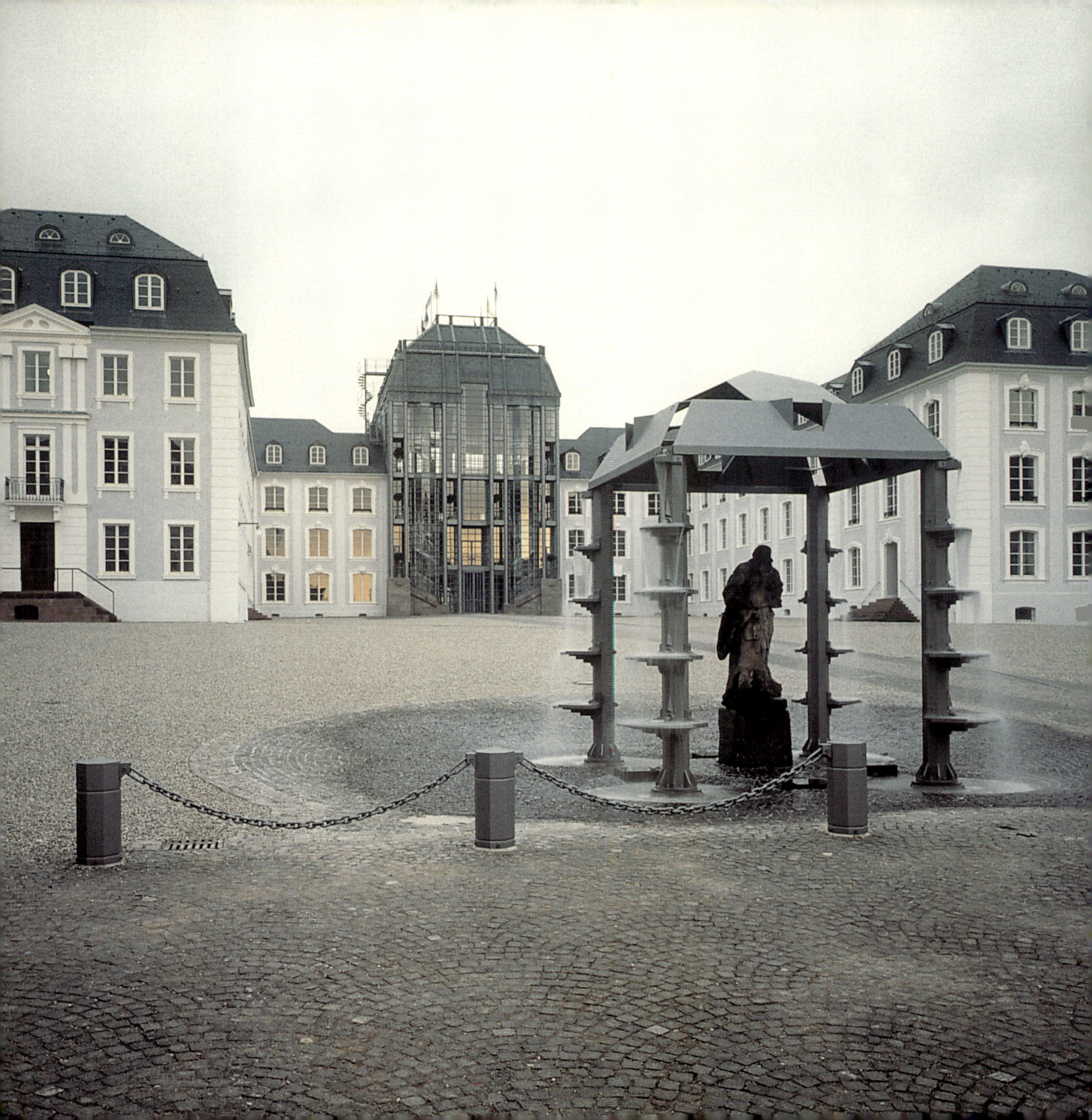

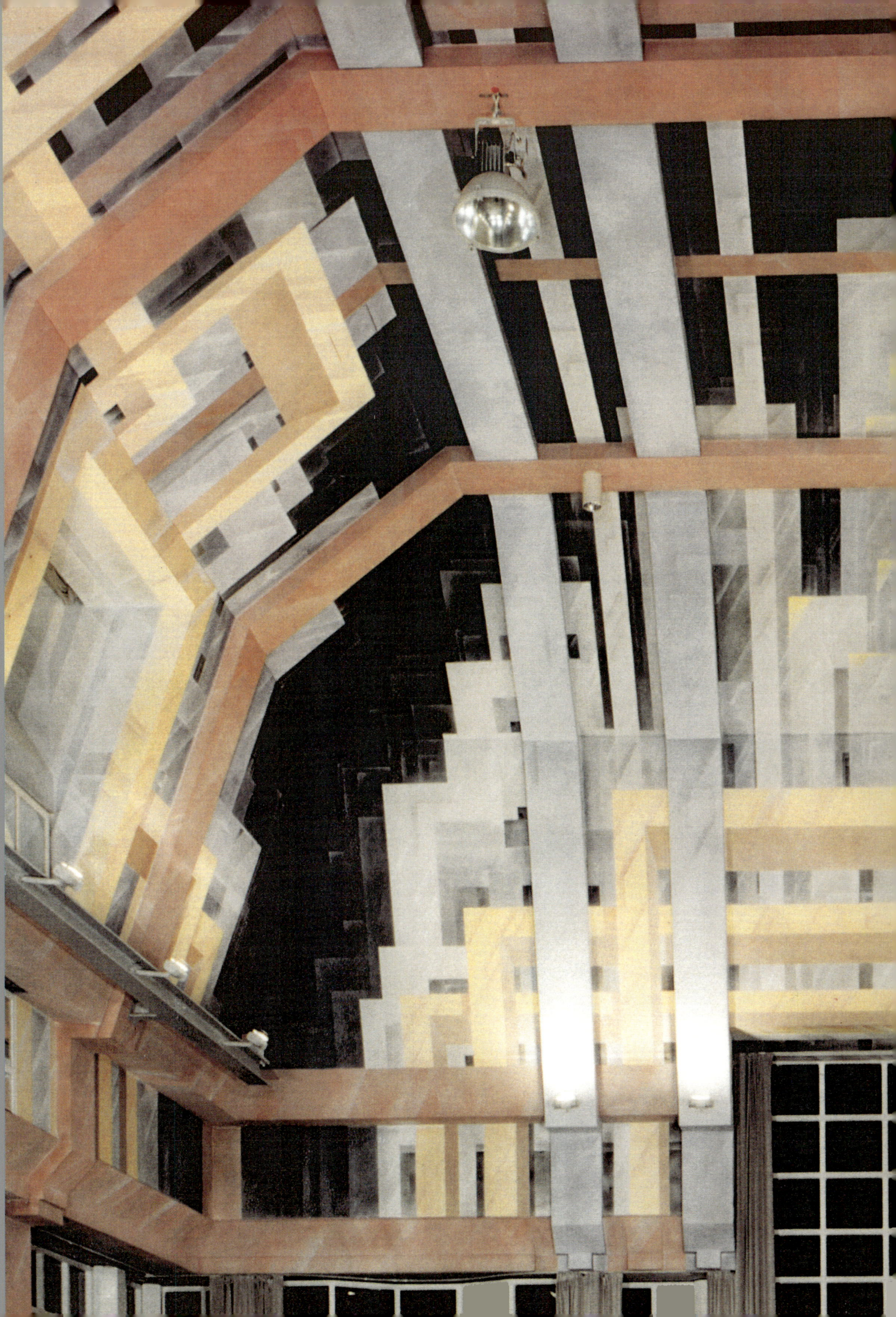

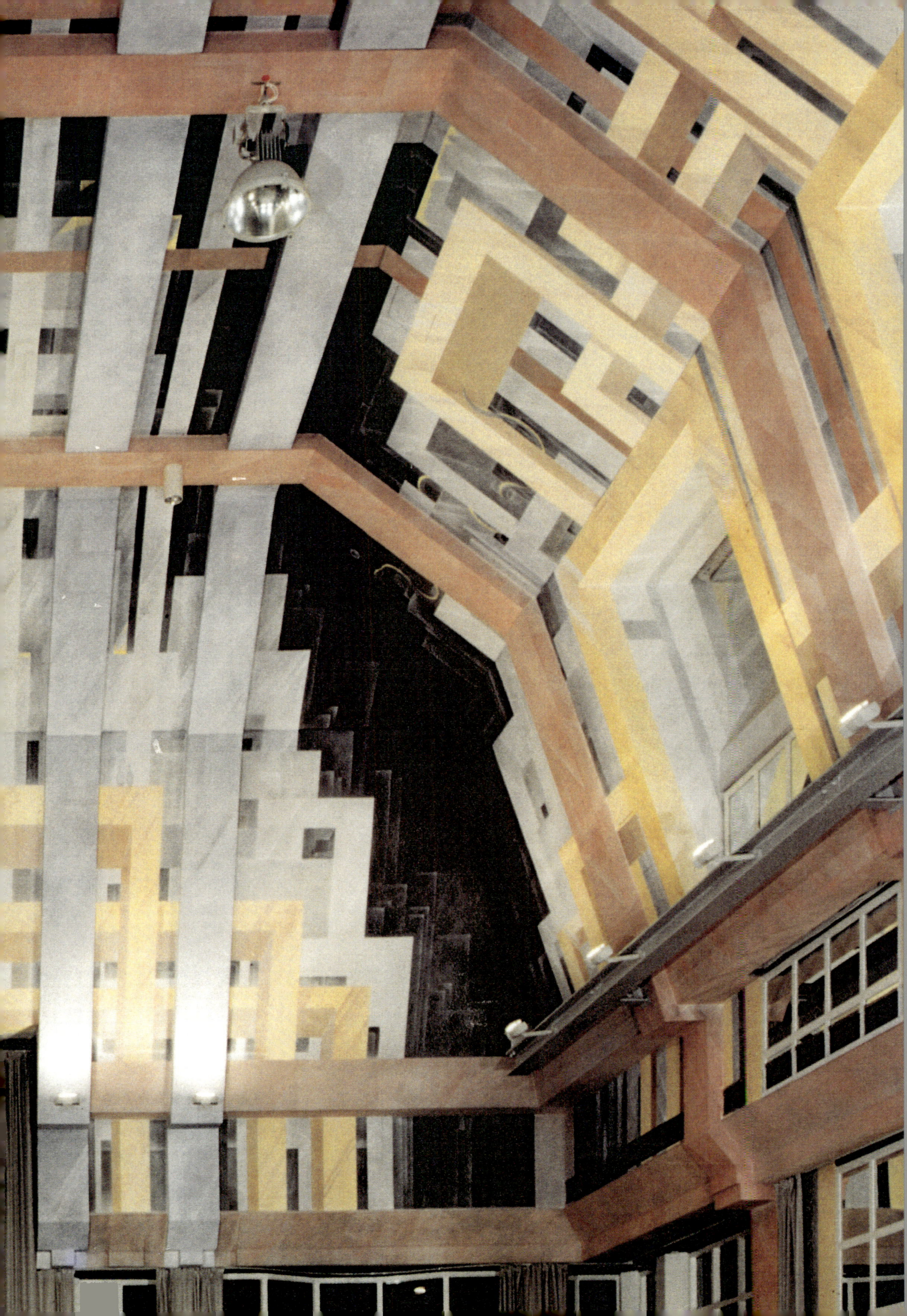

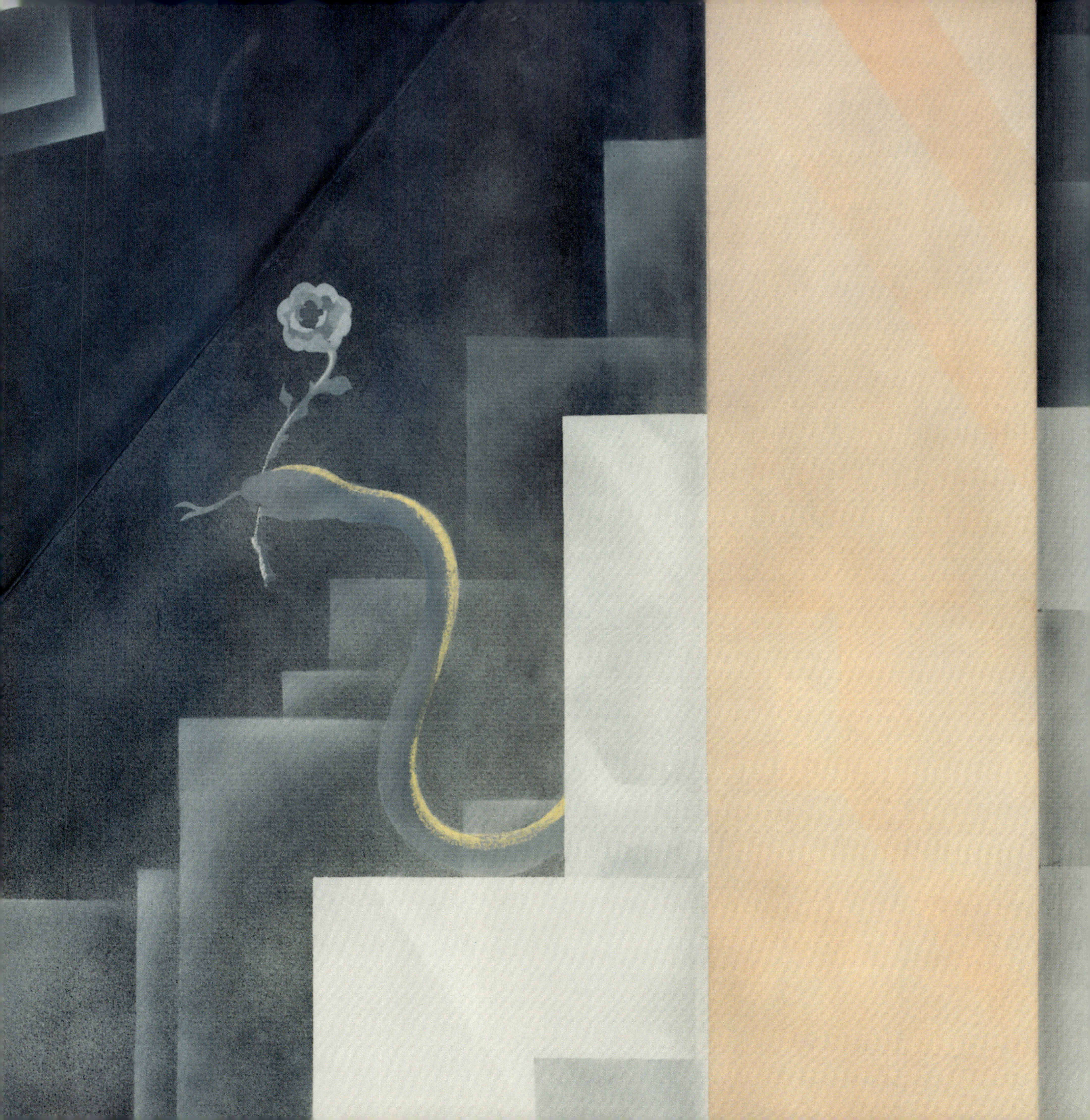

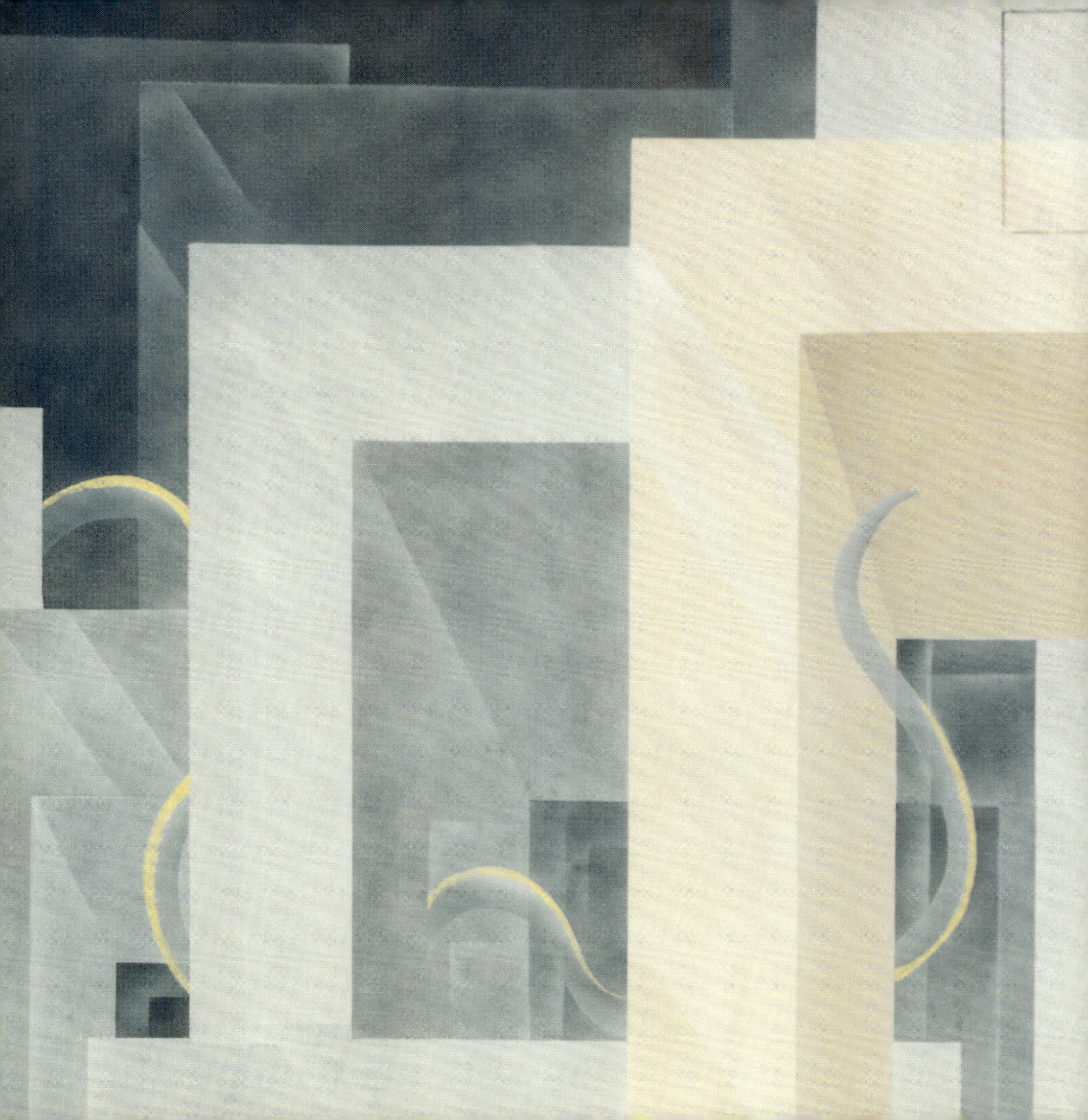

STUTTGART, ZÜBLINHAUS
MIT / WITH DÖRTHE GATTERMANN
1985

DIE HALLE IST BEGEGNUNGSZENTRUM UND WIRD FÜR
VERANSTALTUNGEN VIELFÄLTIGER ART GENUTZT.

THE ENTRANCE HALL IS DESIGNED AS A COMMUNICATION ZONE
IN WHICH A WIDE RANGE OF EVENTS CAN BE HELD.

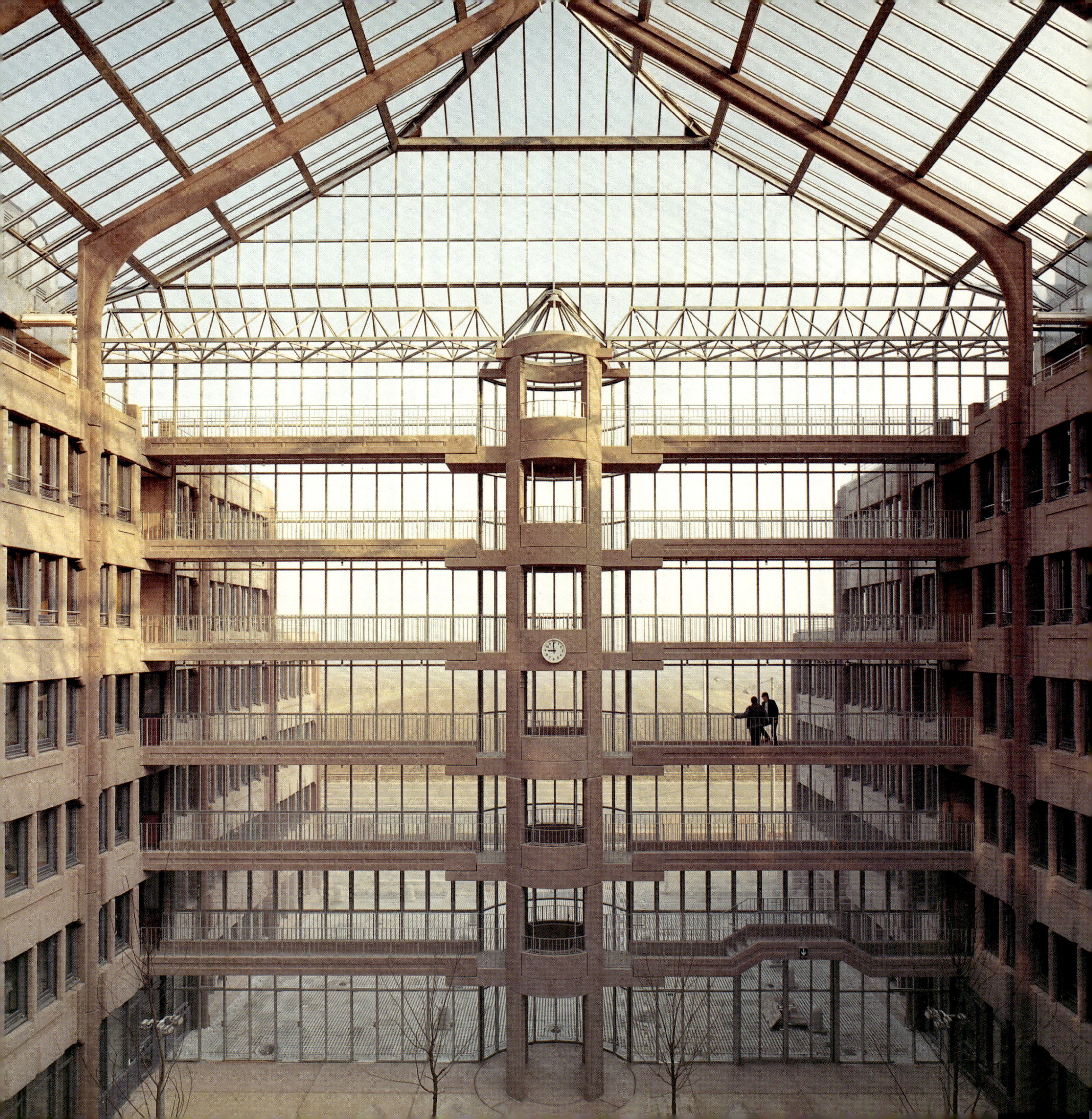

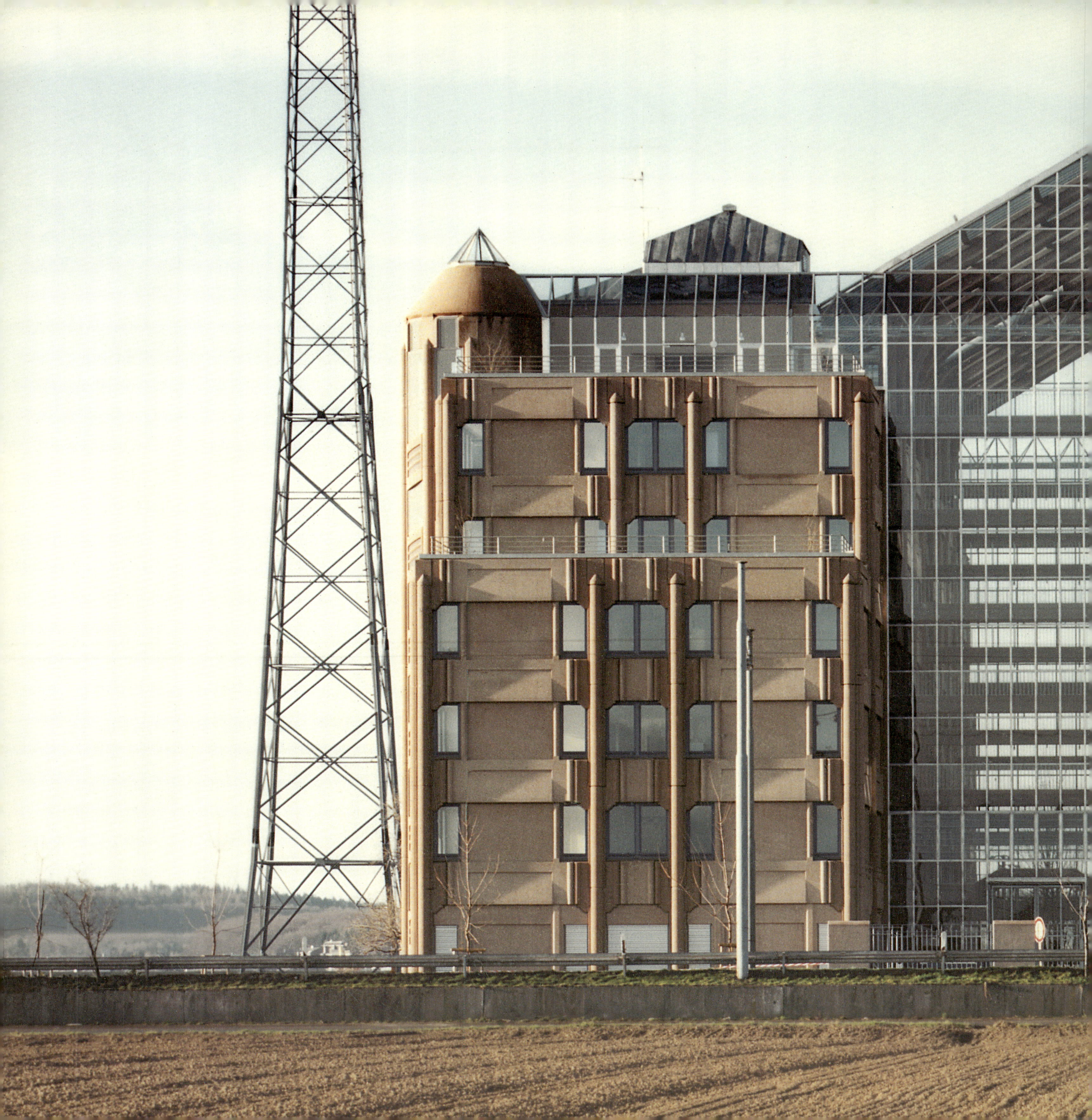

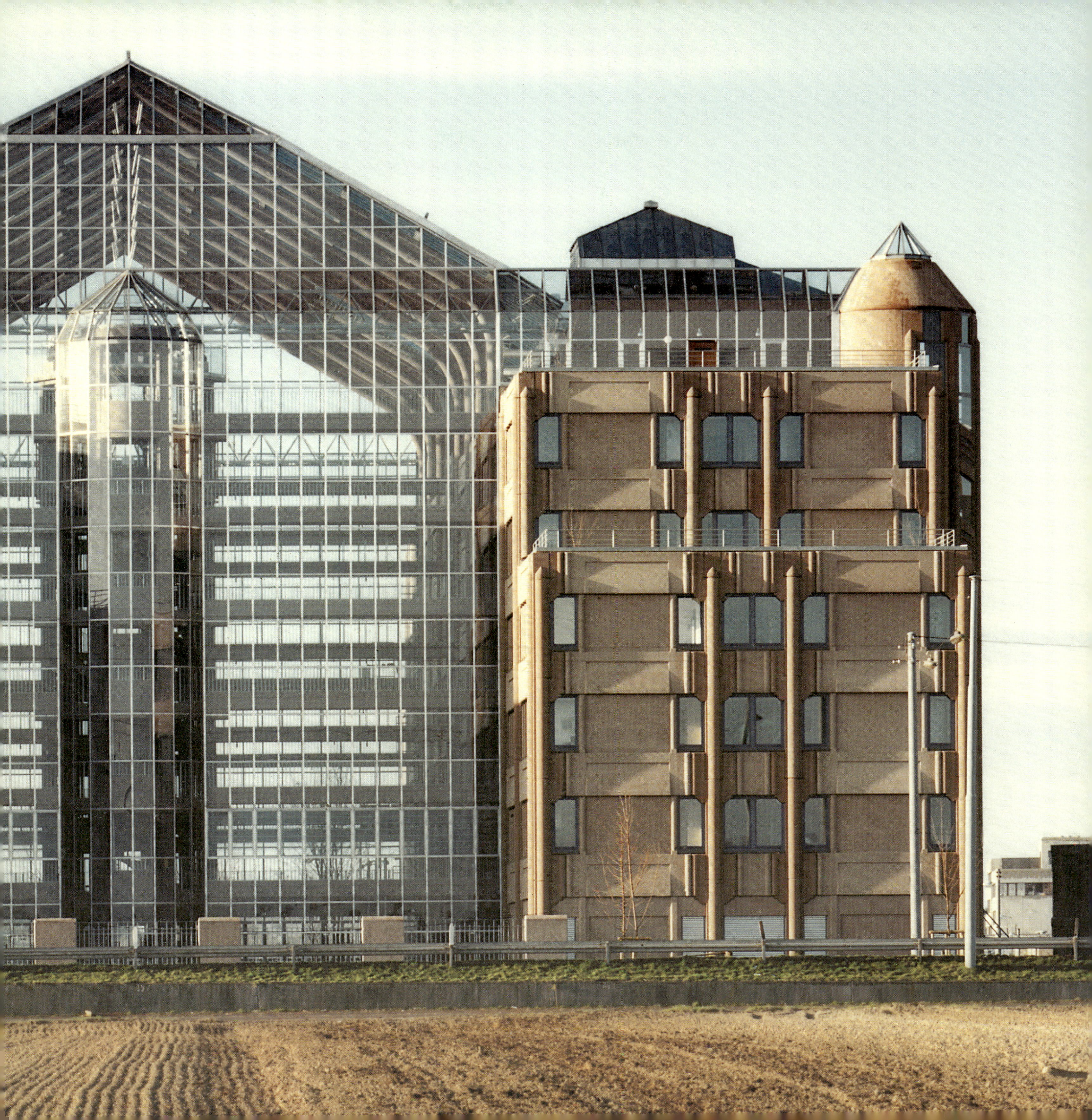

ESTRICHFUSSBODEN DER HALLE

SCREED FLOOR IN THE ENTRANCE HALL

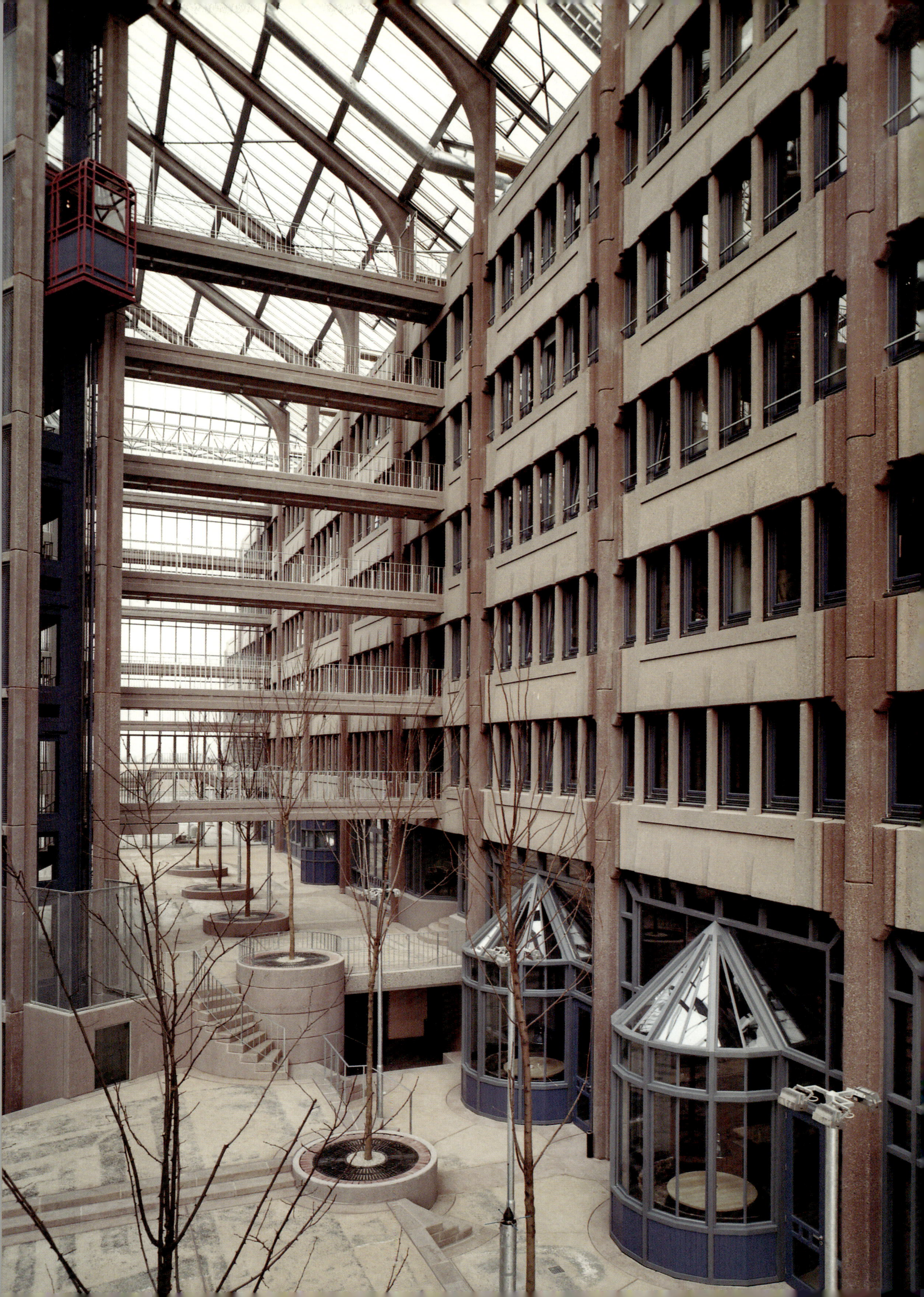

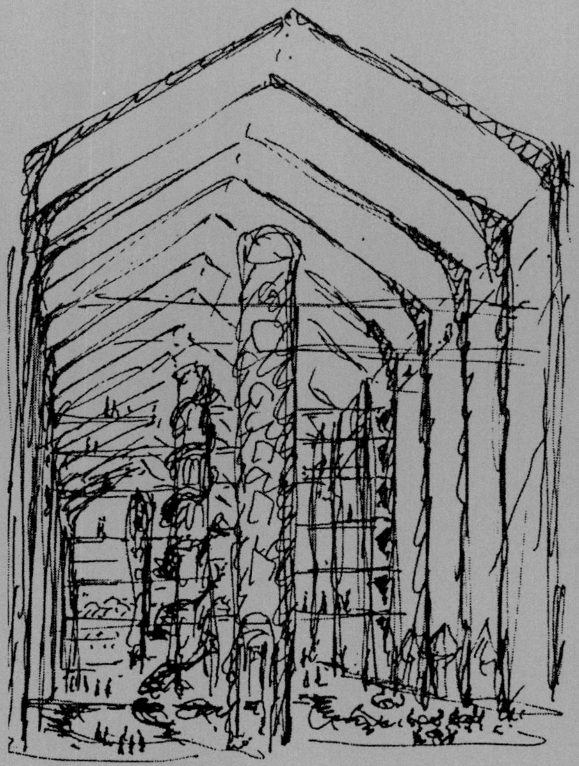

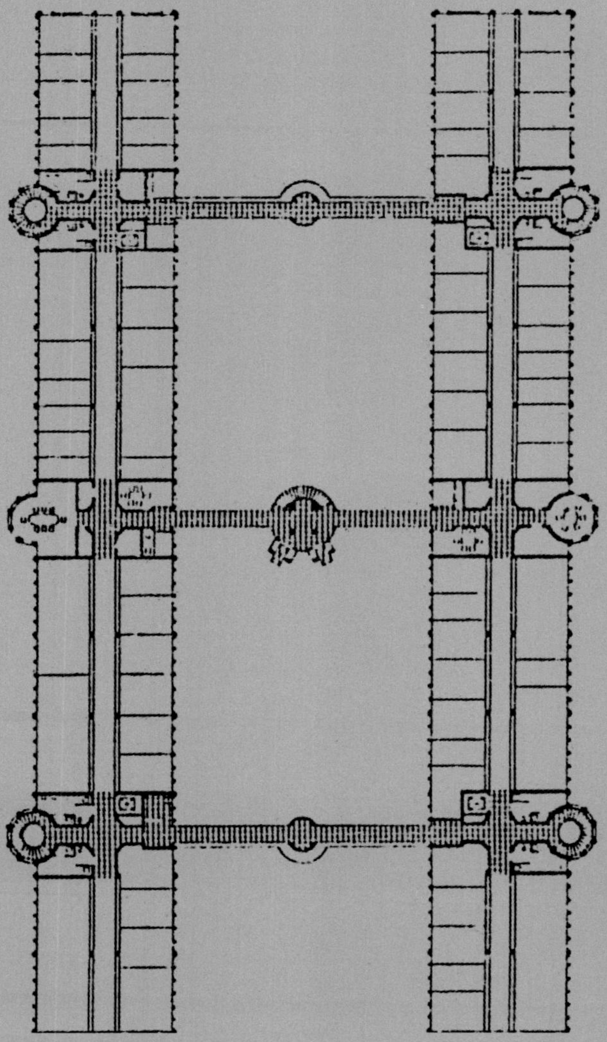

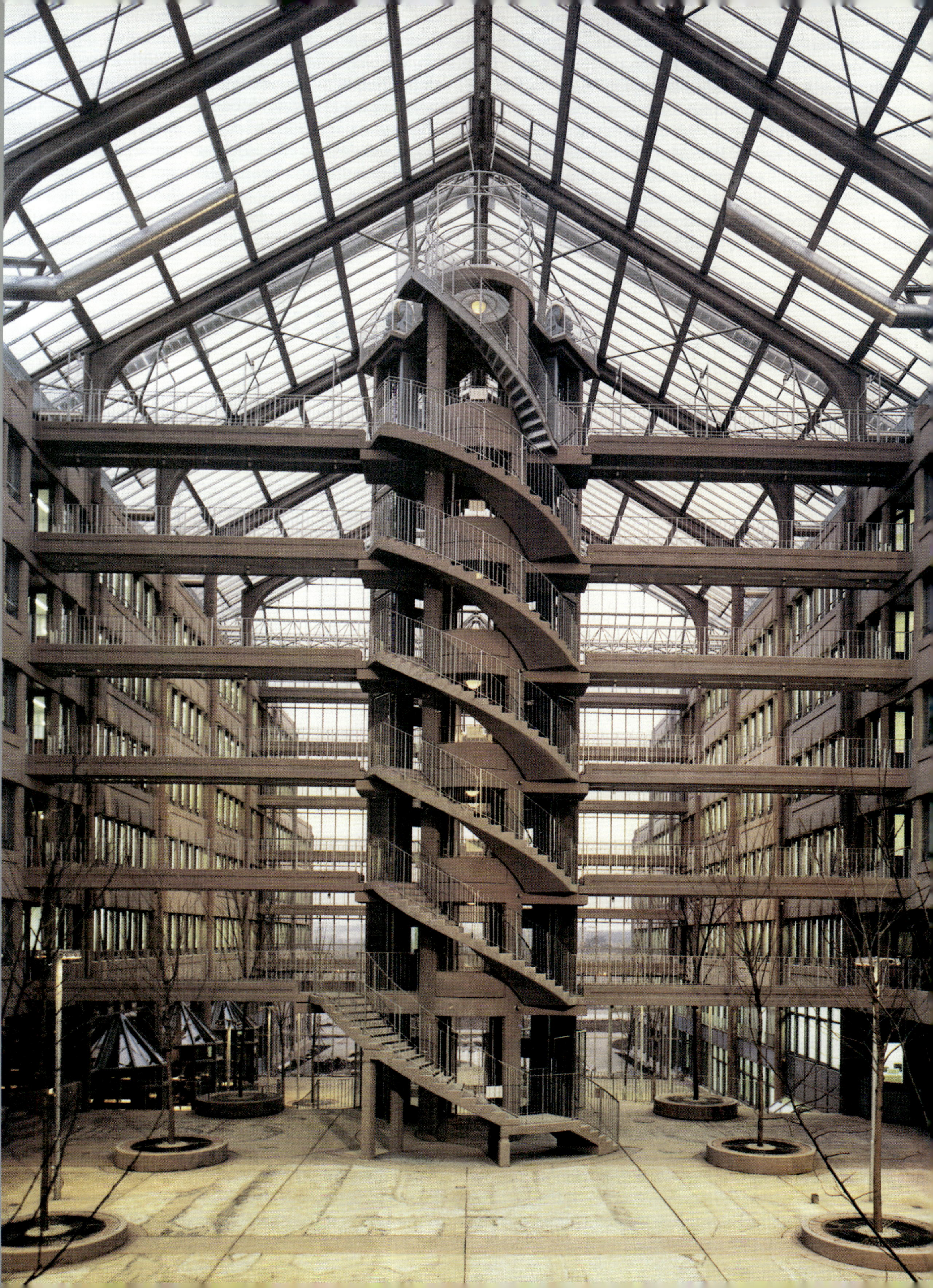

HAMBURG, MUSEUM FÜR MODERNE KUNST
HAMBURG, MUSEUM OF MODERN ART

MIT / WITH JÜRGEN MINKUS

WETTBEWERB / COMPETITION, 1986

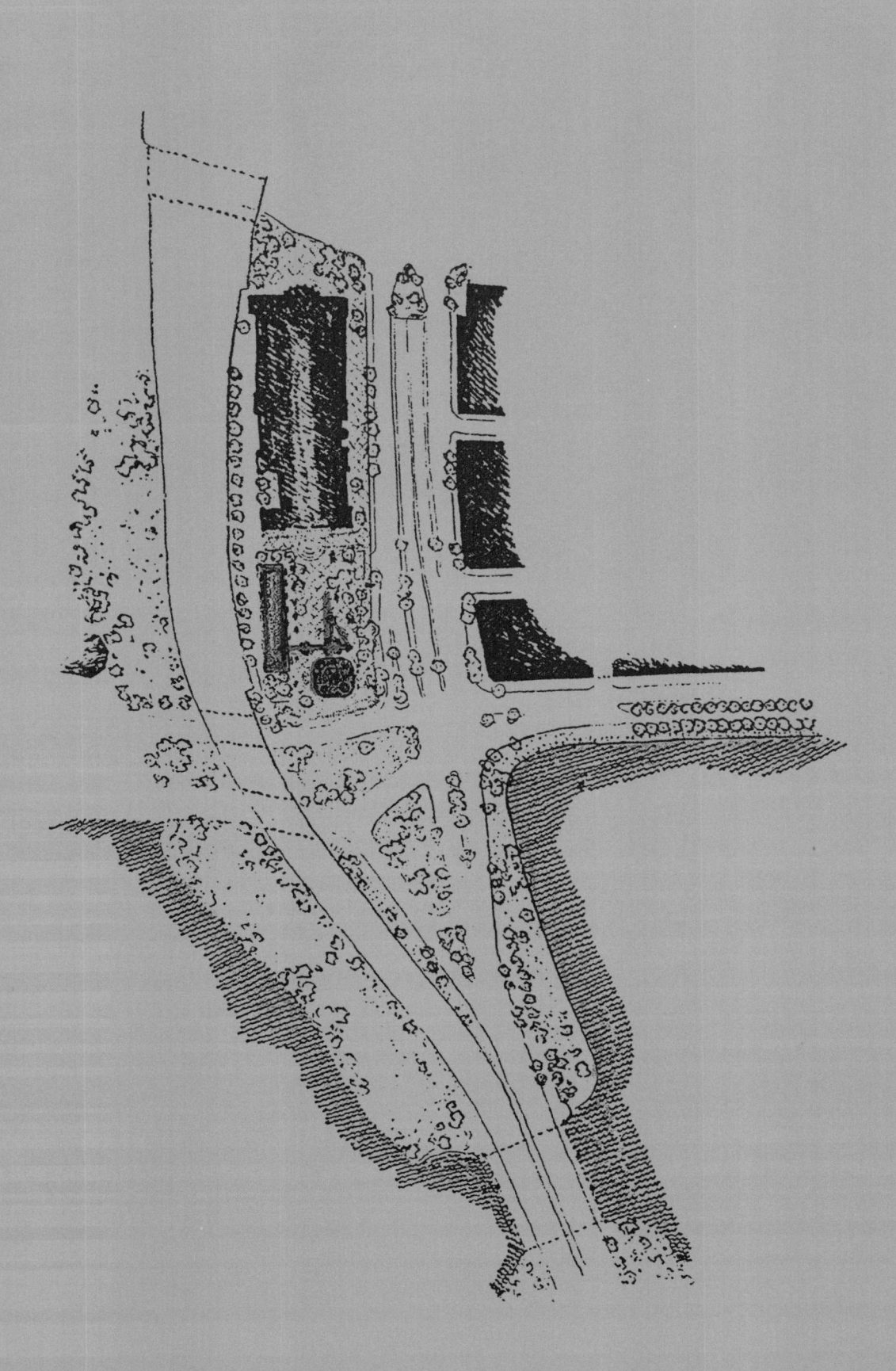

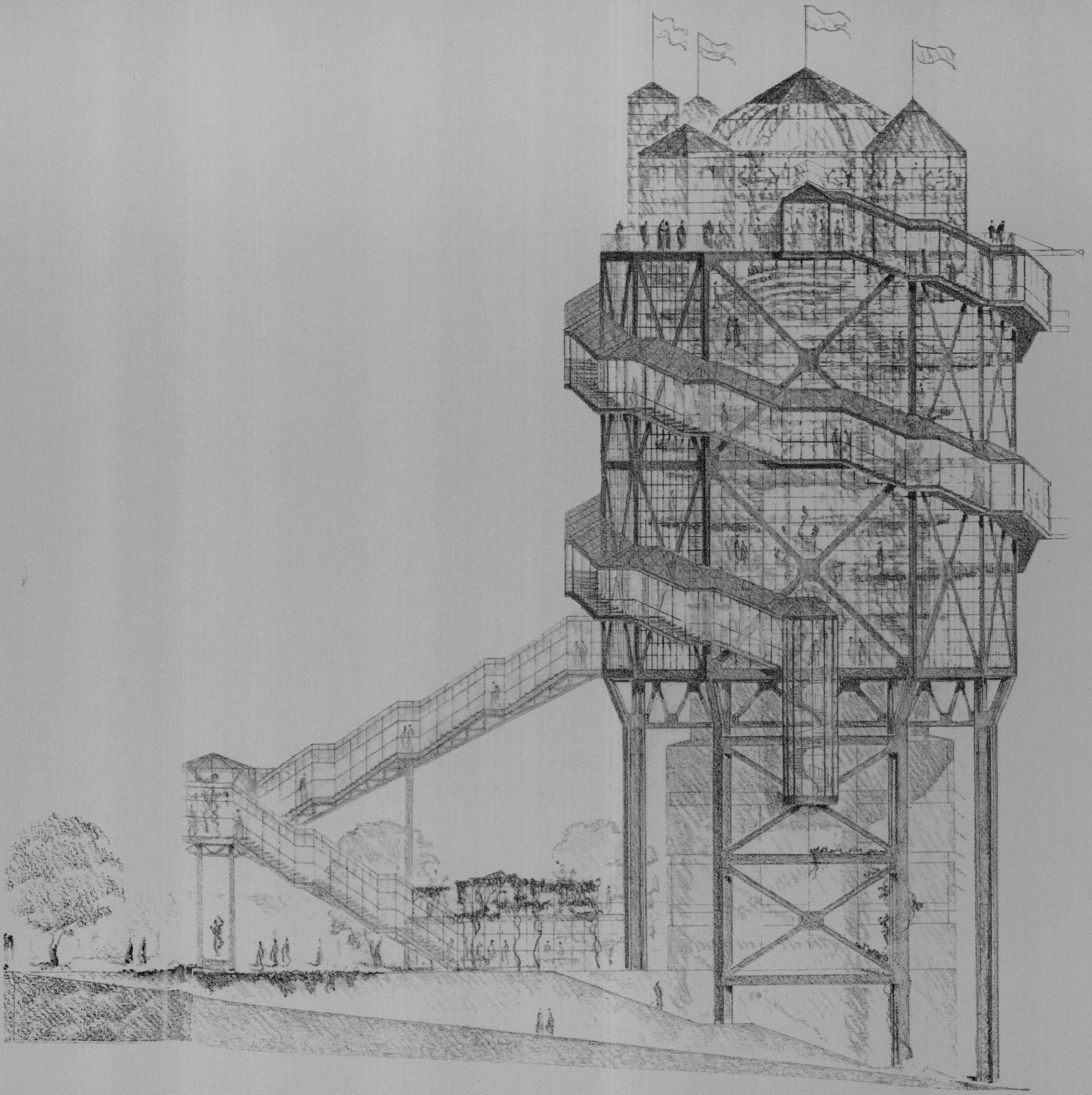

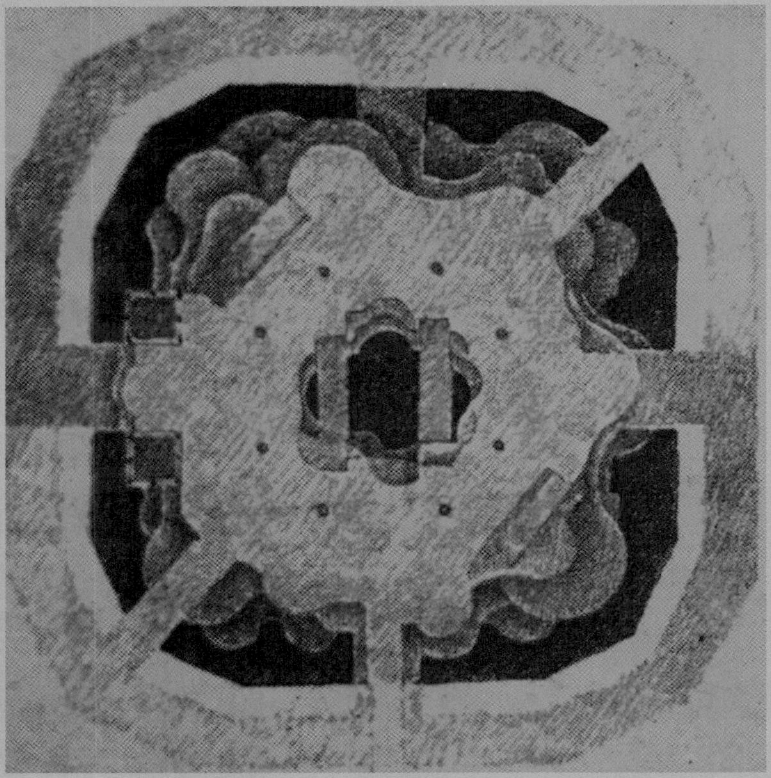

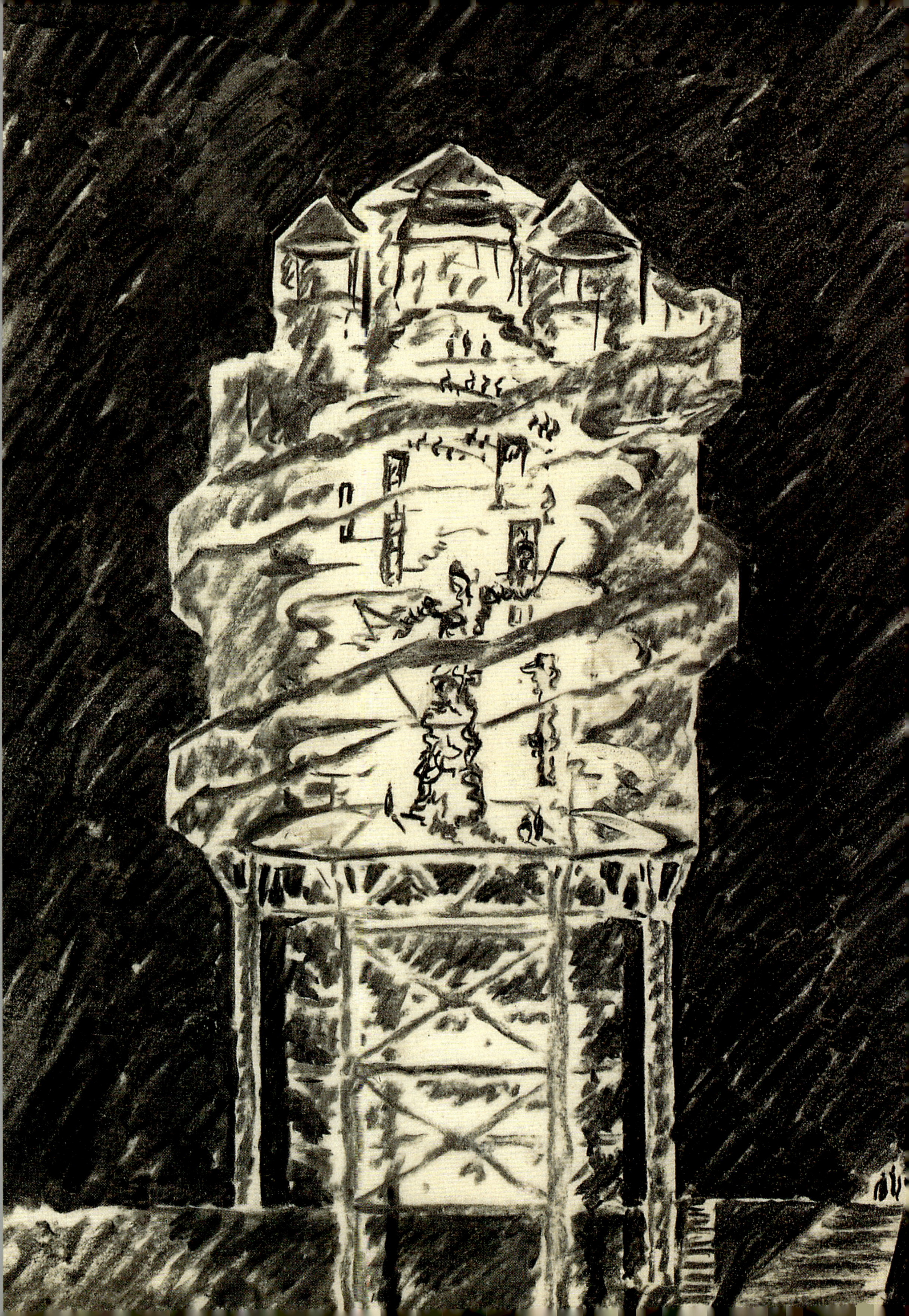

STUTTGART, MUSEUM FÜR MODERNE KUNST
STUTTGART, MUSEUM OF MODERN ART
MIT / WITH FRIEDER STEINIGEWEG
WETTBEWERB / COMPETITION, 1988

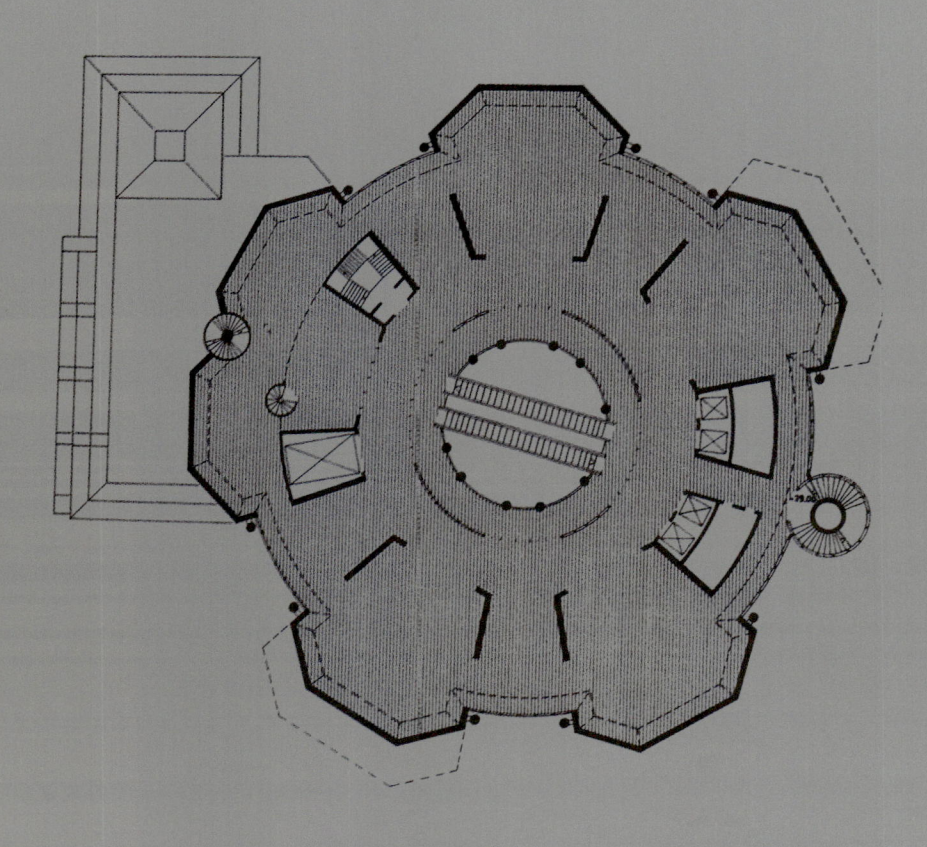

77

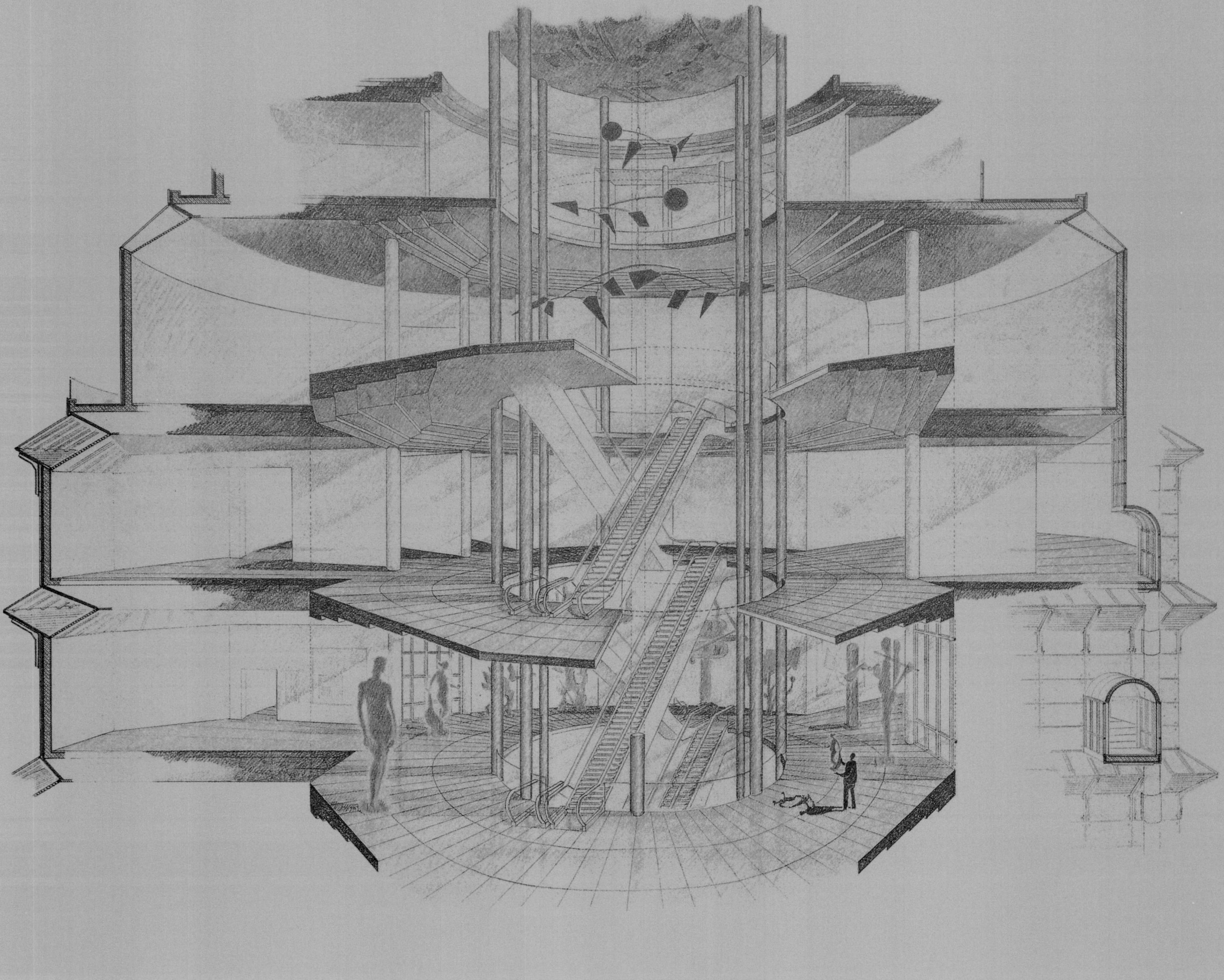

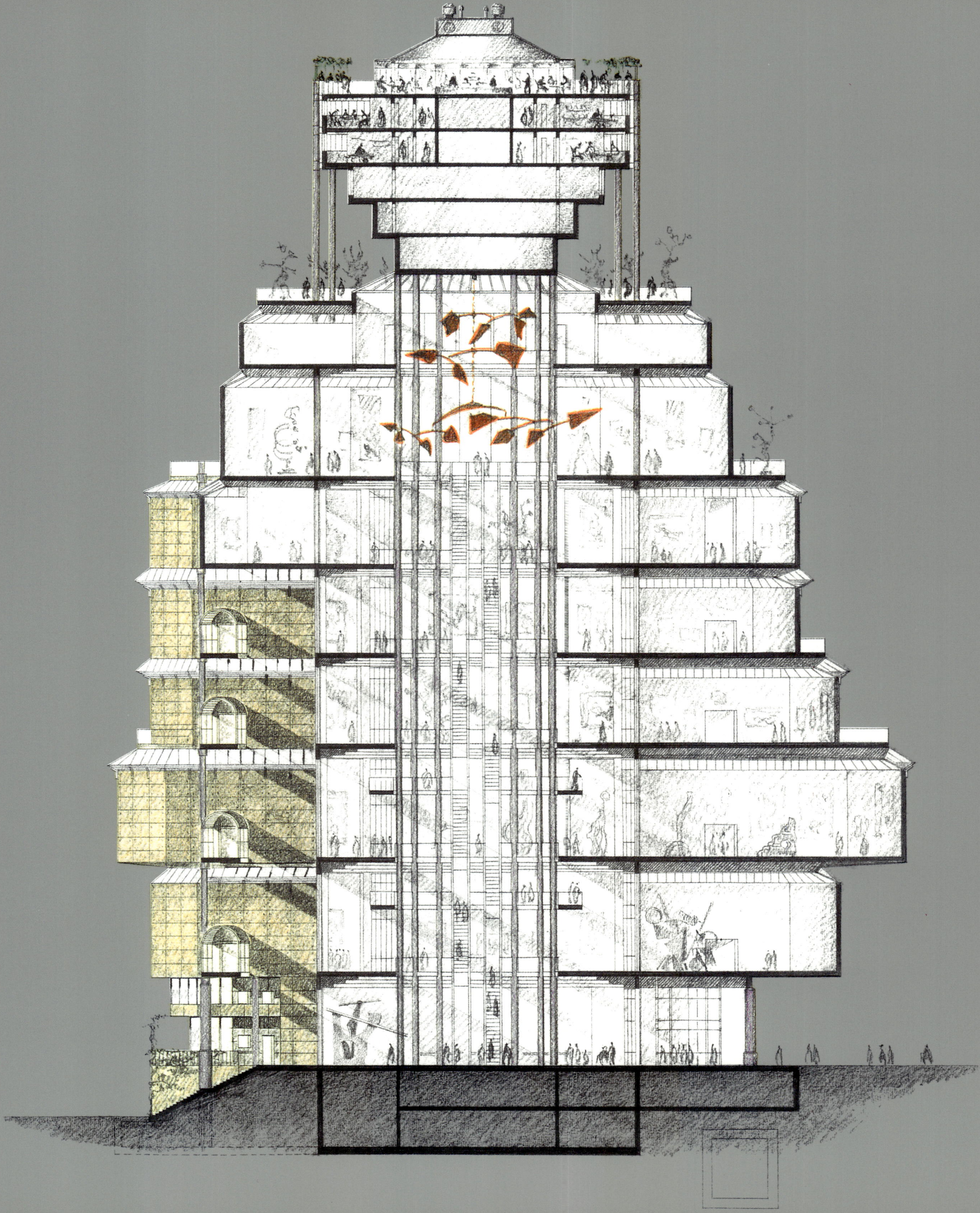

SEVILLA, DEUTSCHER PAVILLON FÜR DIE EXPO 1992
SEVILLE, GERMAN PAVILION FOR EXPO 1992

MIT / WITH FRIEDER STEINIGEWEG

WETTBEWERB / COMPETITION, 1989

80

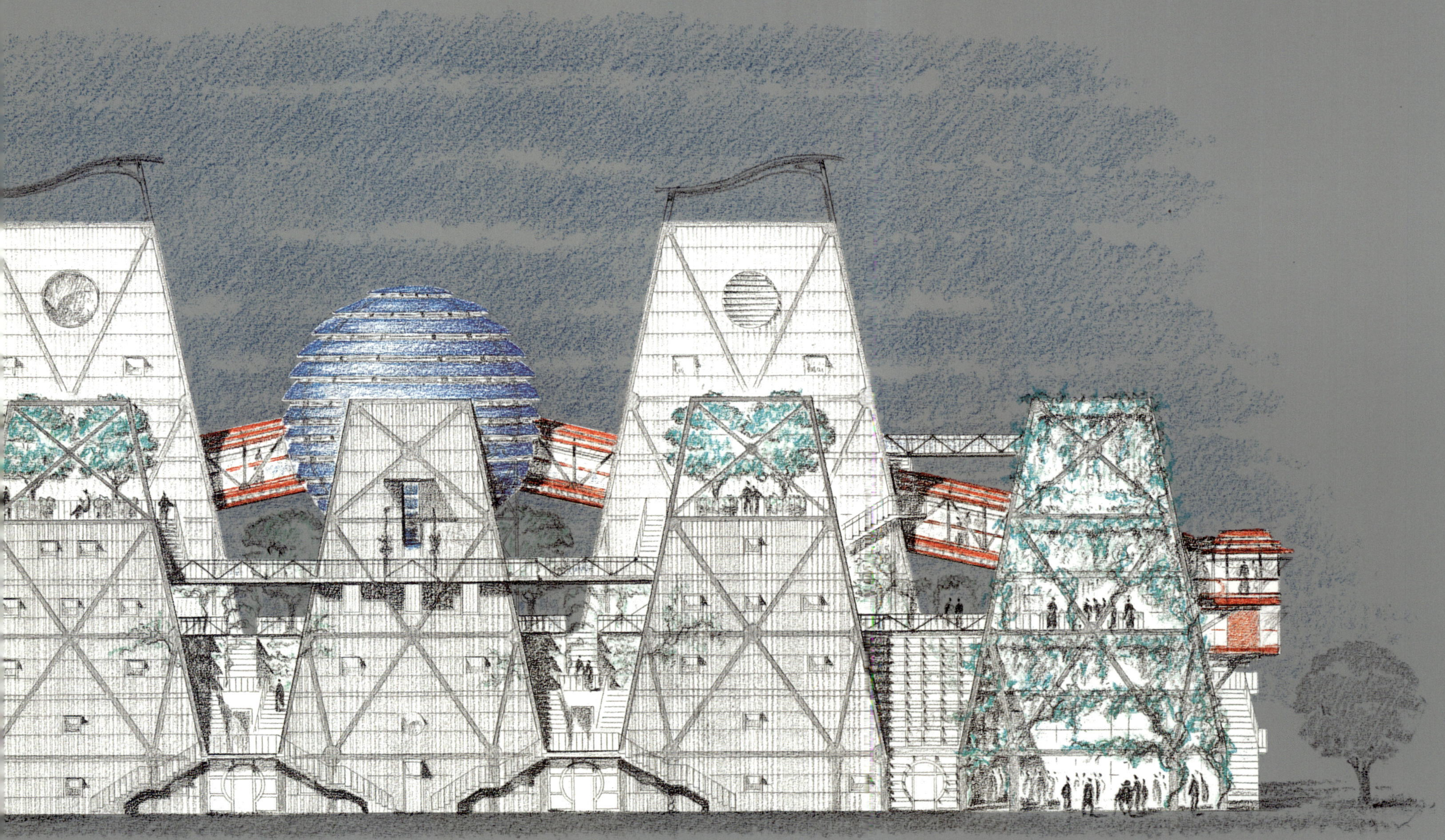

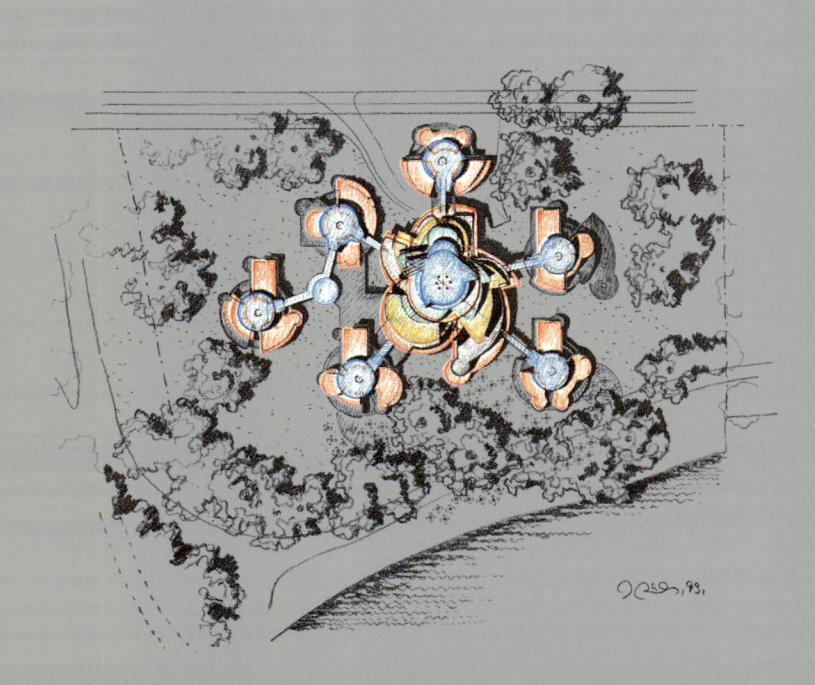

BERLIN-TREPTOW, HOTEL AN DER SPREE
BERLIN-TREPTOW, HOTEL BY THE SPREE

PROJEKT / PROJECT, 1993

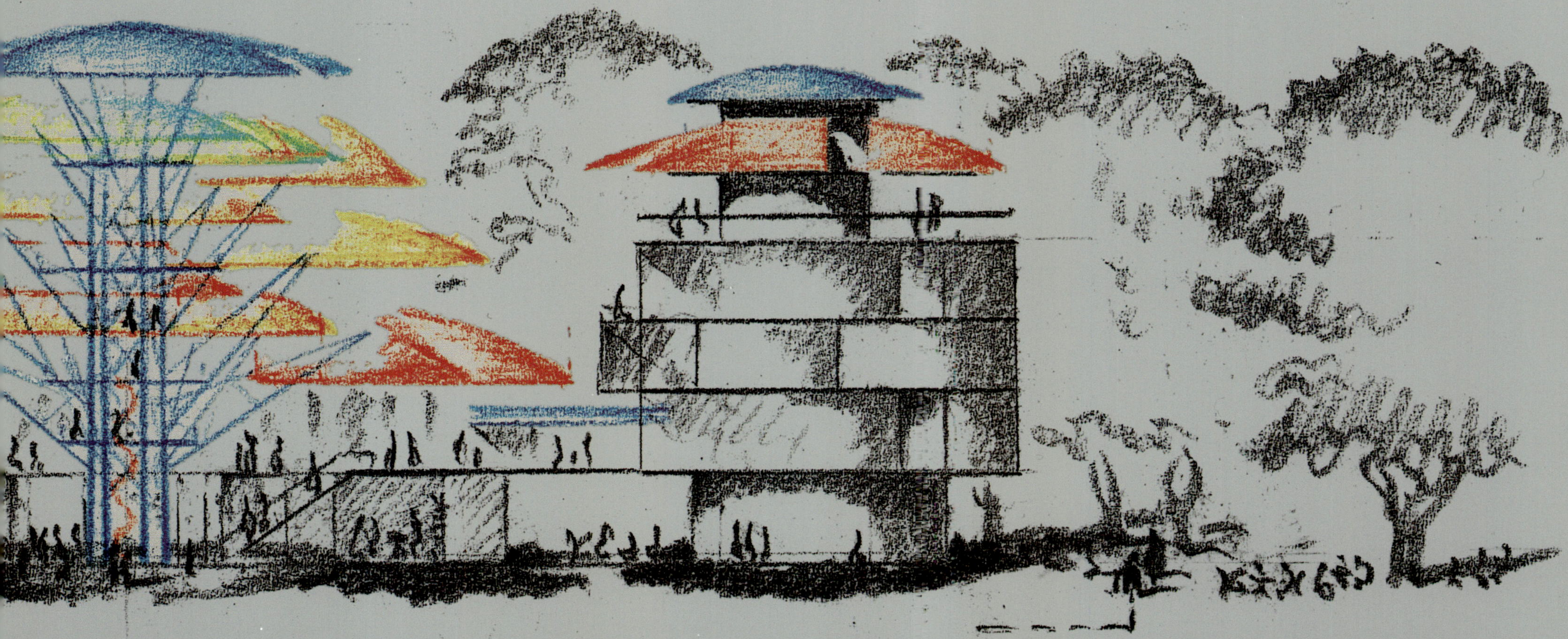

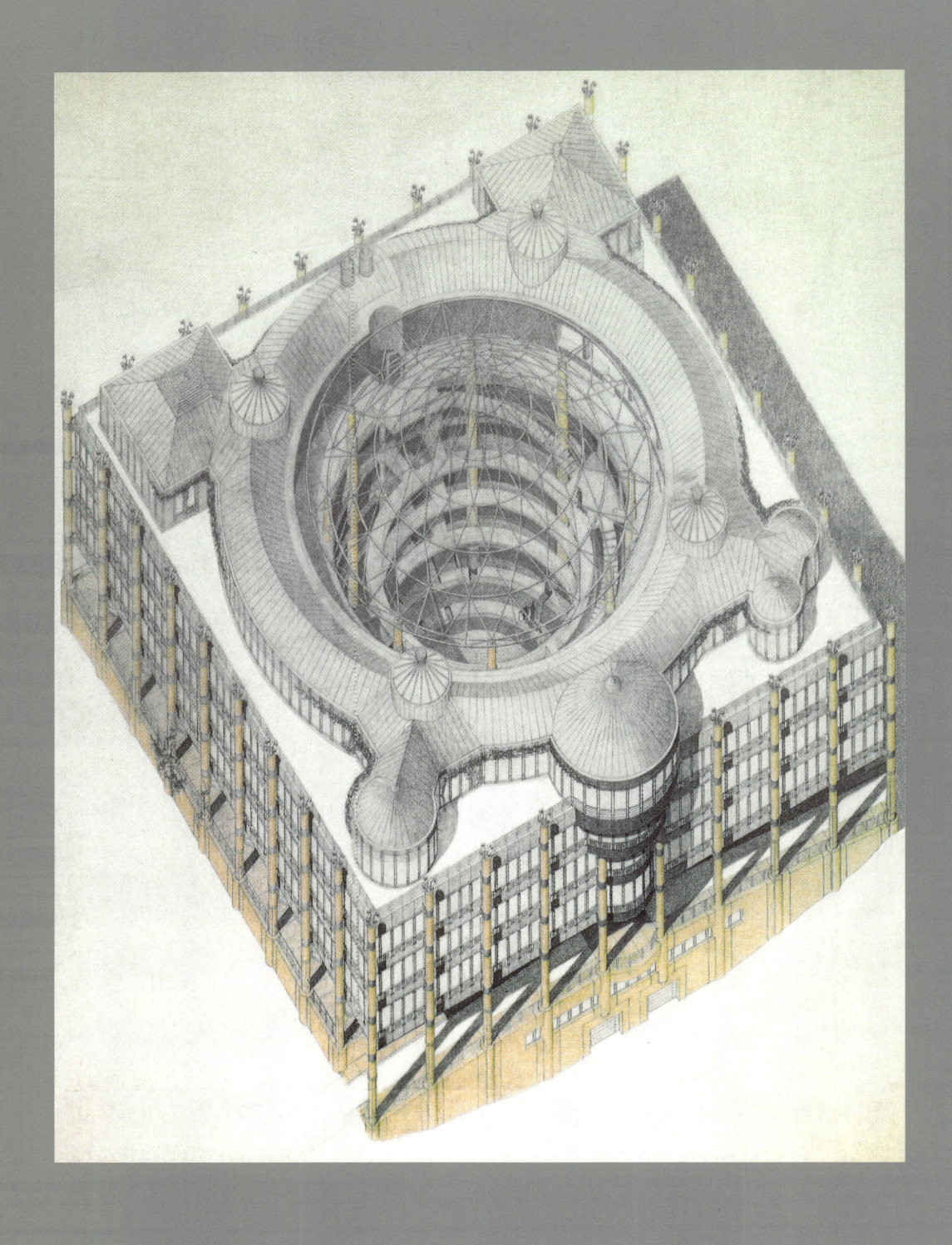

LUXEMBURG, DEUTSCHE BANK
LUXEMBOURG, DEUTSCHE BANK
MIT / WITH JÜRGEN MINKUS
1988

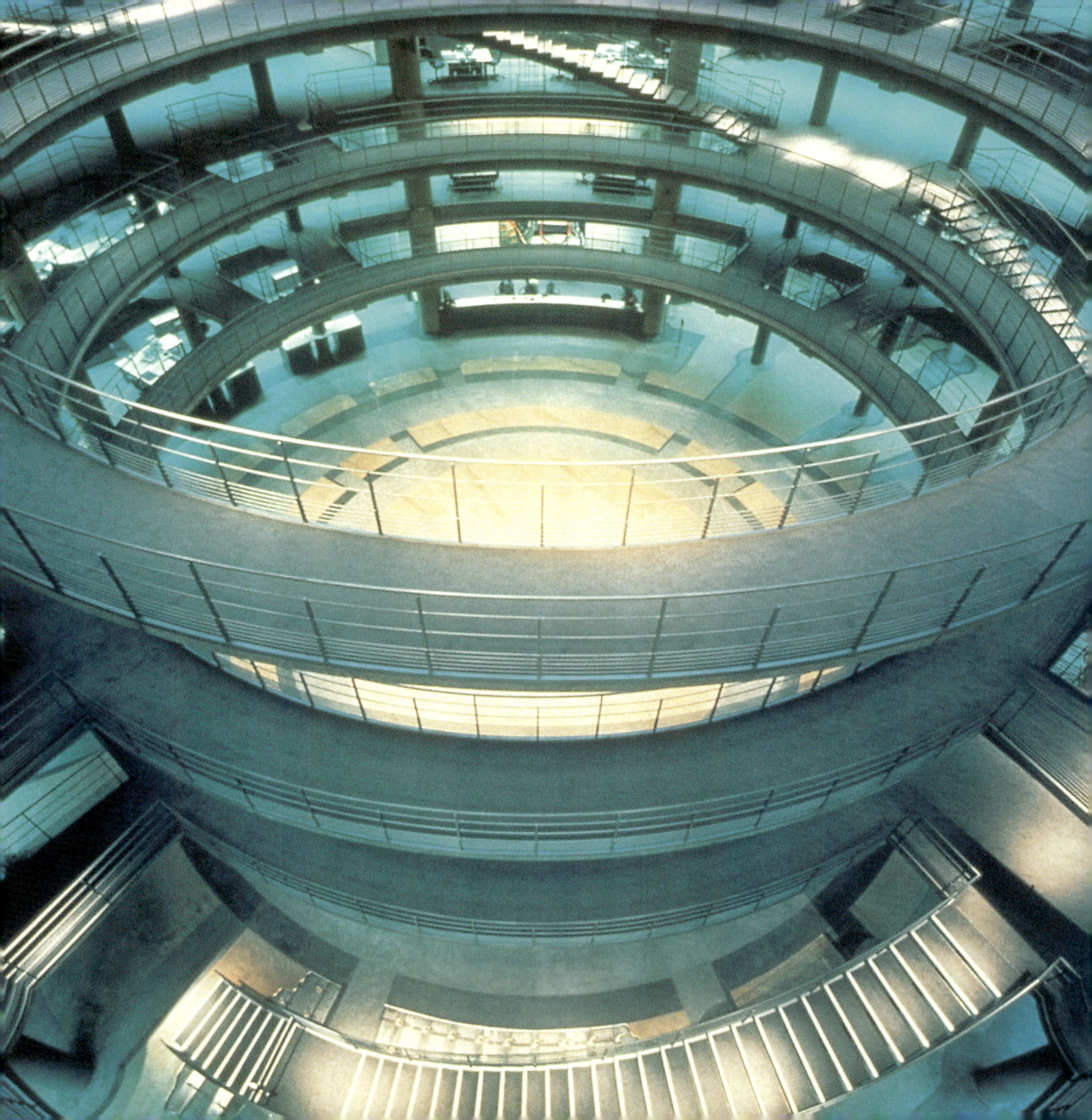

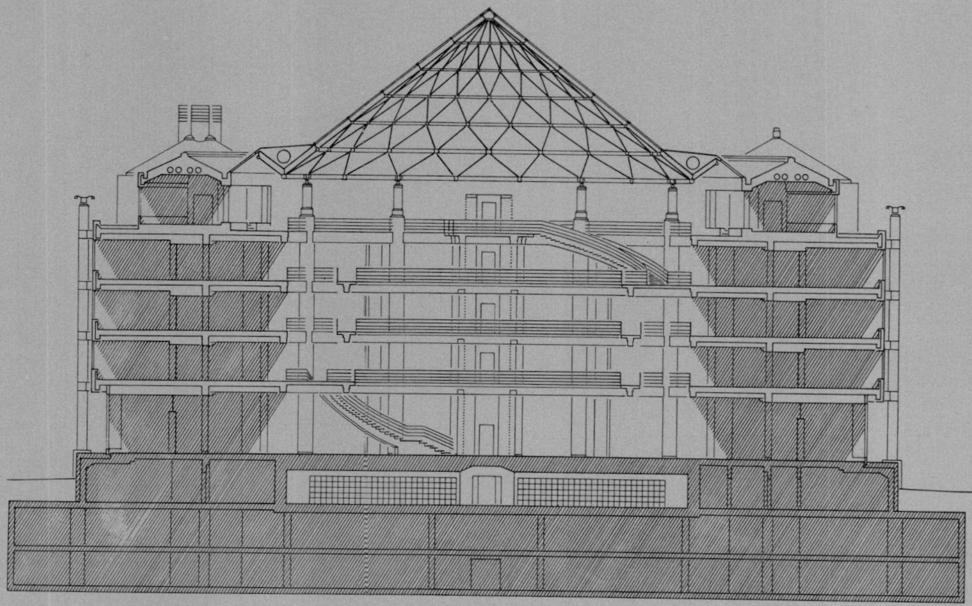

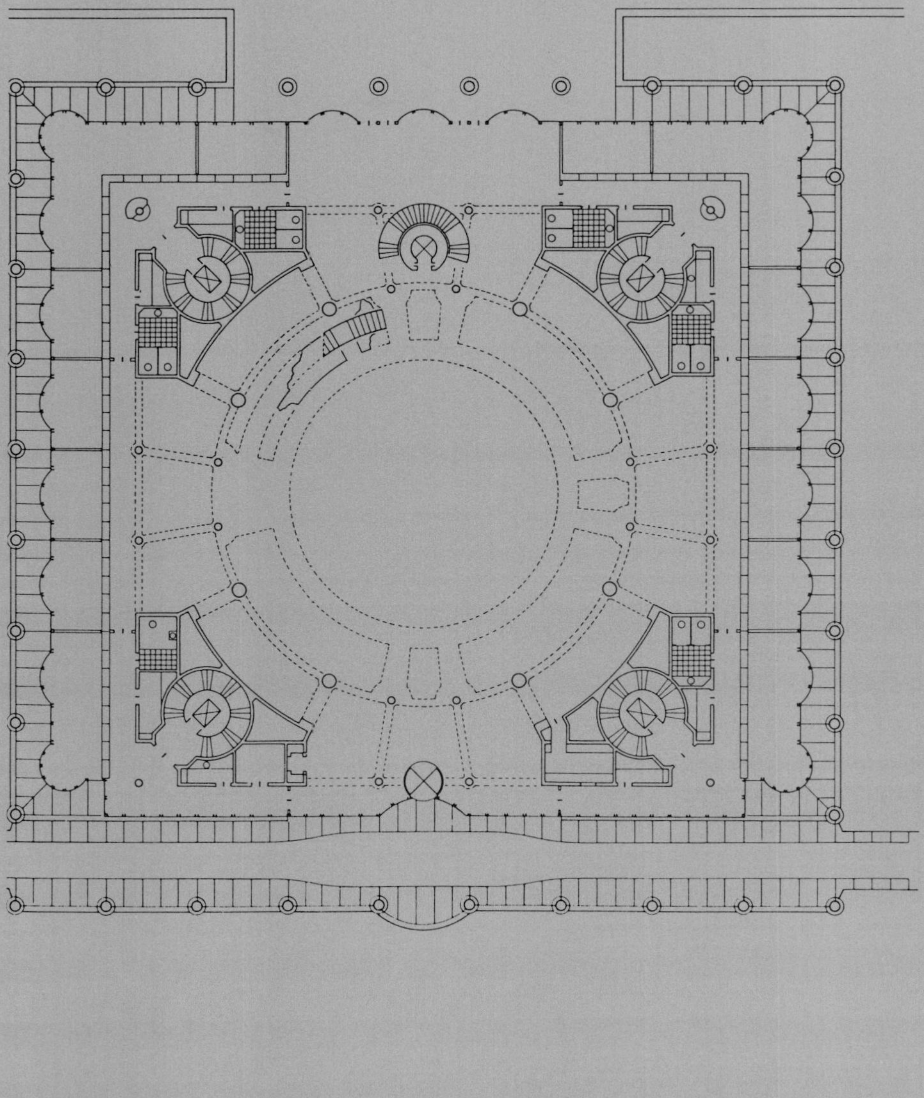

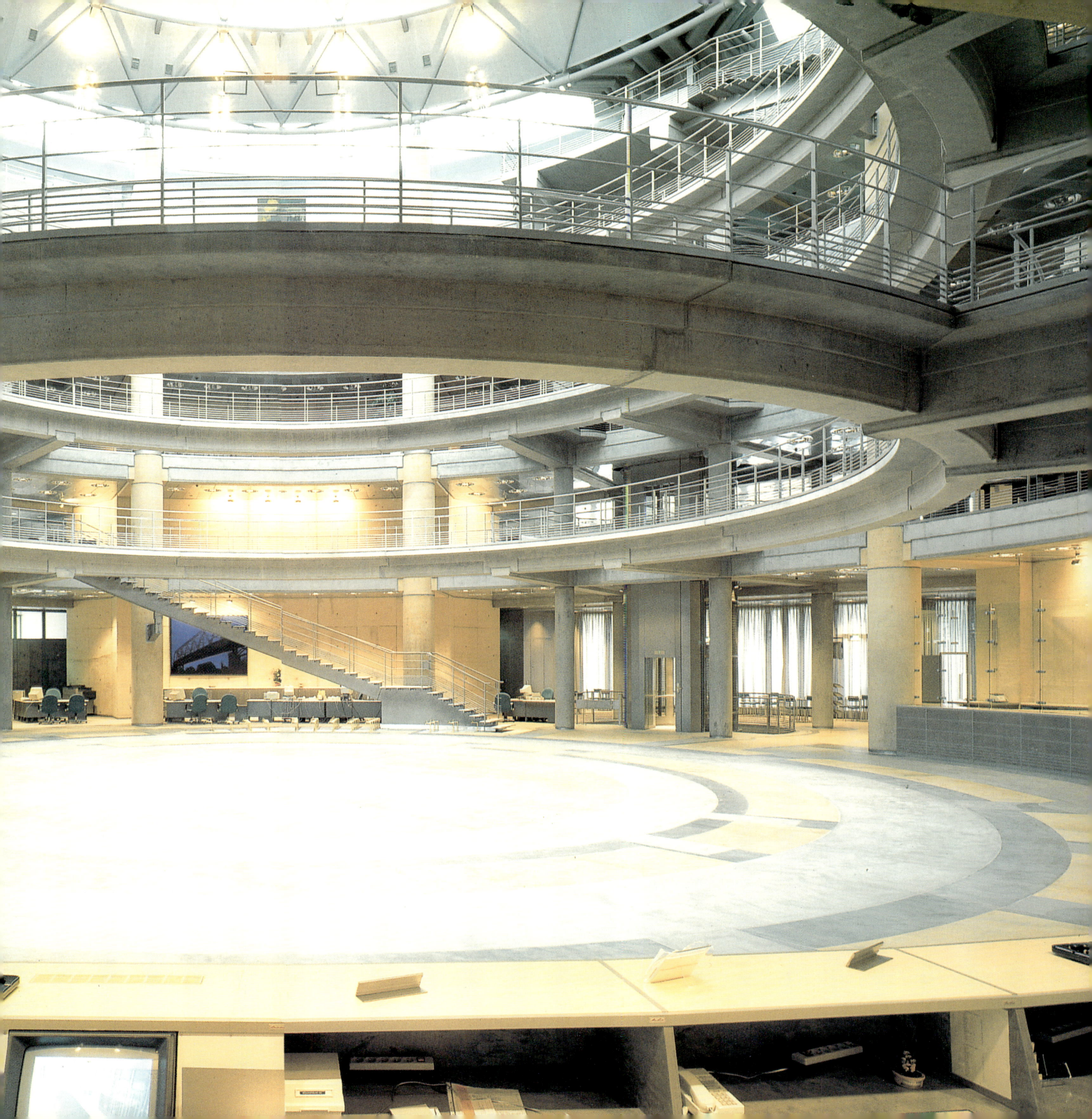

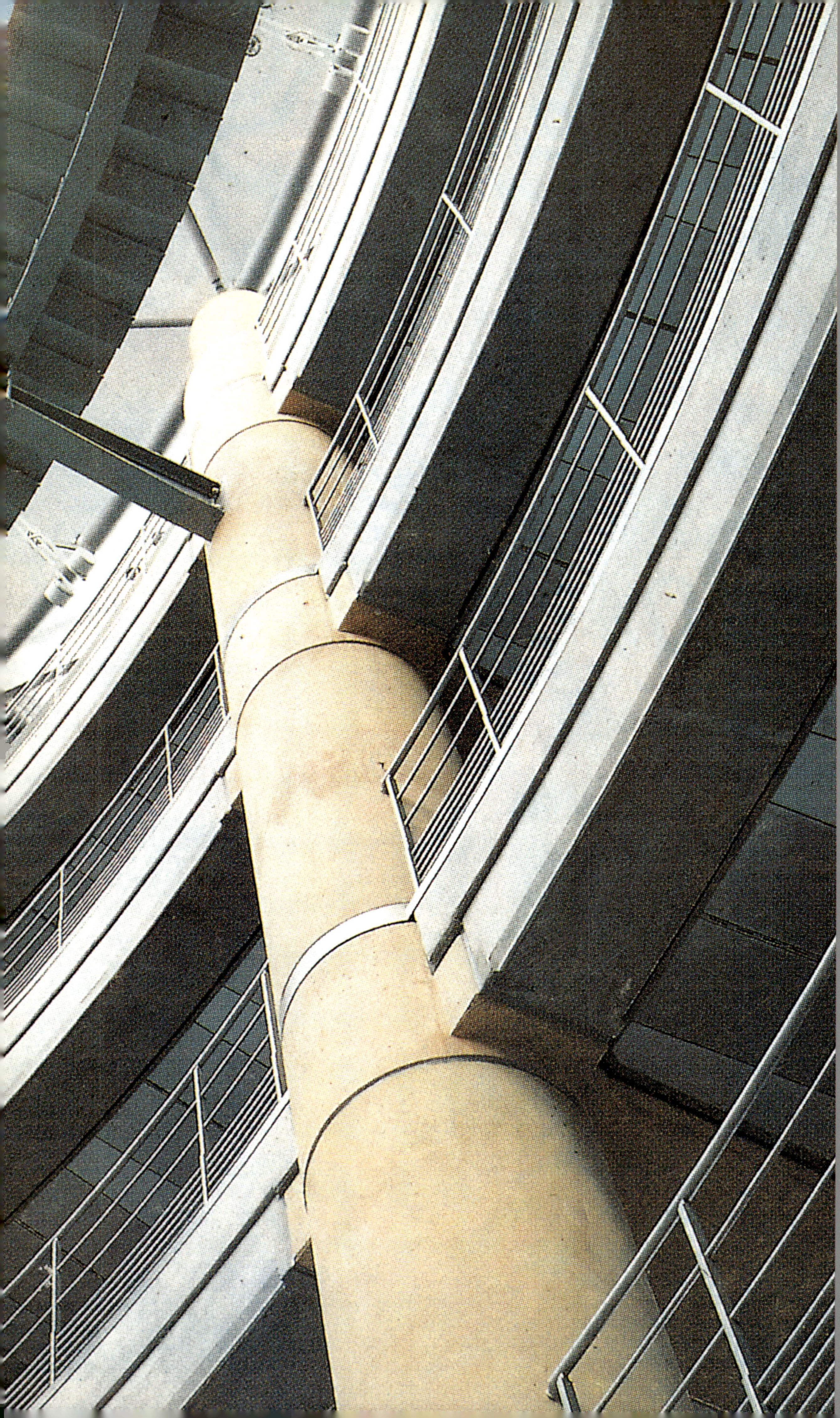

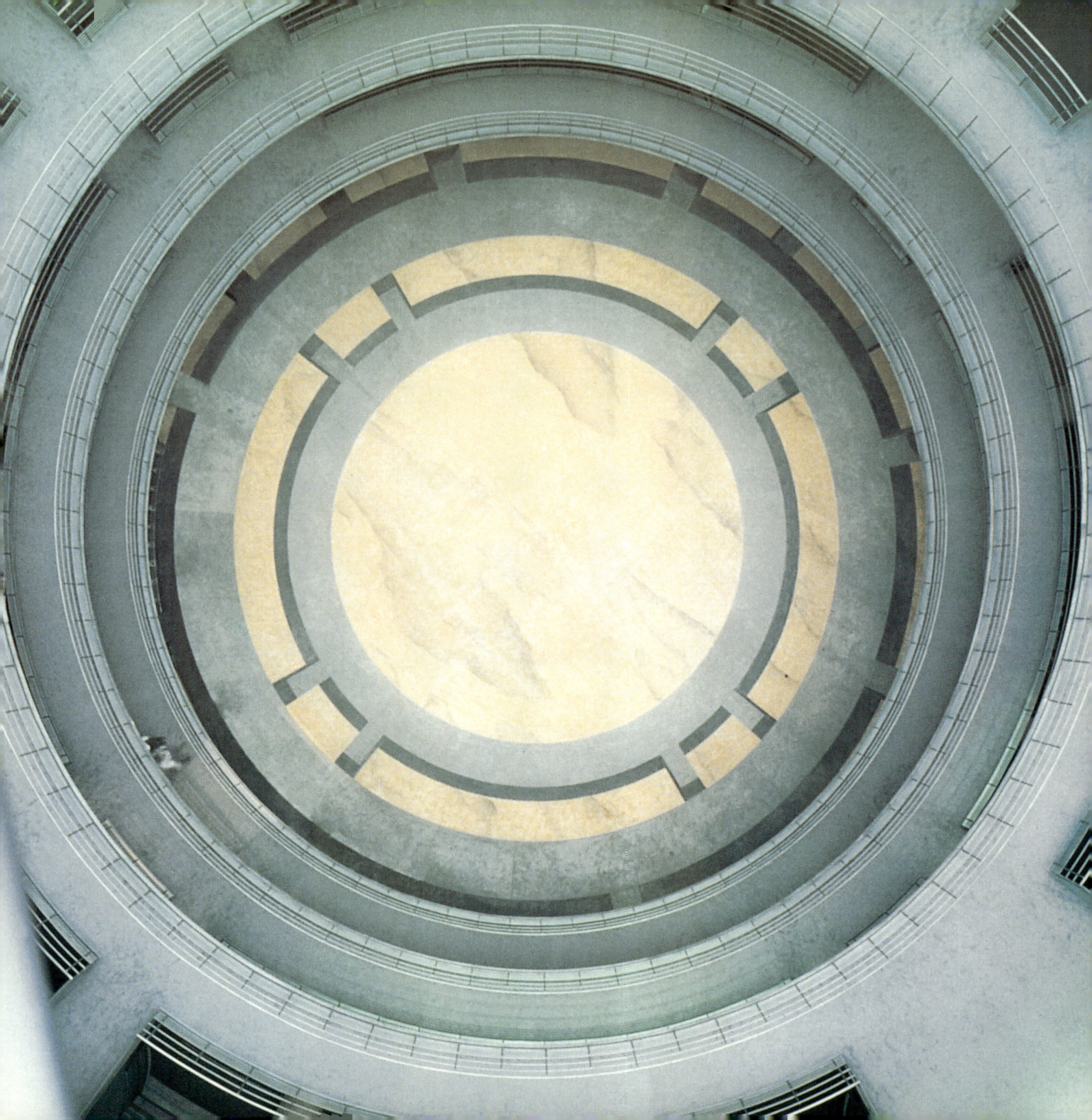

LUXEMBURG-ESCH, ARBED S. A. HAUPTVERWALTUNG
LUXEMBOURG-ESCH, ADMINISTRATIVE HEADQUARTERS OF ARBED S. A.

MIT / WITH JÜRGEN MINKUS

1994

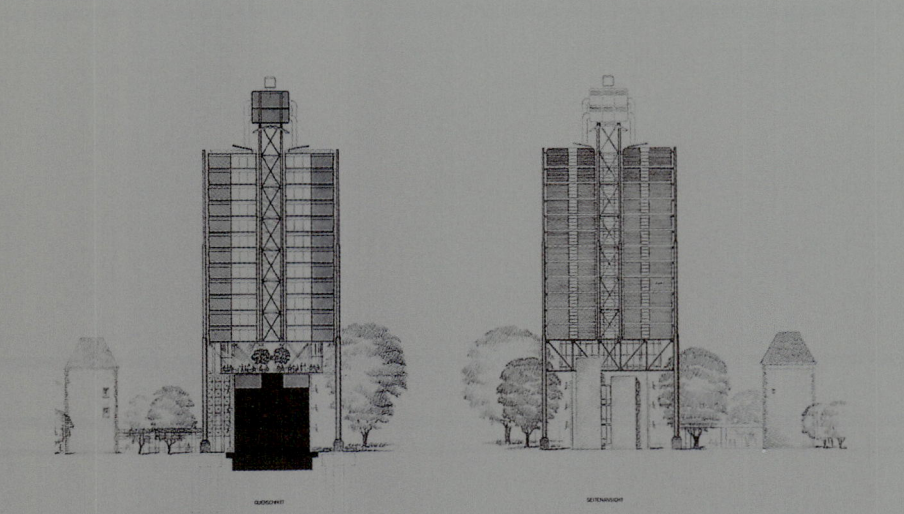

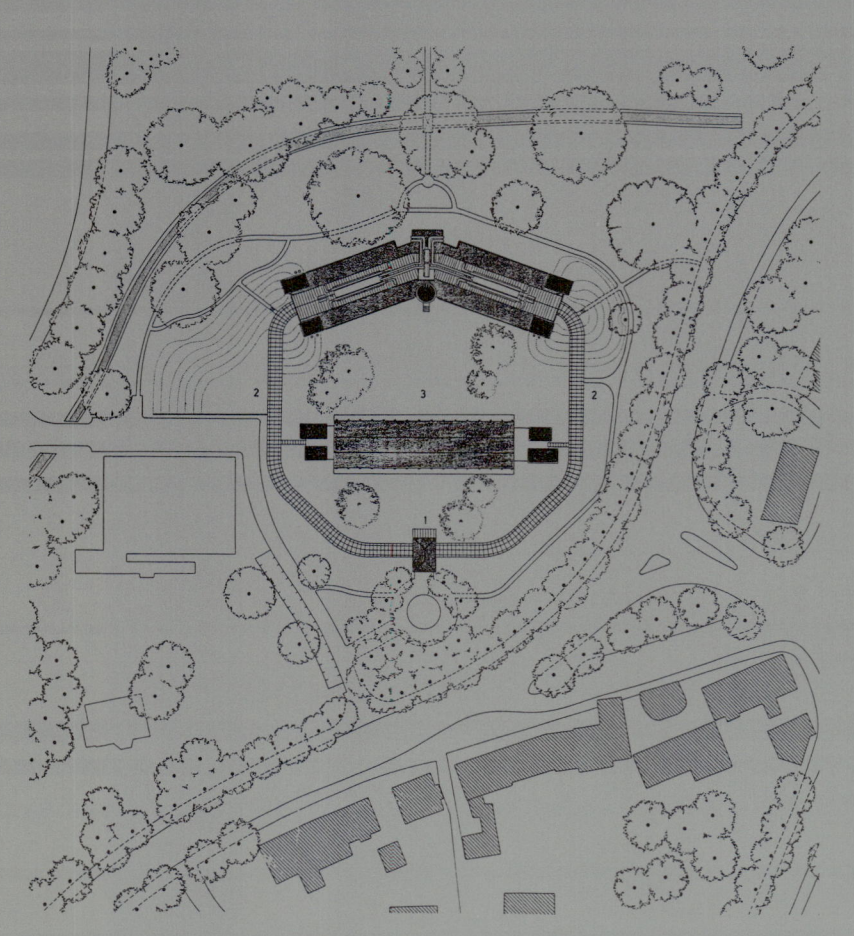

ERHALTUNG UND INTEGRATION
ALTEN BAUBESTANDS

RETENTION AND INCLUSION OF
THE BUILDING'S HISTORIC
STRUCTURES

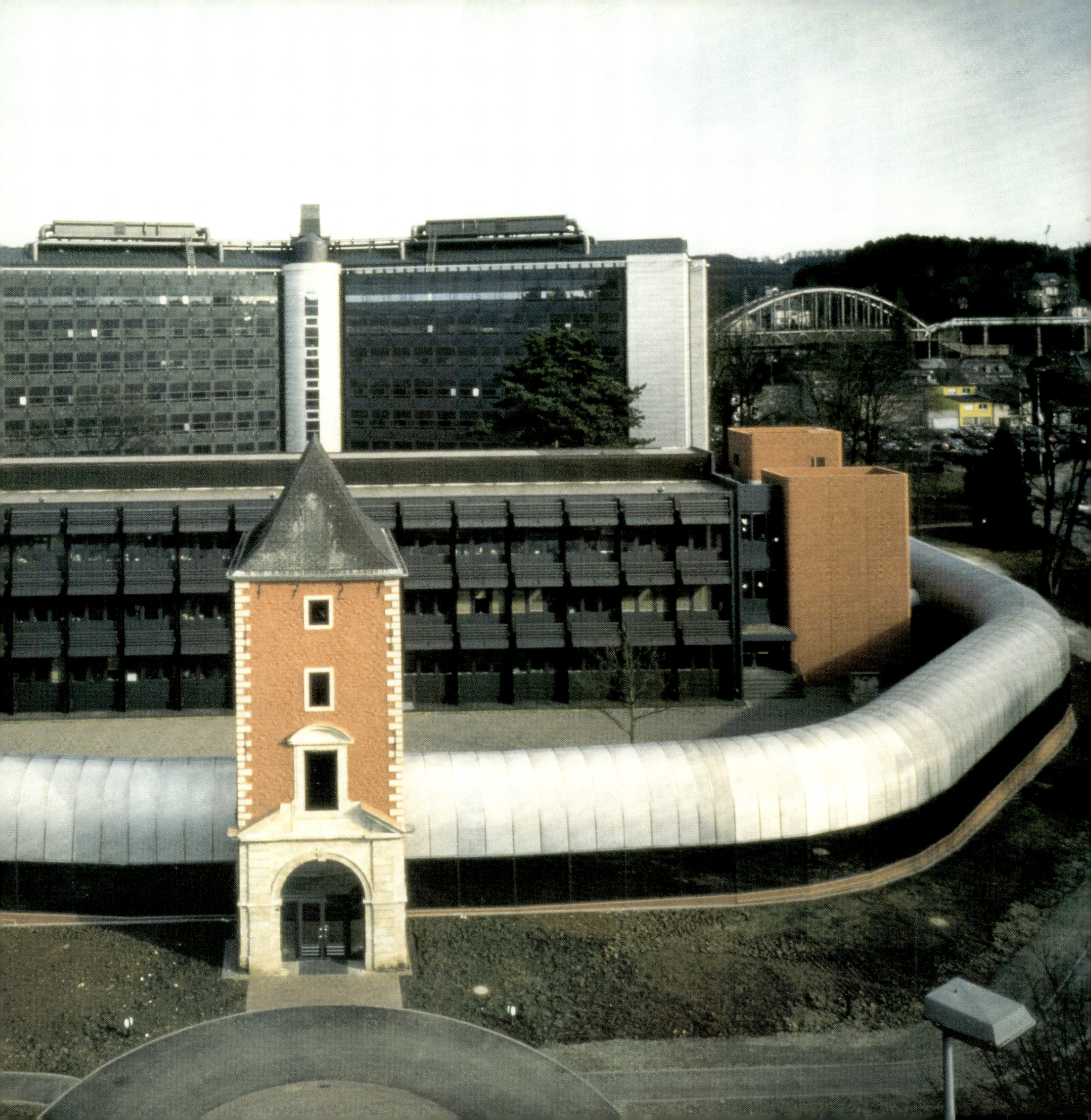

VERBINDUNGSGANG MIT
AUSSTELLUNG

COVERED CORRIDOR SERVING
AS AN EXHIBITION AREA

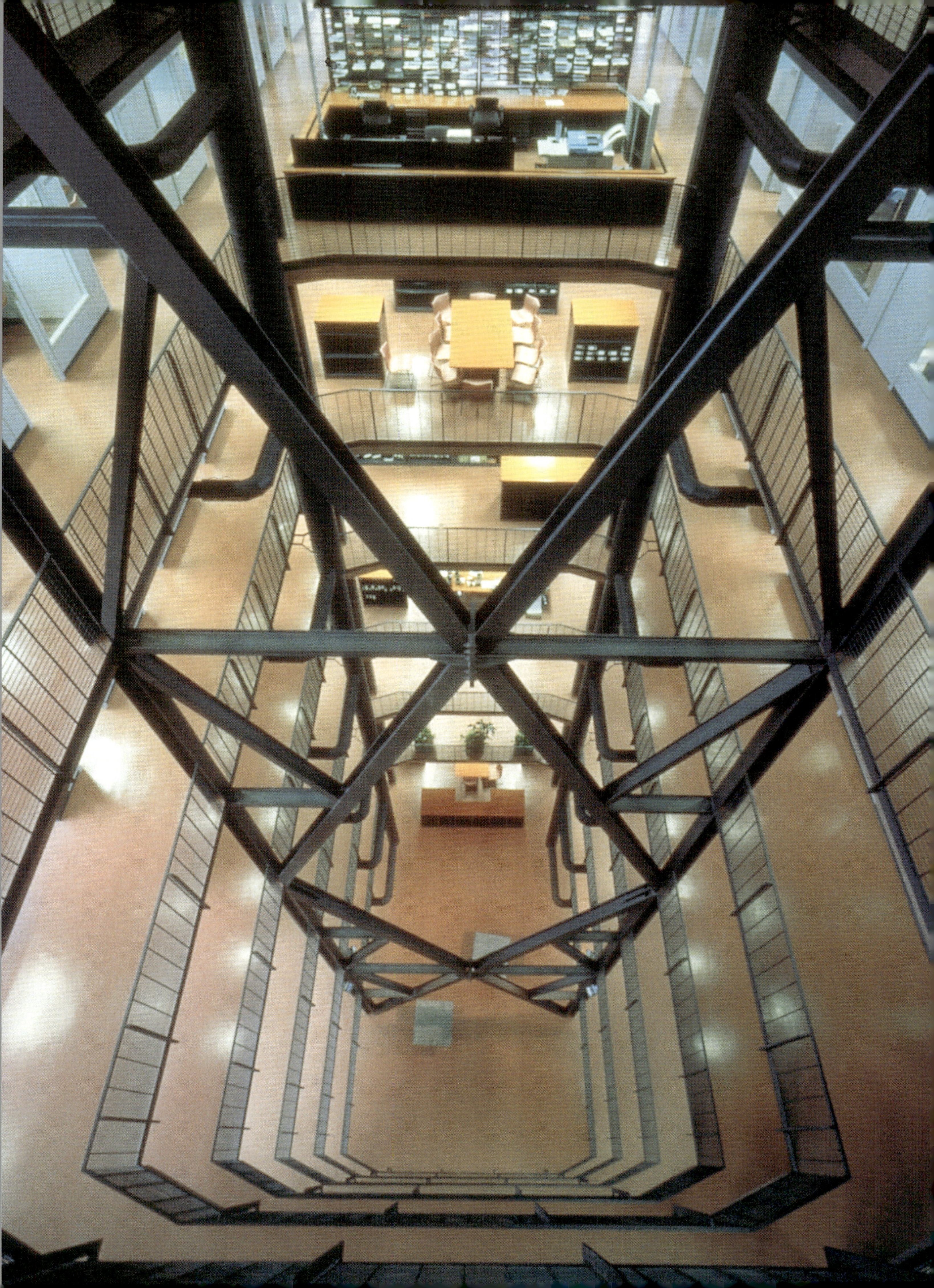

MANNHEIM, UNIVERSITÄTSBIBLIOTHEK UND AUDITORIUM
MANNHEIM, UNIVERSITY LIBRARY AND AUDITORIUM

MIT / WITH JÜRGEN MINKUS

1987

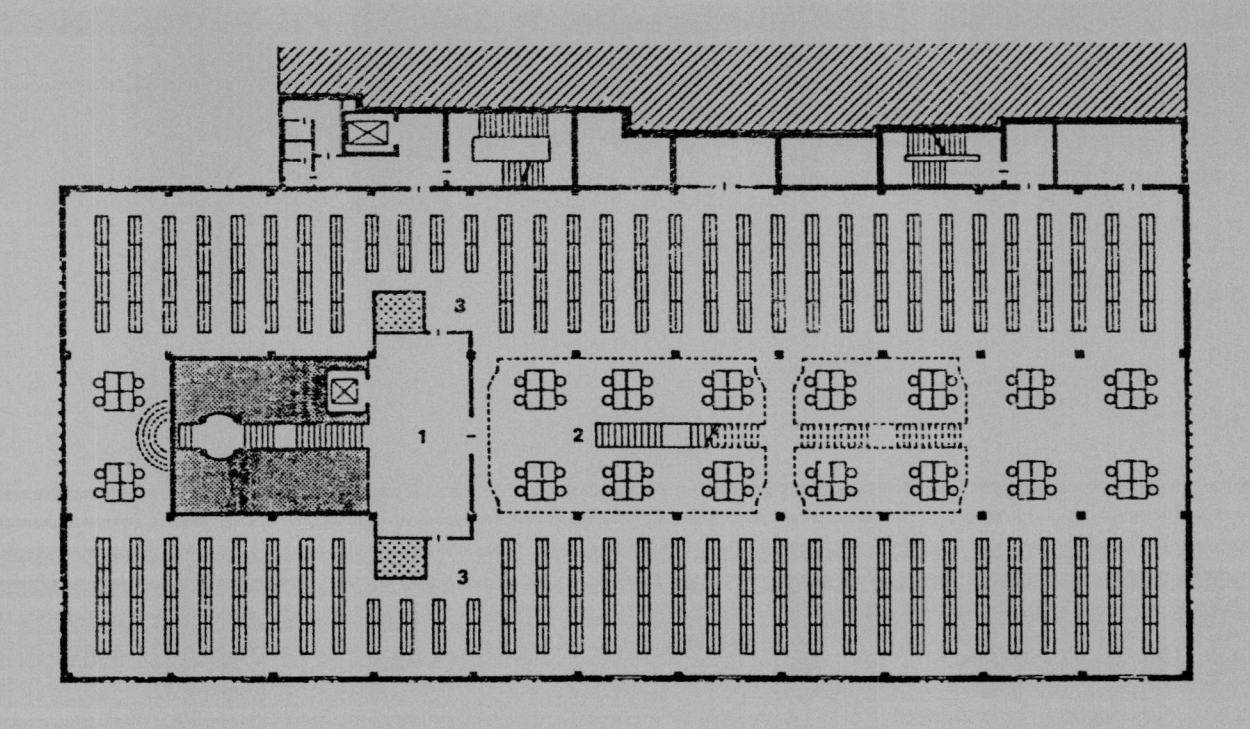

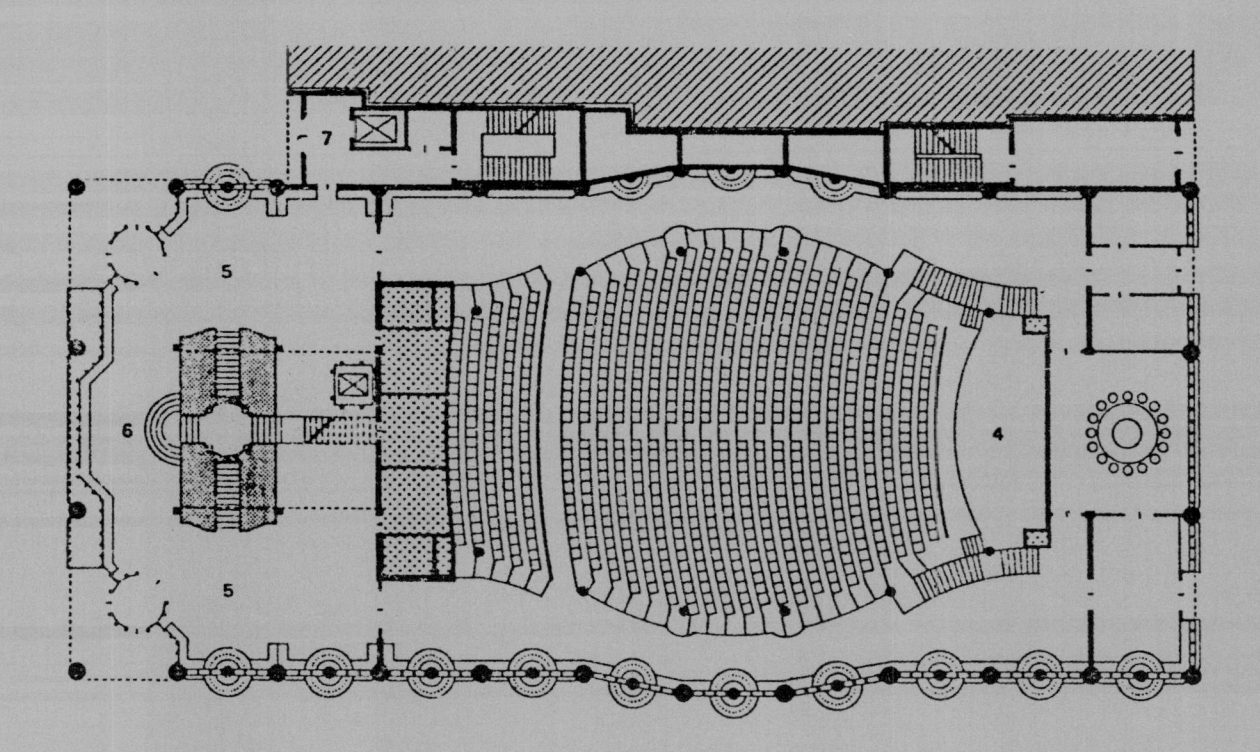

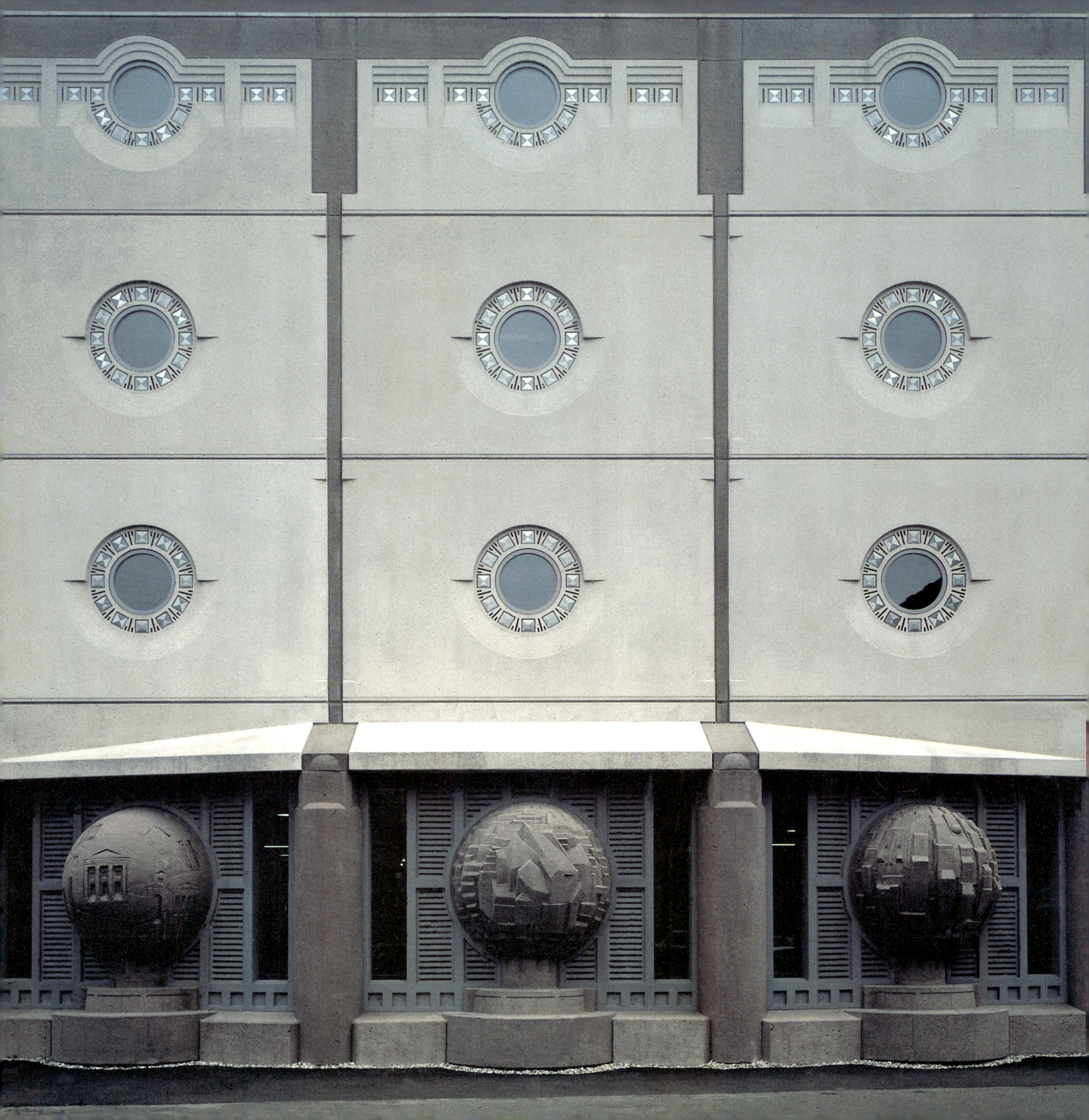

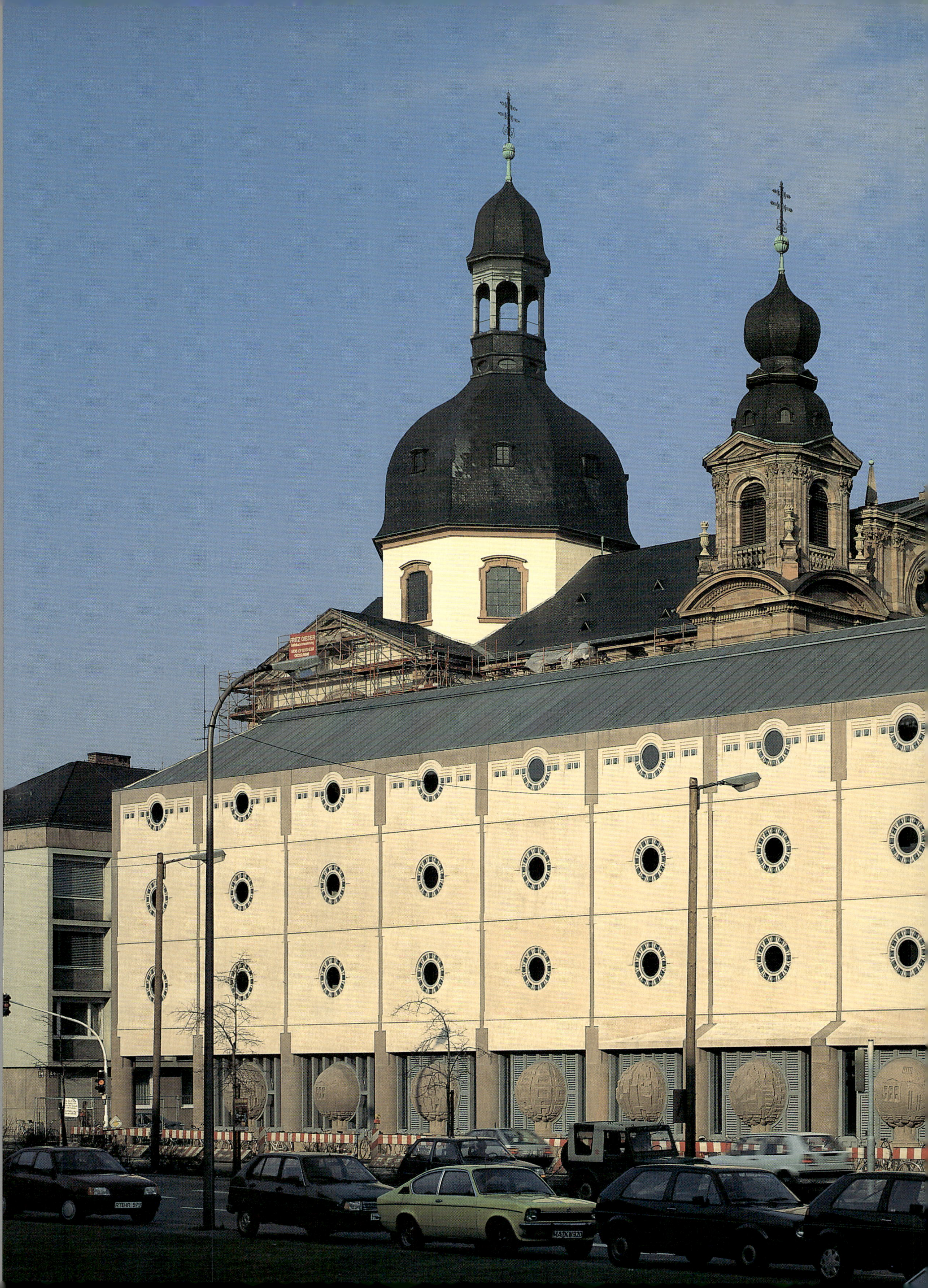

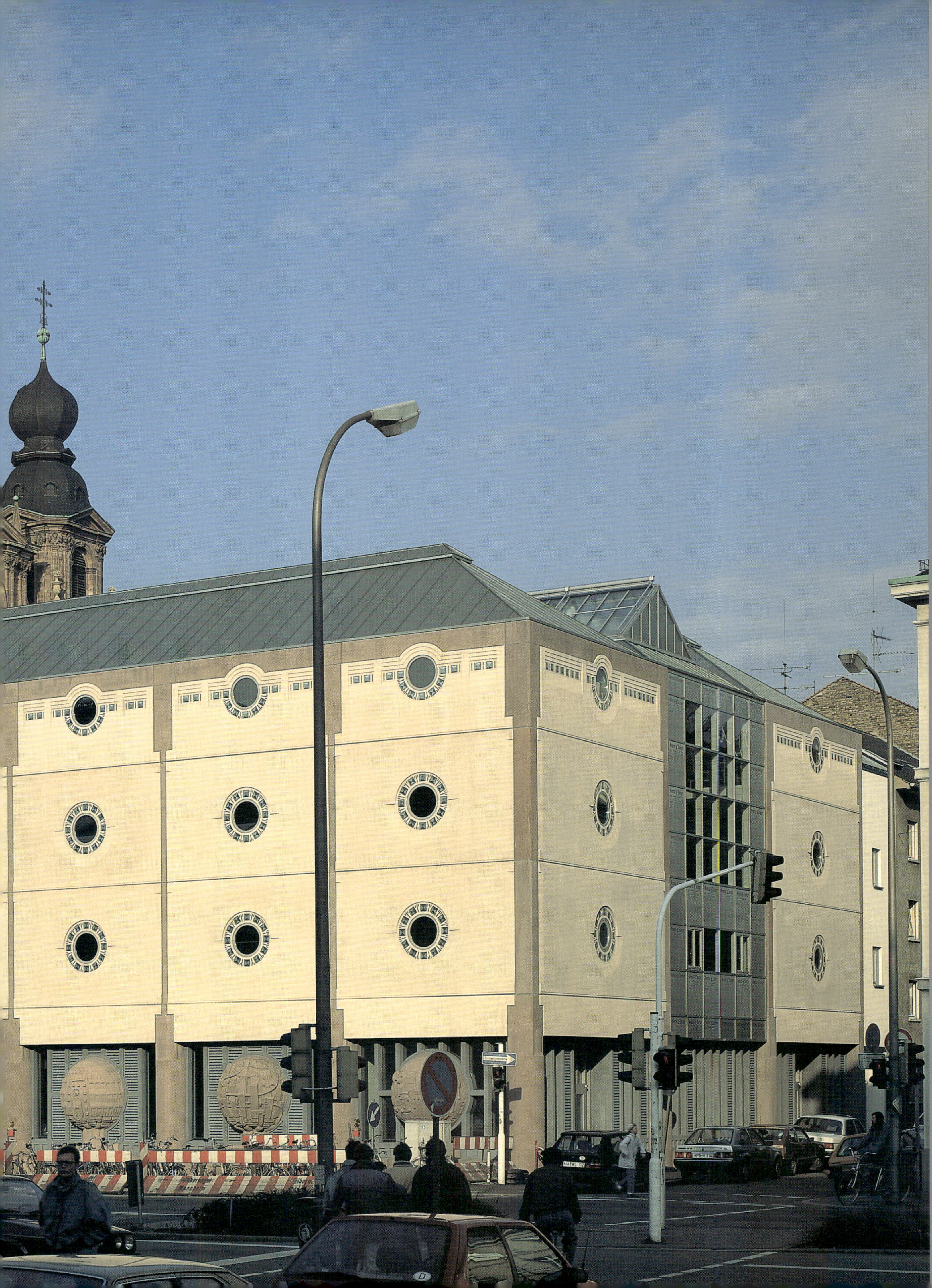

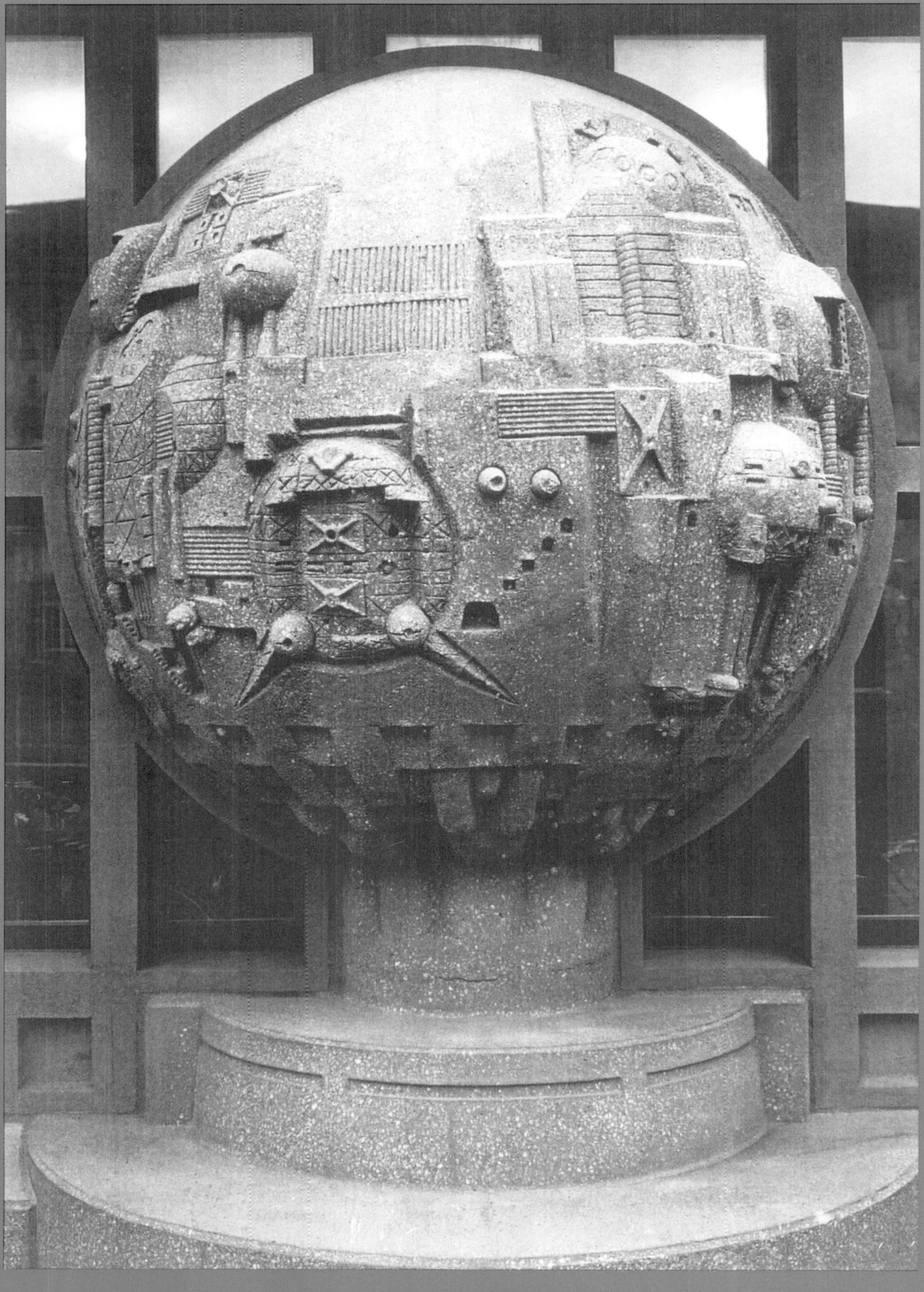

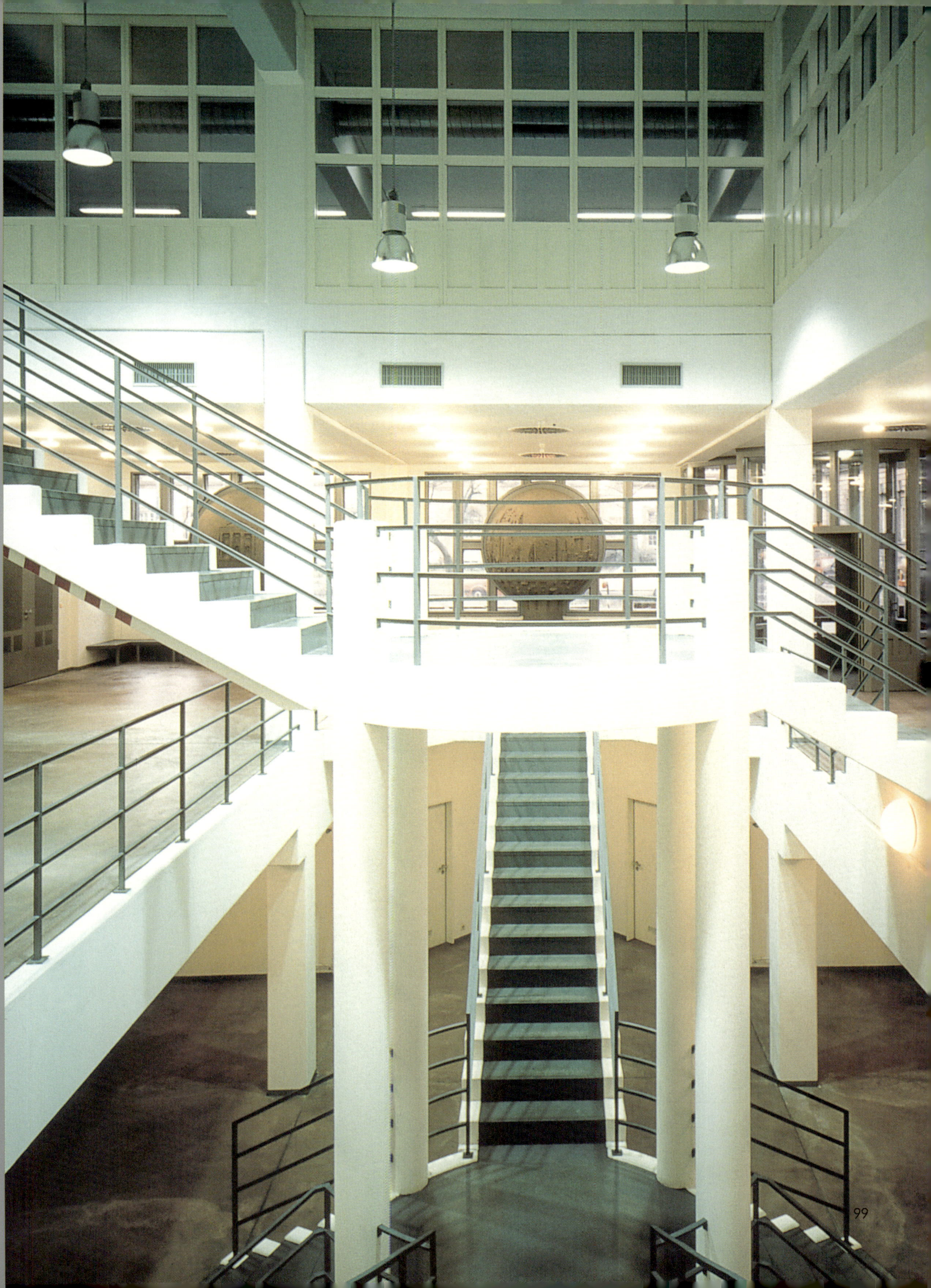

ULM, STADTBIBLIOTHEK
ULM, CITY LIBRARY
MIT / WITH SEVERIN HEIERMANN
PROJEKT / PROJECT, 1999–2000

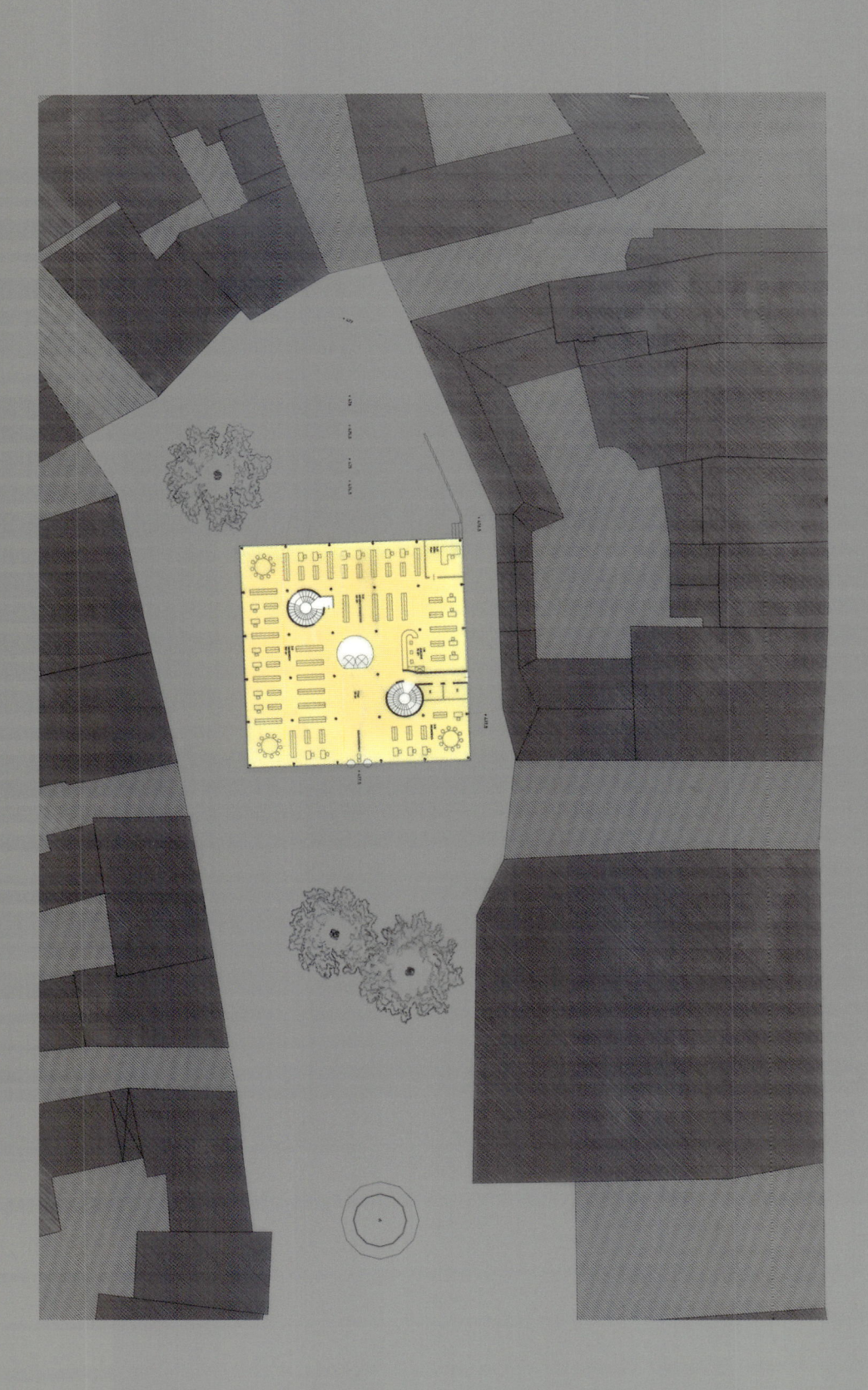

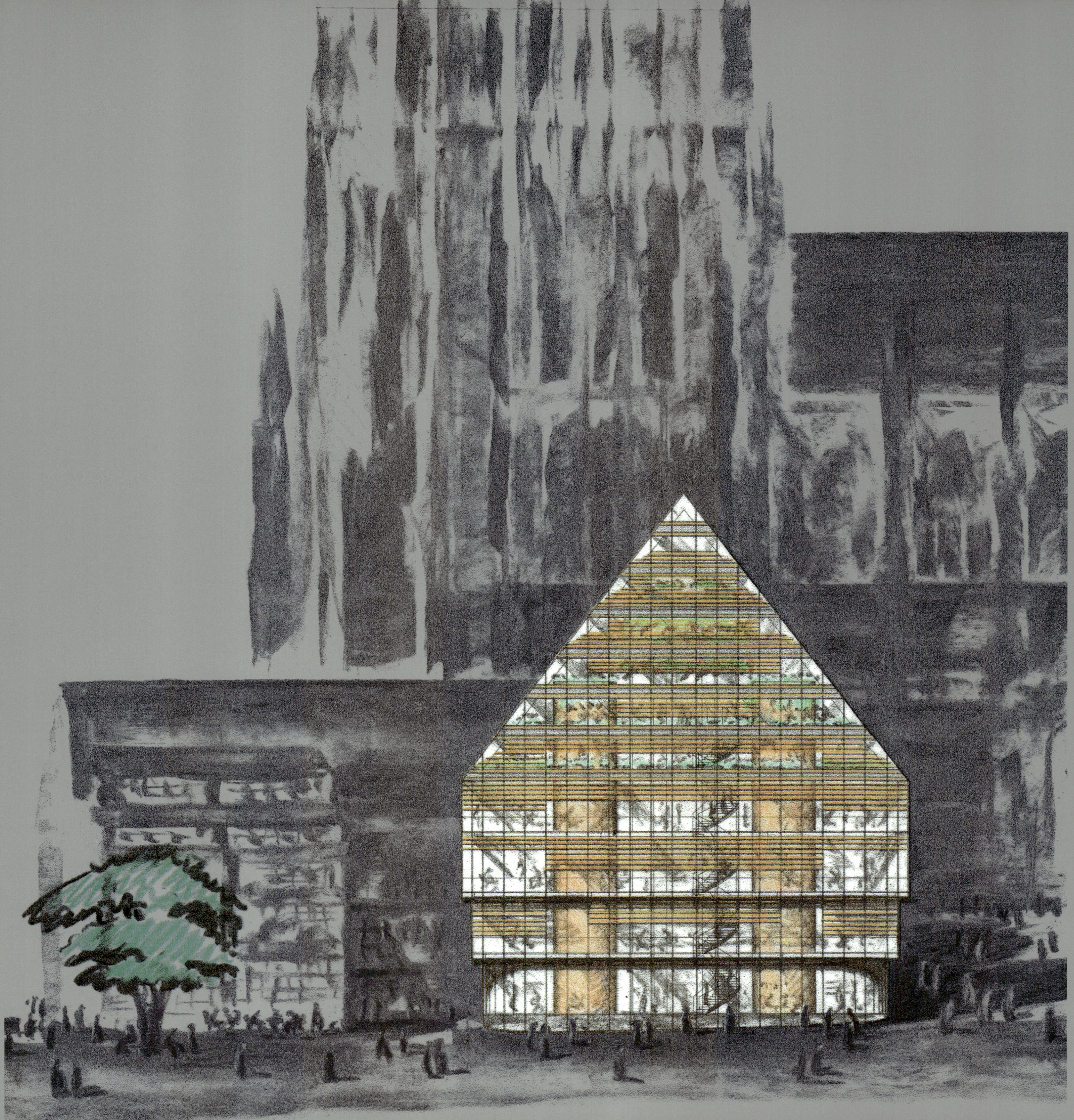

102

103

BERLIN, KAUFHAUS PEEK & CLOPPENBURG
BERLIN, PEEK & CLOPPENBURG DEPARTMENT STORE
MIT / WITH JÜRGEN MINKUS
1993

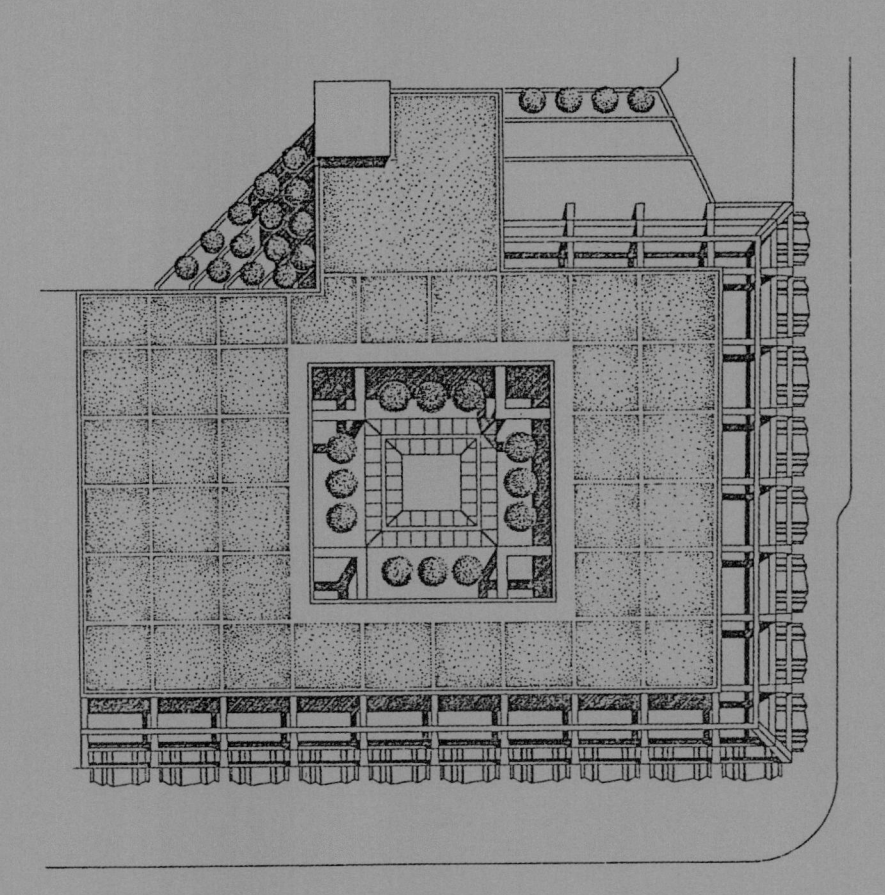

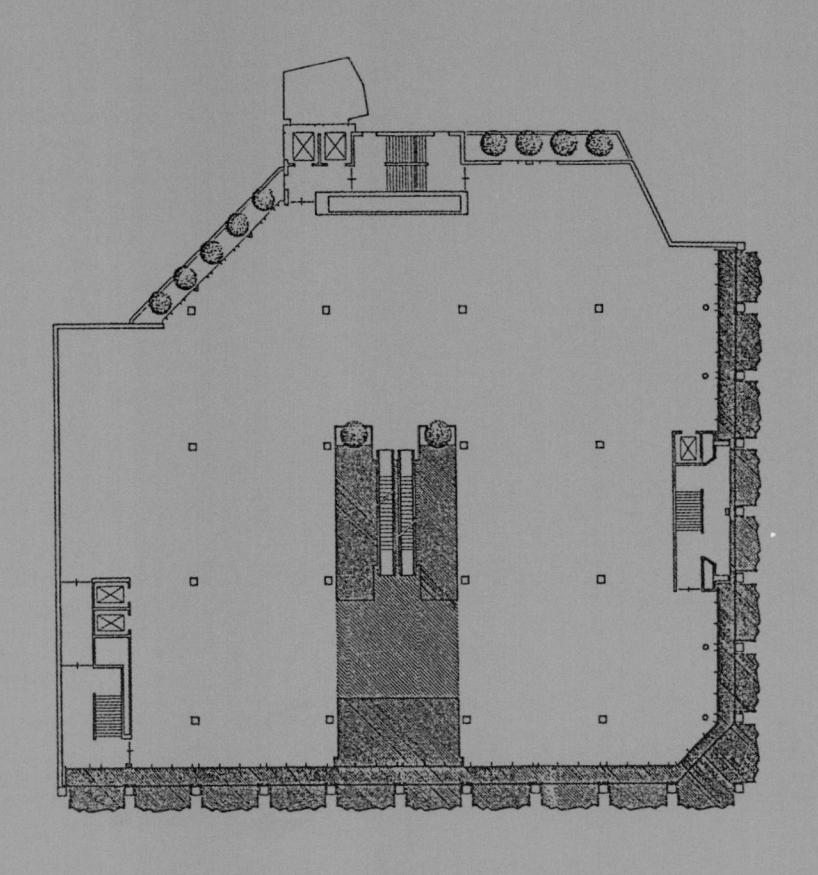

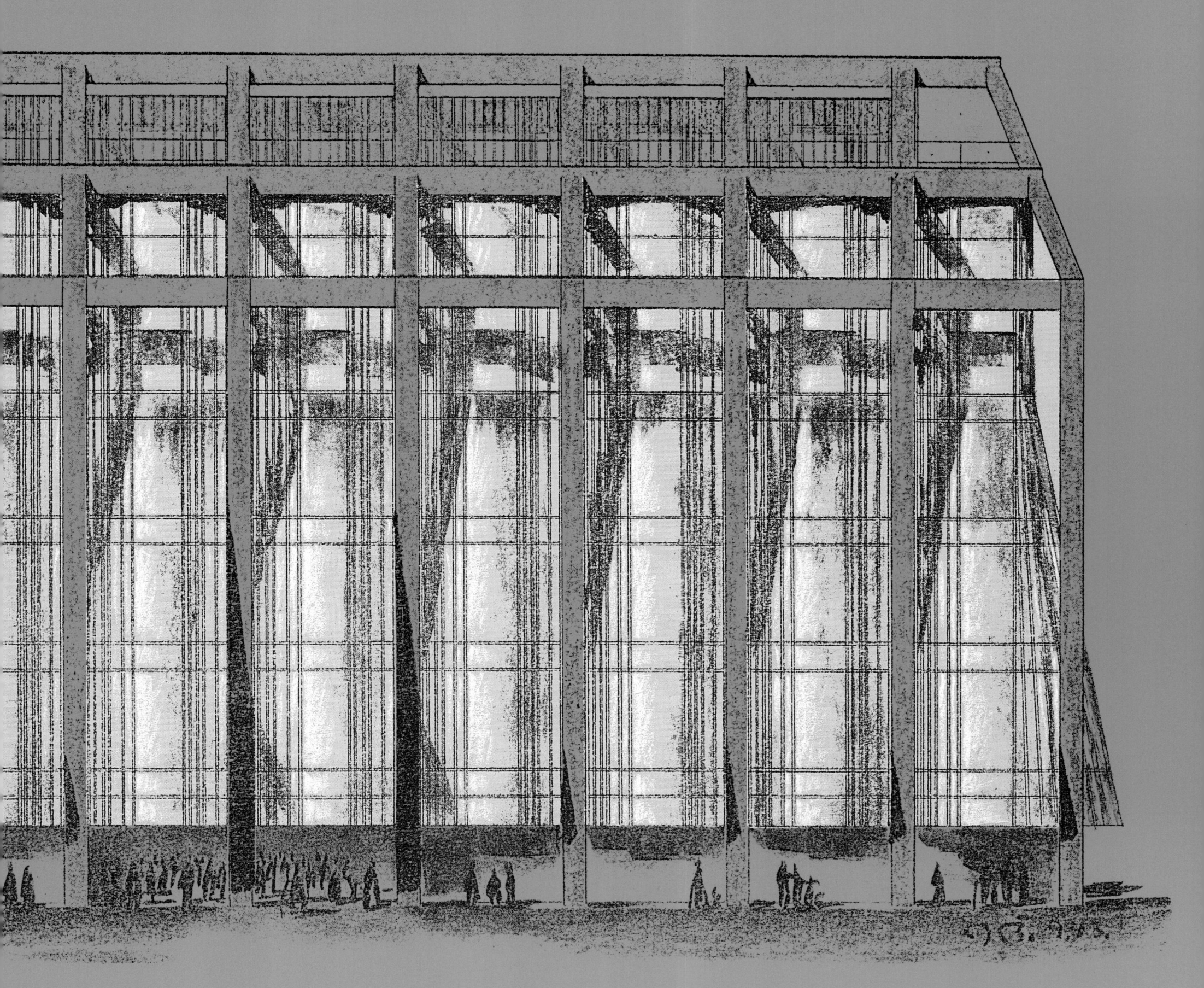

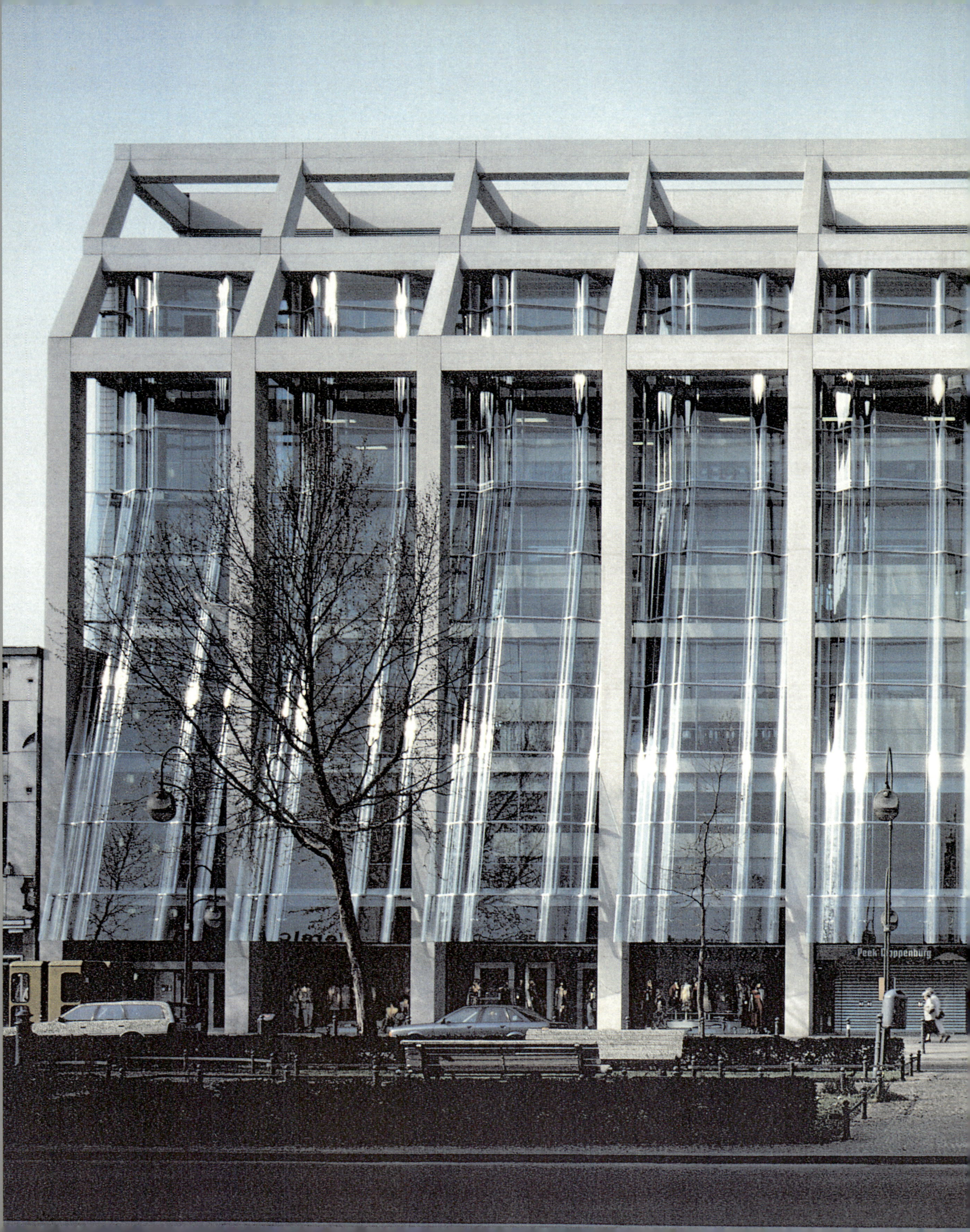
Peek Cloppenburg

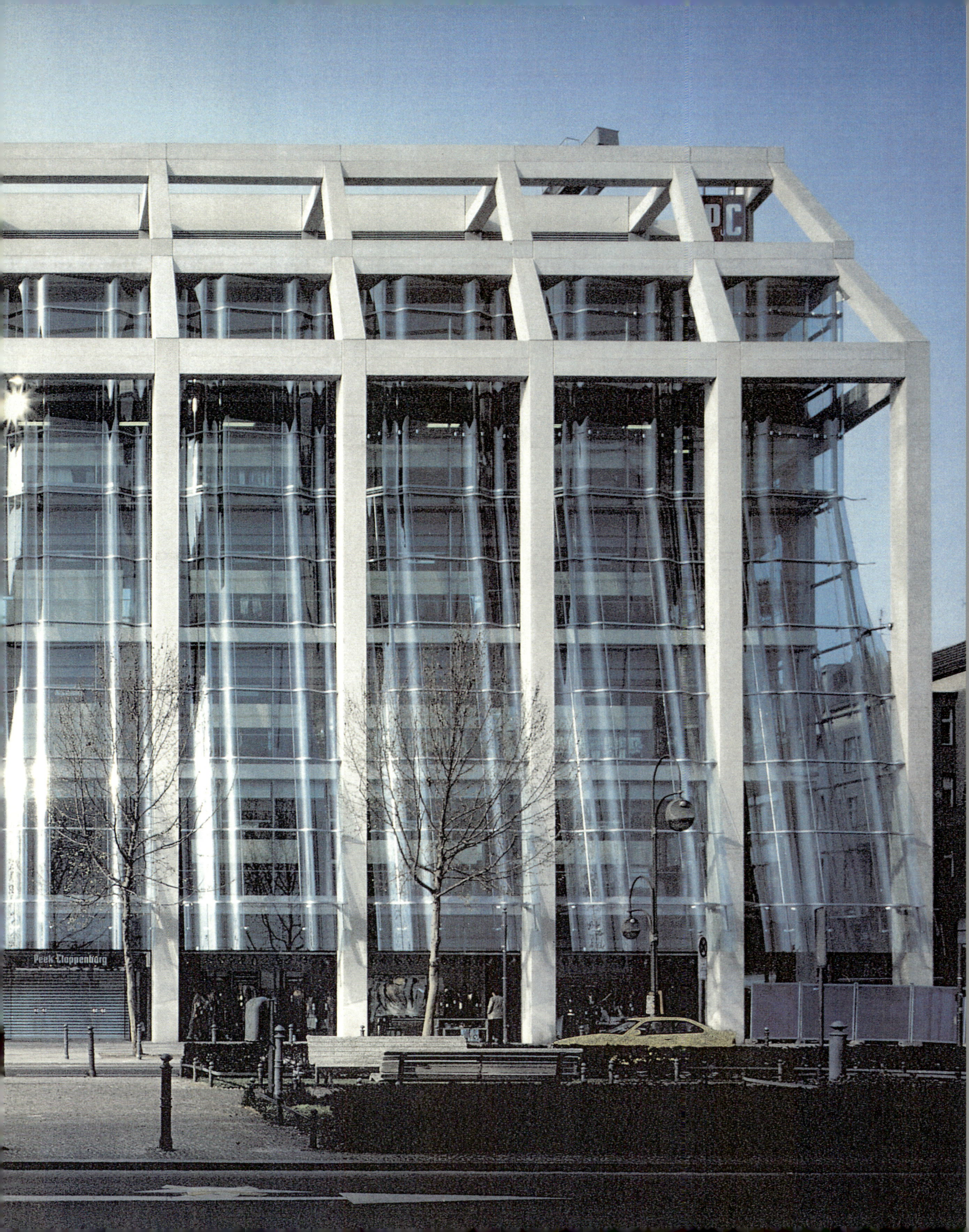

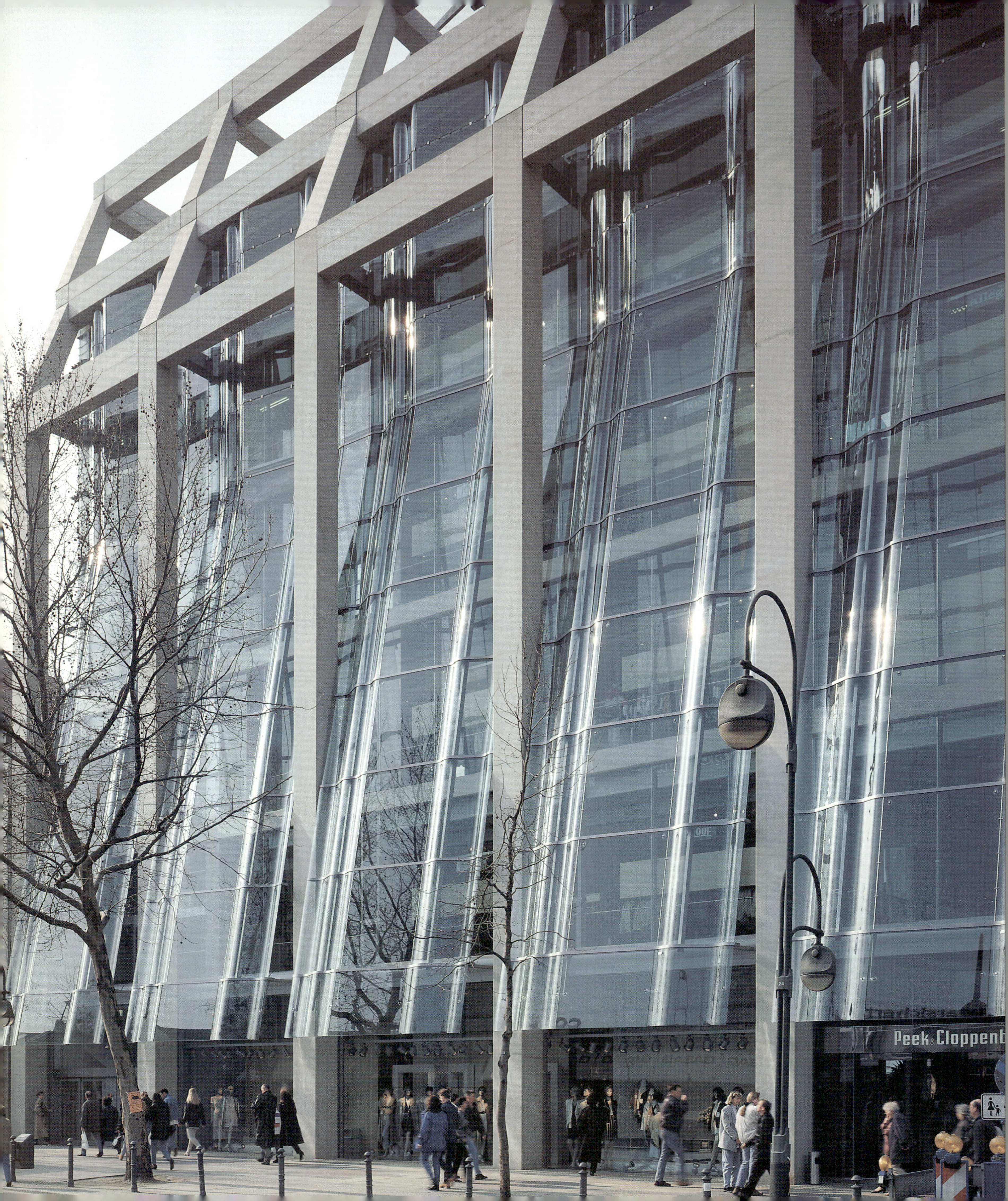
Peek&Cloppenb

DECKENMALEREI
MARKUS BÖHM

PAINTED DECORATION
BY MARKUS BÖHM

ITZEHOE, STADTTHEATER
ITZEHOE, MUNICIPAL THEATRE

MIT / WITH GEORG ADOLPHI

1992

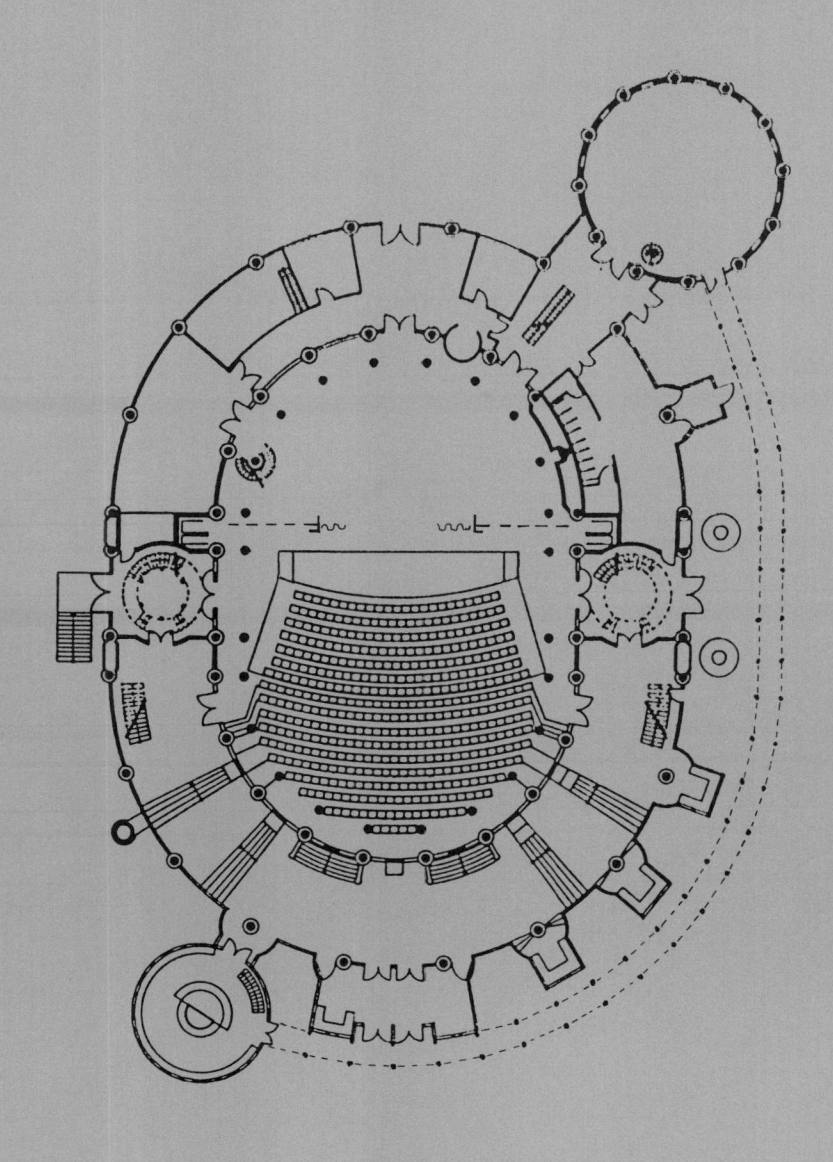

MEHRZWECKPLATZ MIT EINSCHIEBBARER BÜHNE –
„DIE FREIE BÜHNE AUF DEM ÜBERDACHTEN STÄDTISCHEN PLATZ"

MULTIFUNCTIONAL SPACE WITH REMOVABLE STAGE -
"AN OPEN-AIR STAGE ON A COVERED URBAN SQUARE"

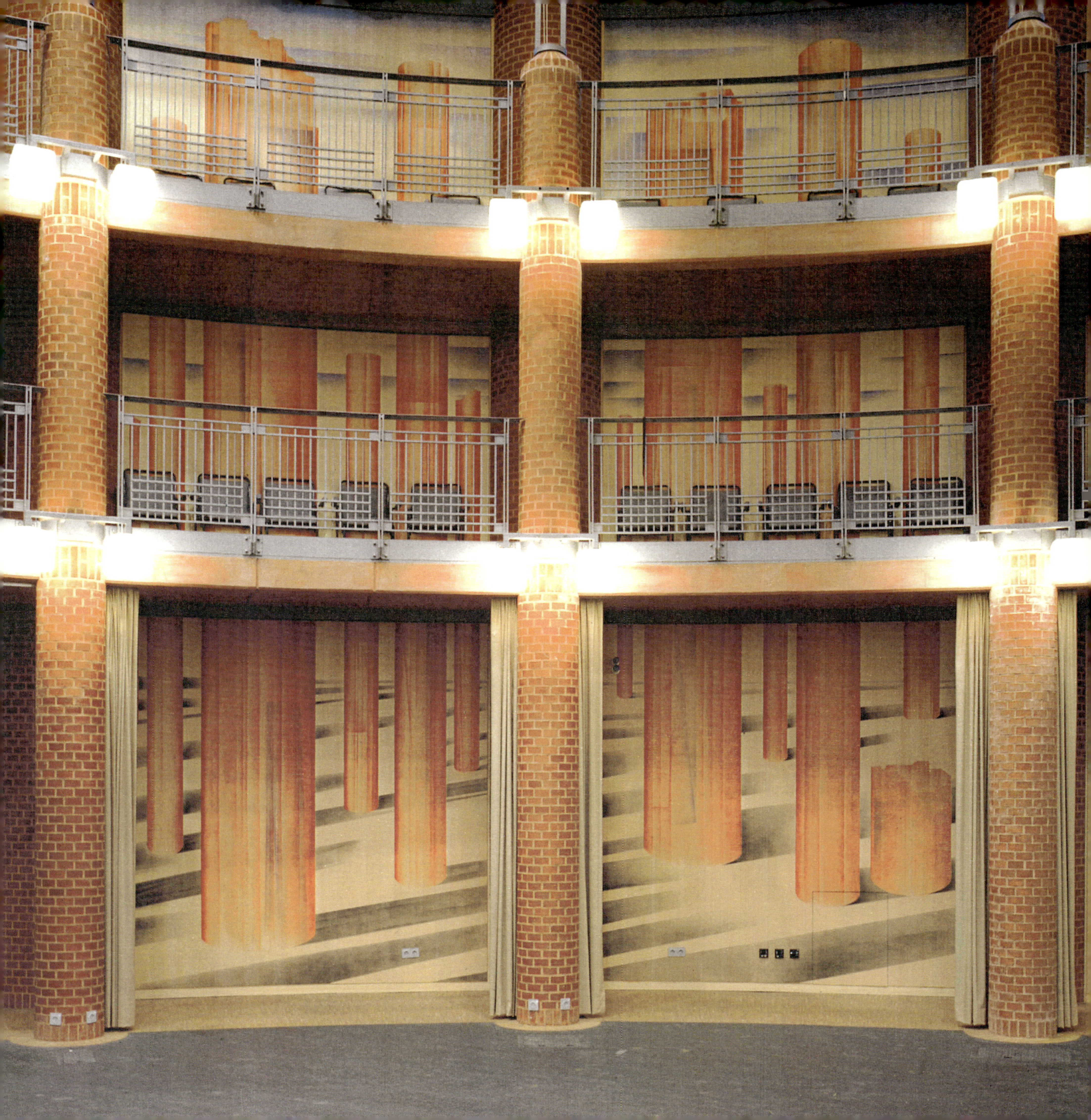

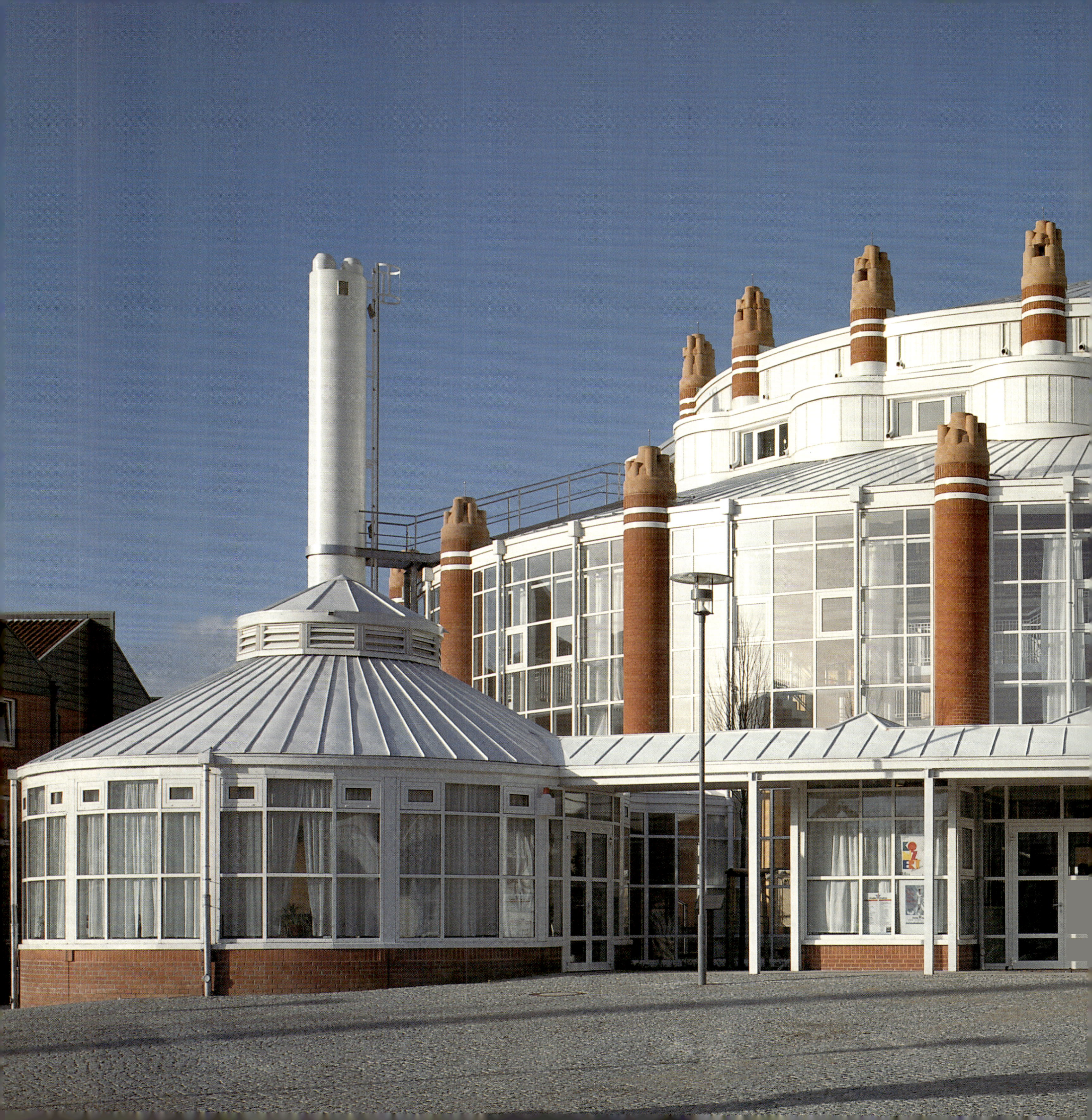

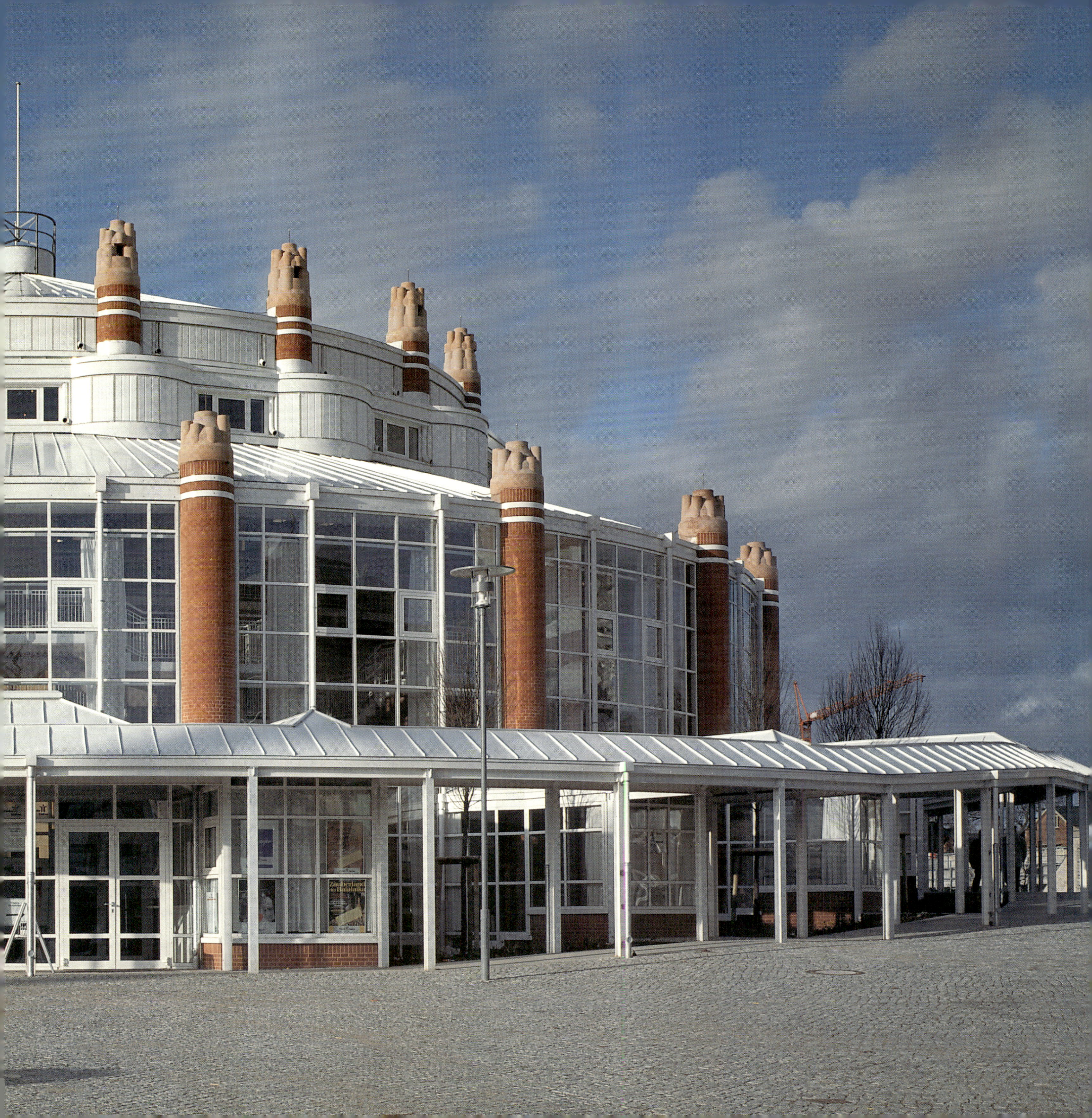
Zauberland

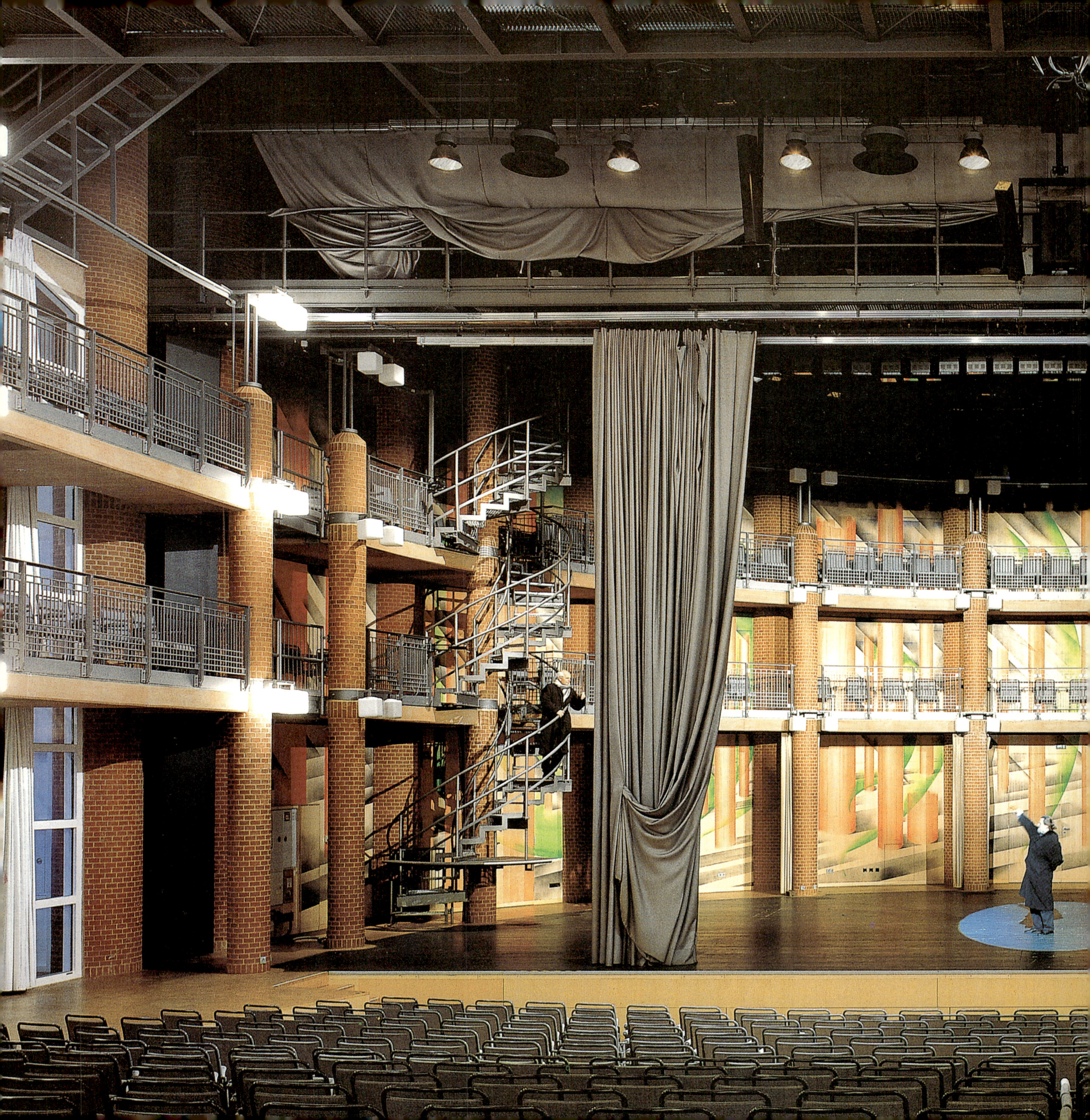

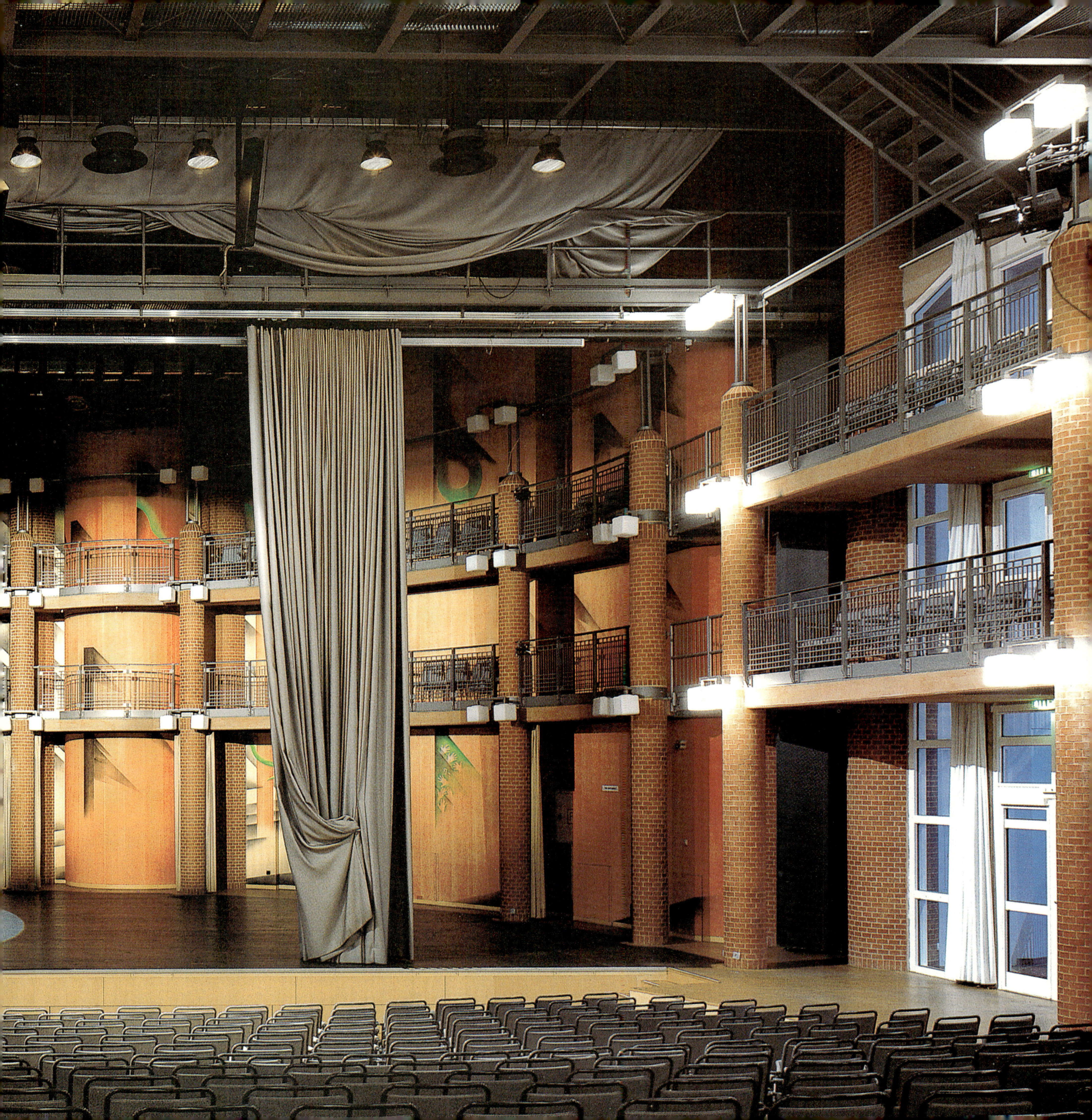

AACHEN, NEUGESTALTUNG DES BAHNHOFSPLATZES
AACHEN, REDEVELOPMENT OF THE STATION SQUARE

MIT / WITH PAUL BÖHM

WETTBEWERB / COMPETITION, 1997

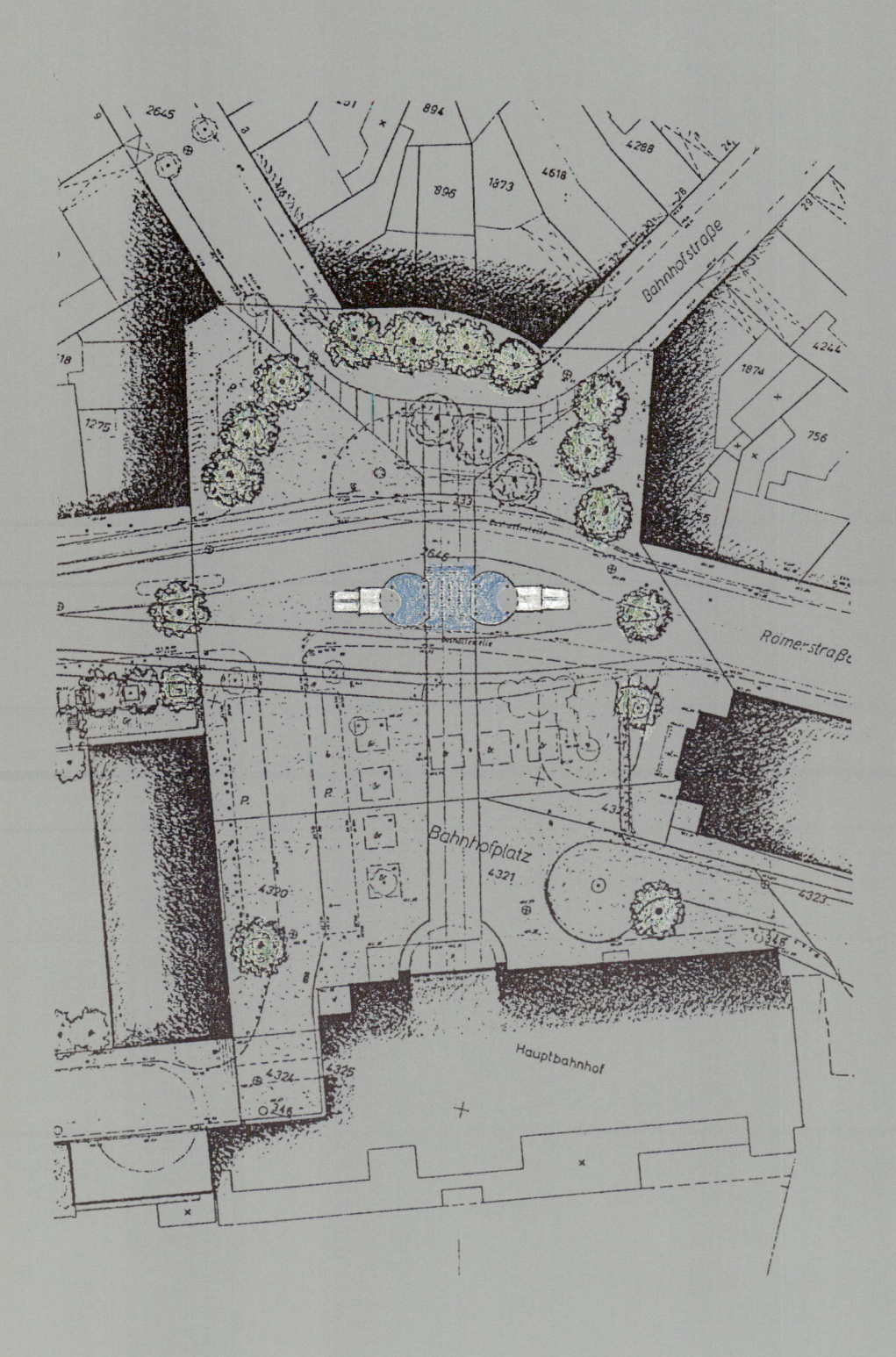

EIN TORHAUS, ANALOG ZU AACHENS ALTEN STADTTOREN, RAHMT DEN ZUGANG ZUR INNENSTADT.

A GATEHOUSE, SIMILAR TO AACHEN'S OLD CITY GATES, FRAMES THE ENTRANCE TO THE OLD TOWN.

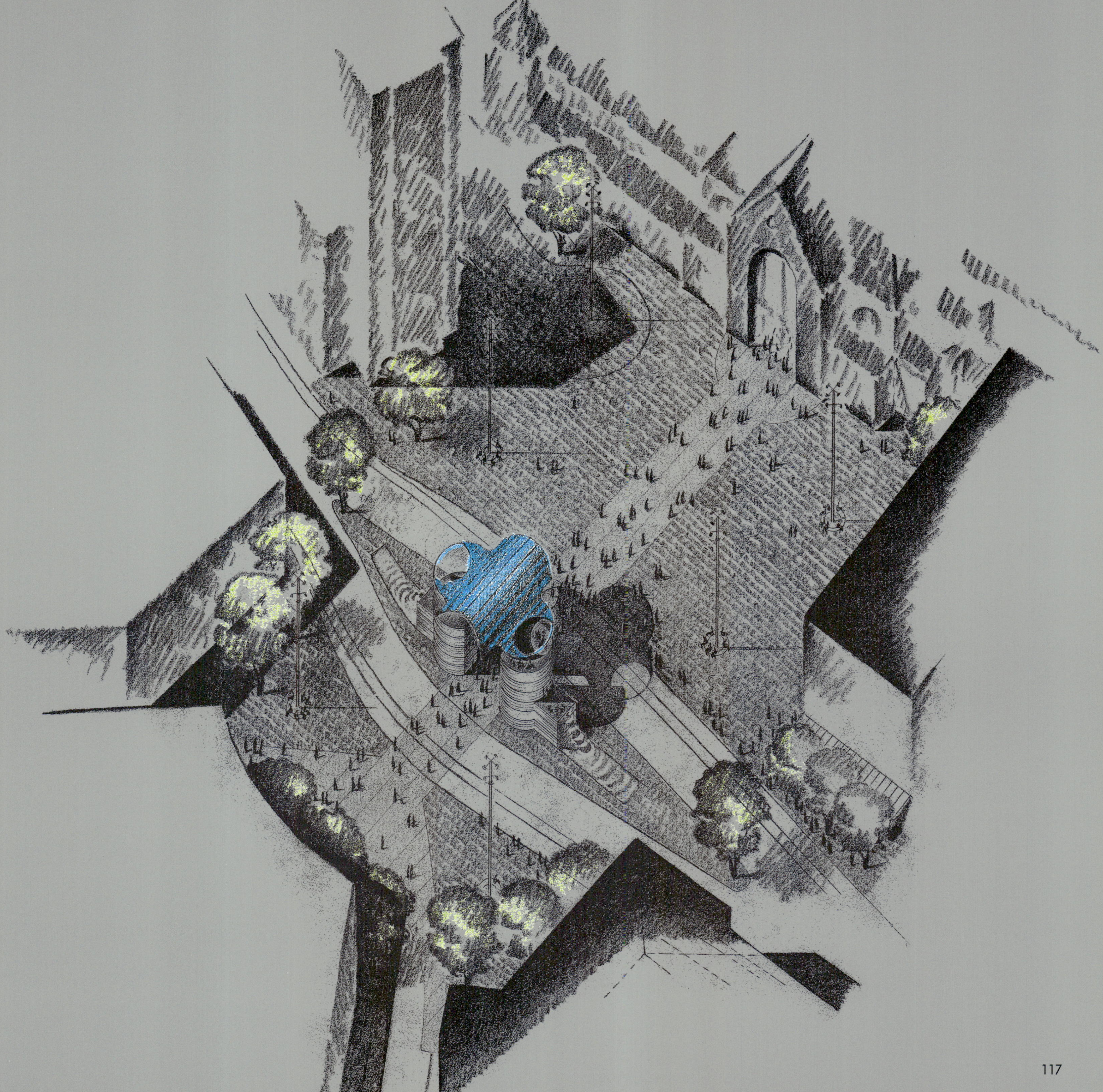

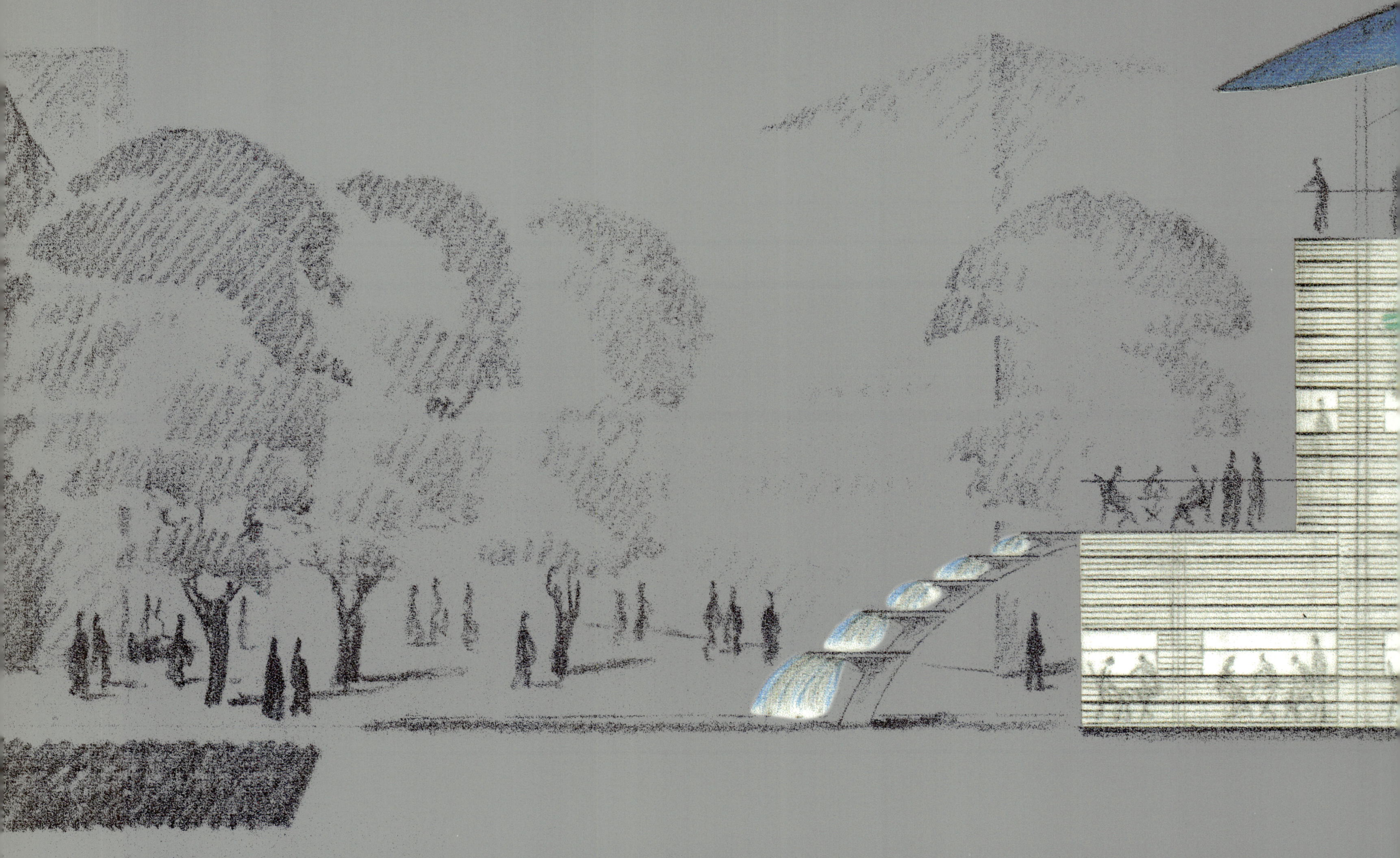

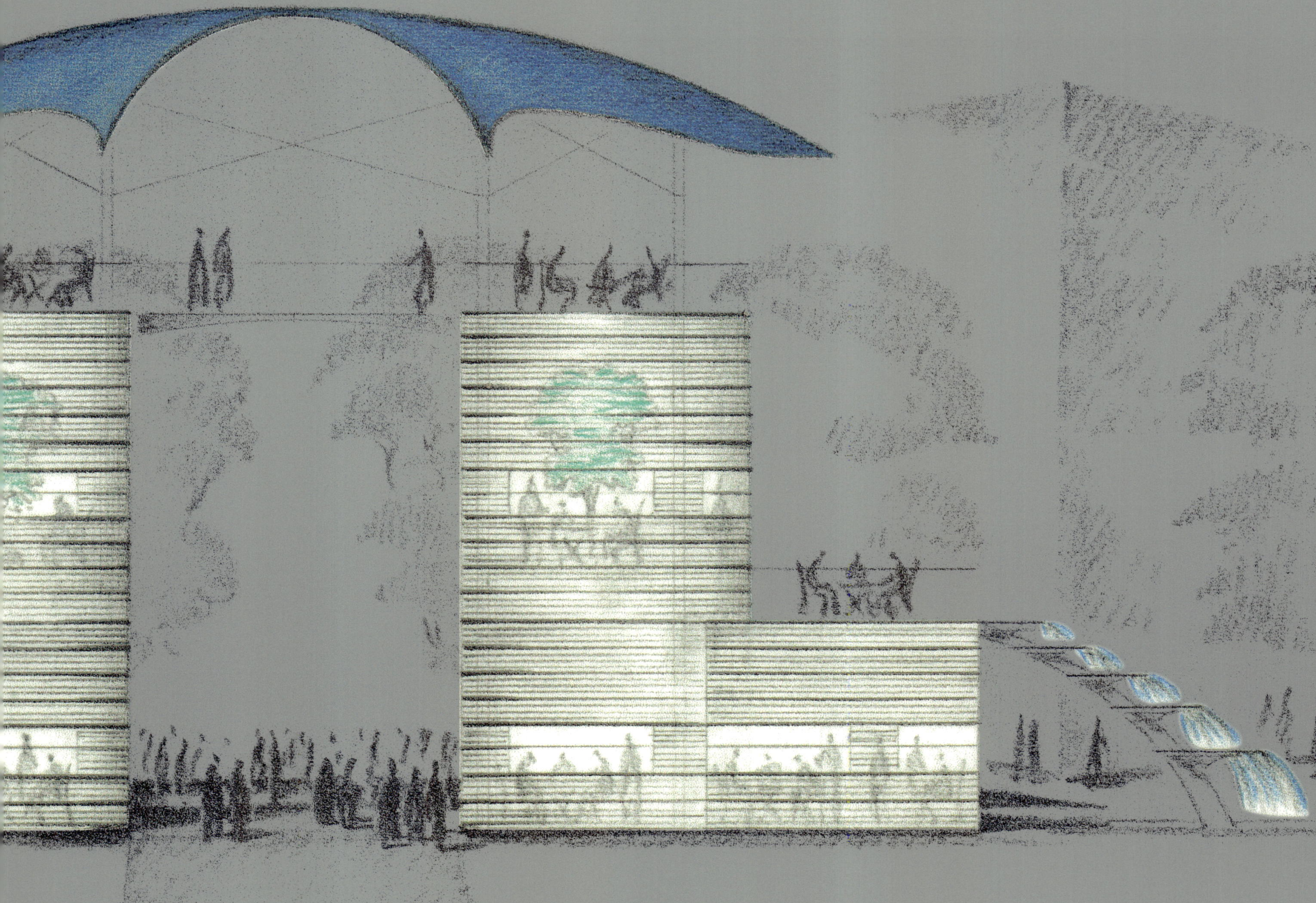

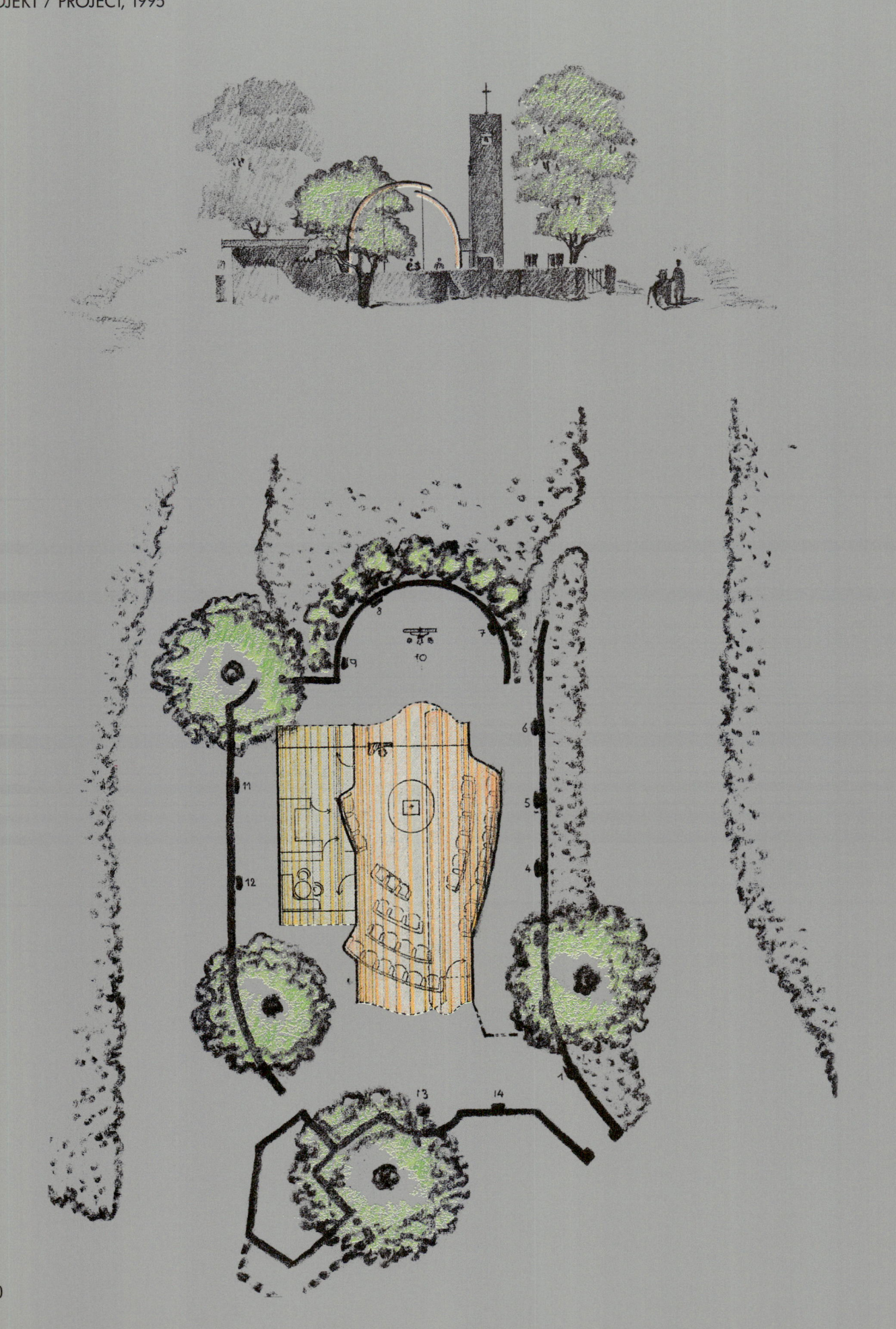

BERNKASTEL-KUES, KAPELLE
BERNKASTEL-KUES, CHAPEL
PROJEKT / PROJECT, 1995

120

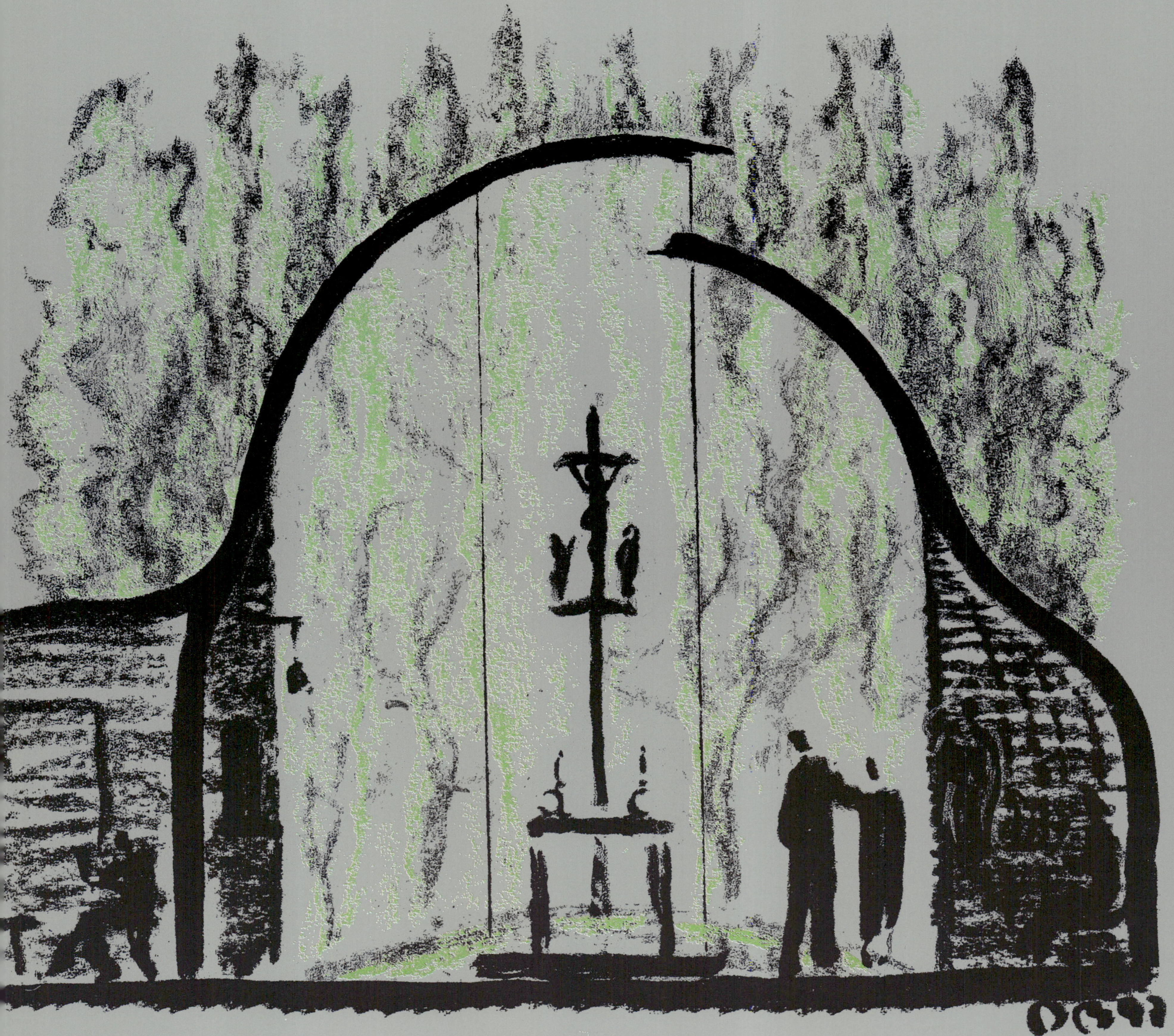

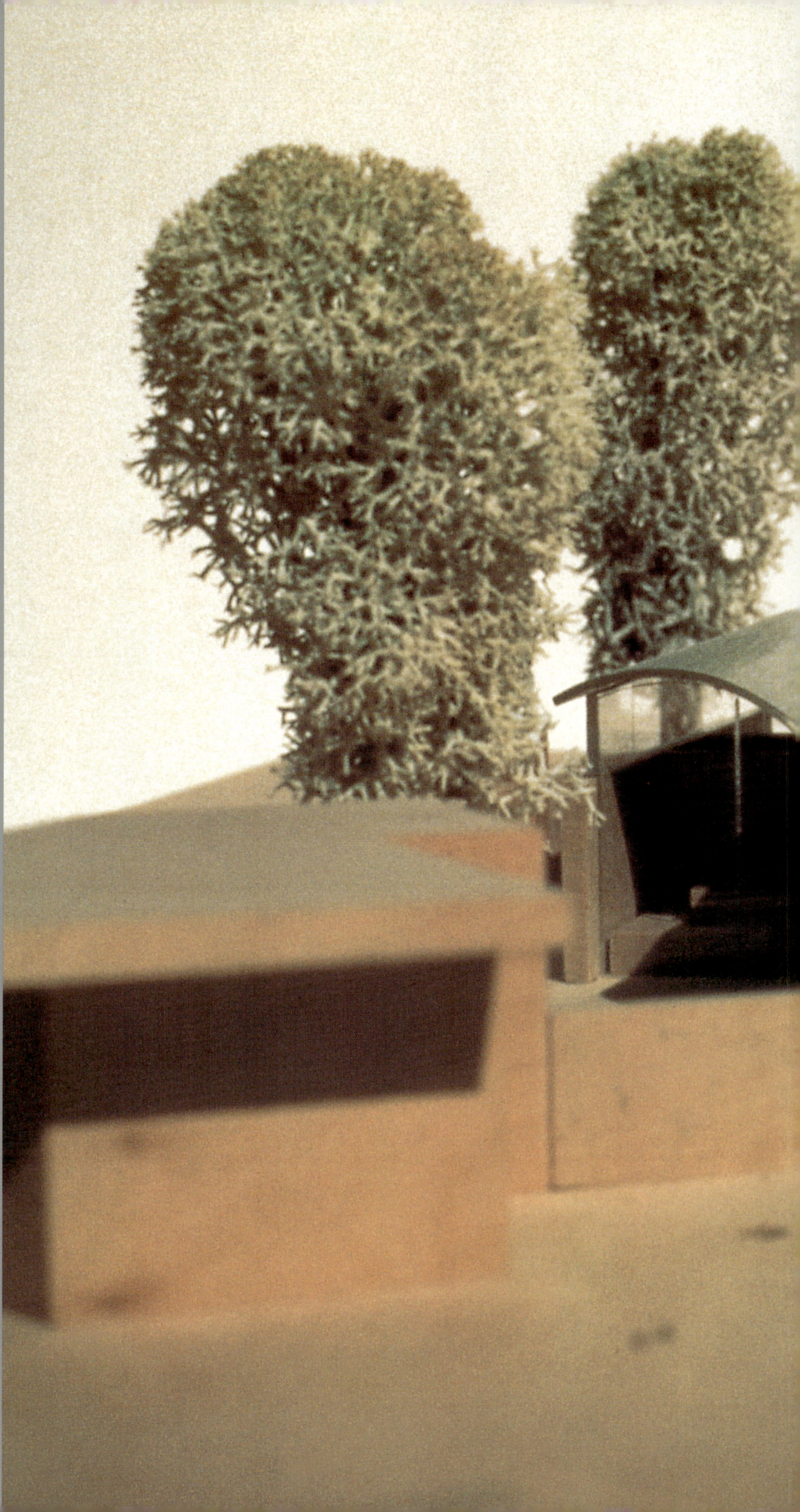

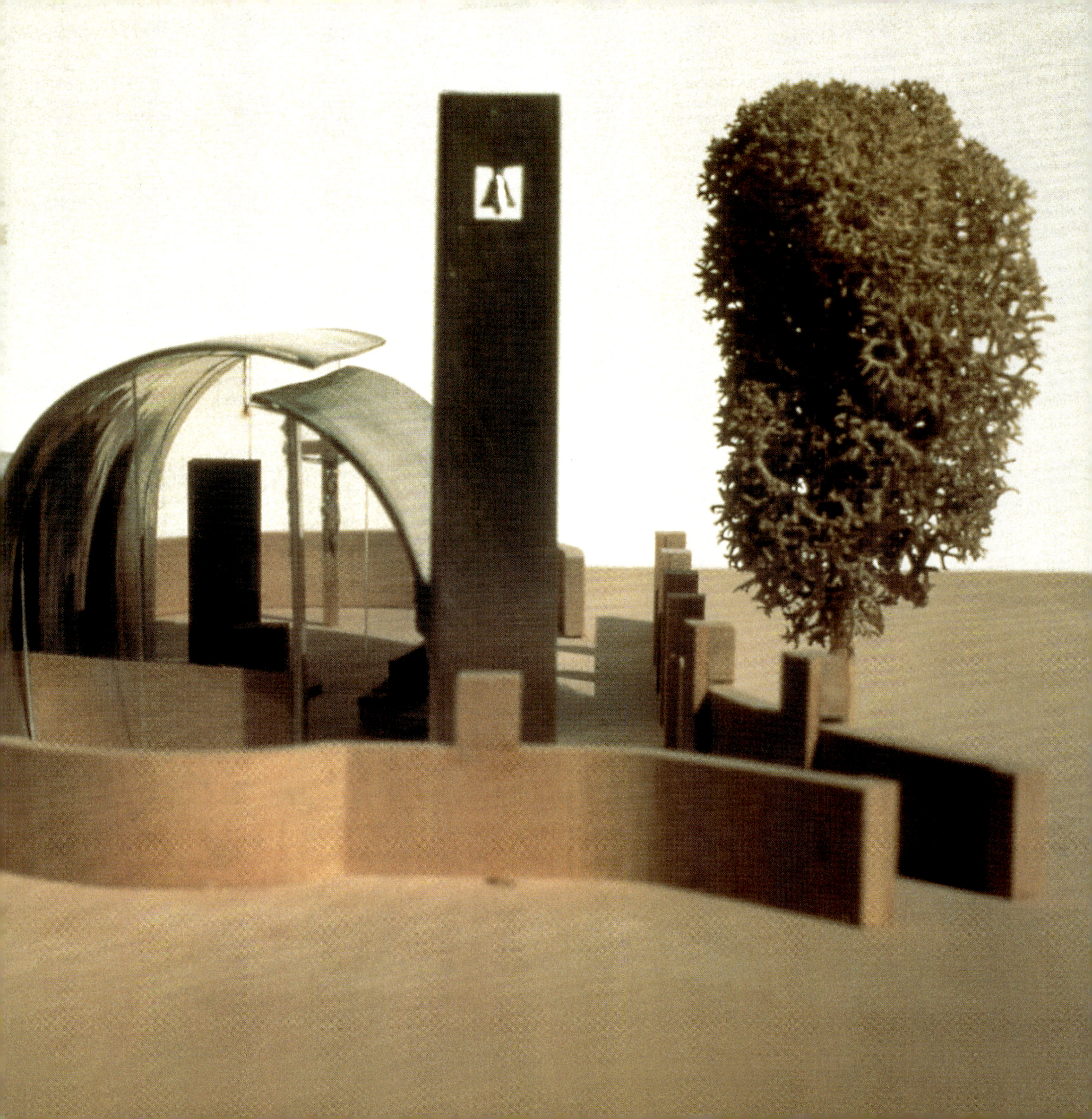

ROM, DENKMAL FÜR KÖNIG VIKTOR EMANUEL II.
ROME, MONUMENT TO KING VICTOR EMMANUEL II

VORSCHLAG / PROPOSAL, 2000

ÜBERLEGUNG, DAS ISOLIERTE MONUMENT INS STADTGEFÜGE EINZUBINDEN. MIT EINER TEILWEISEN ÜBERBAUUNG ENTSTEHT DIE SITUATION EINES 'KLASSISCHEN FORUMS'. ES KÖNNTE ENTSPRECHEND DER BEDEUTUNG DES MONUMENTS DIE VERBINDUNG VON LÄNDERN UND DIE WELTWEITE VERKNÜPFUNG ALLER BEREICHE UNSERER ZEIT SYMBOLISIEREN.

IDEAS ON HOW TO INTEGRATE THE ISOLATED MONUMENT INTO ITS URBAN CONTEXT. BY PARTIALLY EXTENDING BUILDING DEVELOPMENT UP TO THE MONUMENT, A 'CLASSICAL FORUM' SITUATION IS CREATED. IN VIEW OF THE SIGNIFICANCE OF THE MONUMENT, IT COULD ALSO BE SEEN AS A SYMBOL FOR THE COMING TOGETHER OF COUNTRIES AND TODAY'S GLOBAL LINKING OF ALL AREAS.

125

POTSDAM, HANS-OTTO-THEATER
MIT / WITH MARIA MACANU
1995–2000

LAGE IN EINEM ALTEN INDUSTRIEGELÄNDE
IN SCHÖNER UFERSITUATION

SITUATION IN A FORMER INDUSTRIAL ZONE
IN AN ATTRACTIVE RIVERSIDE LOCATION

127

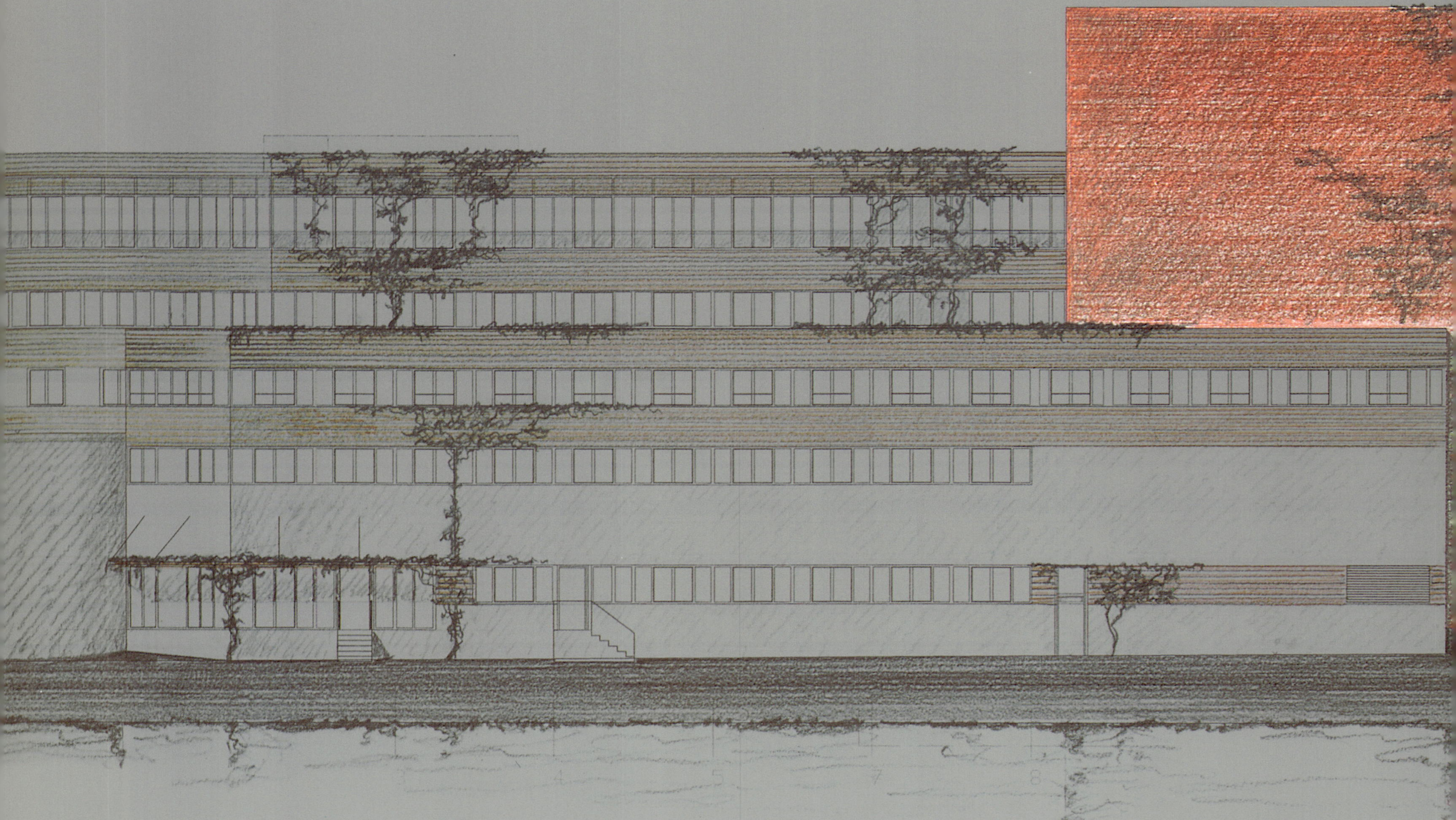

129

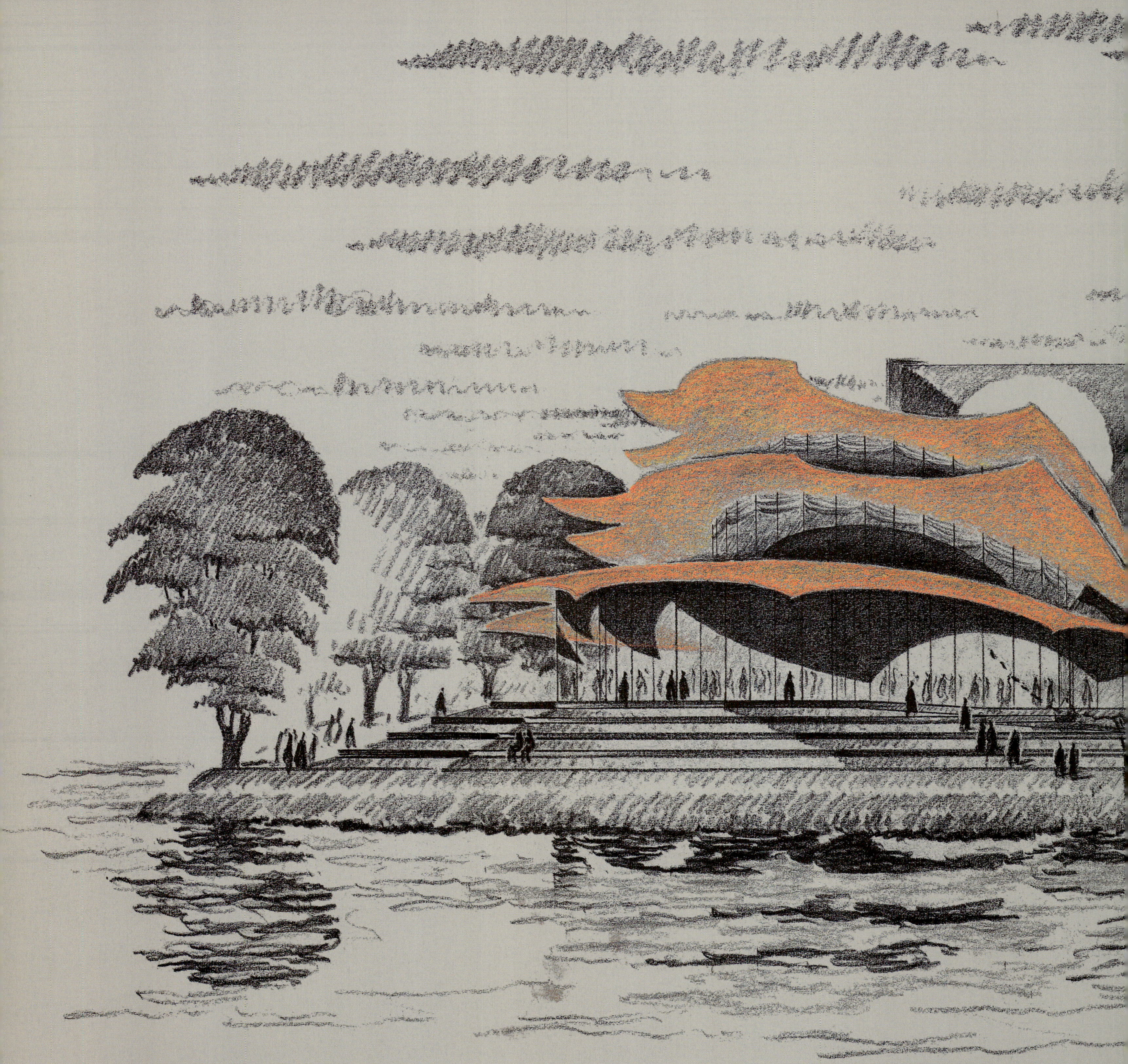

5.12.99

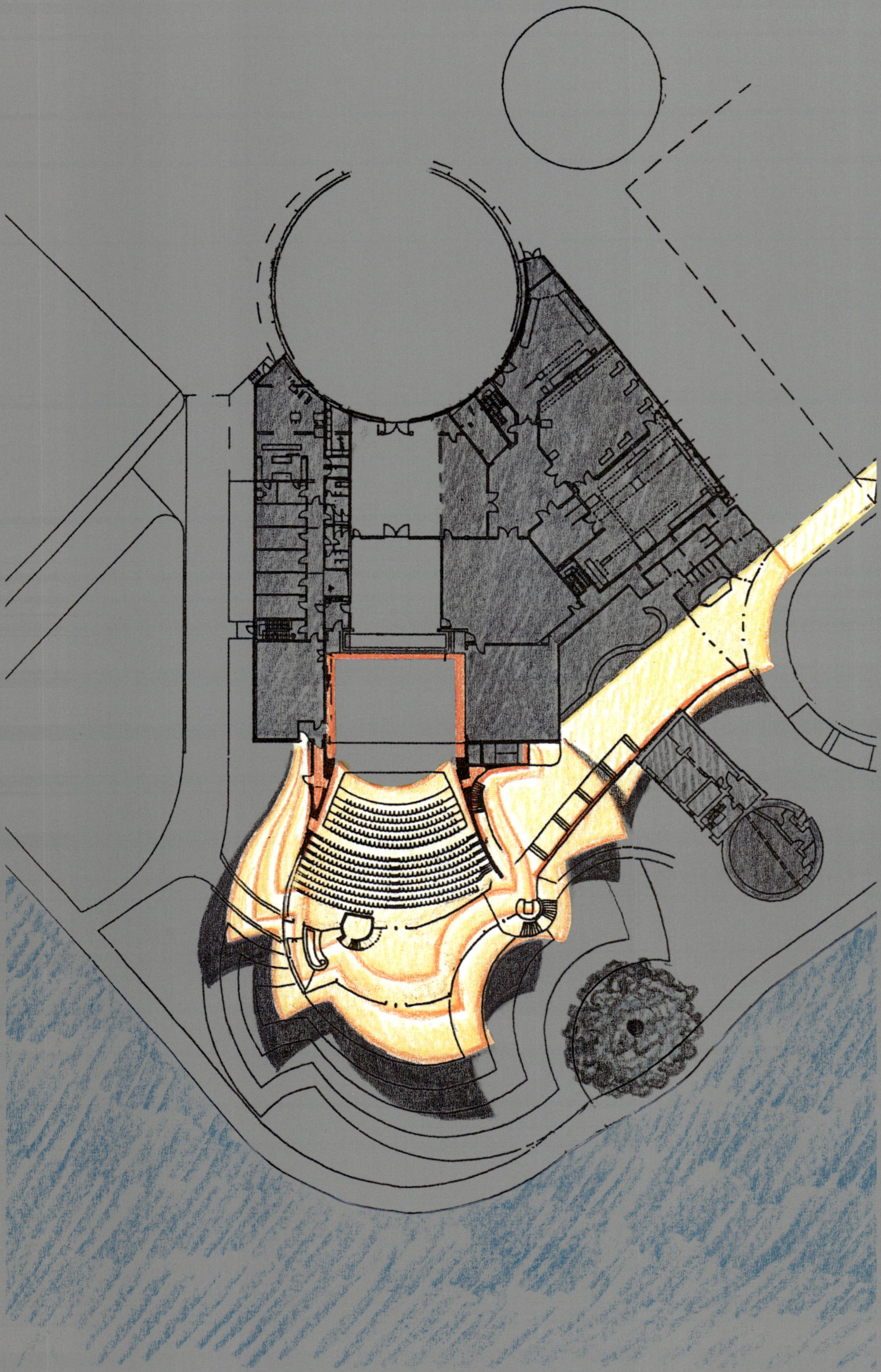

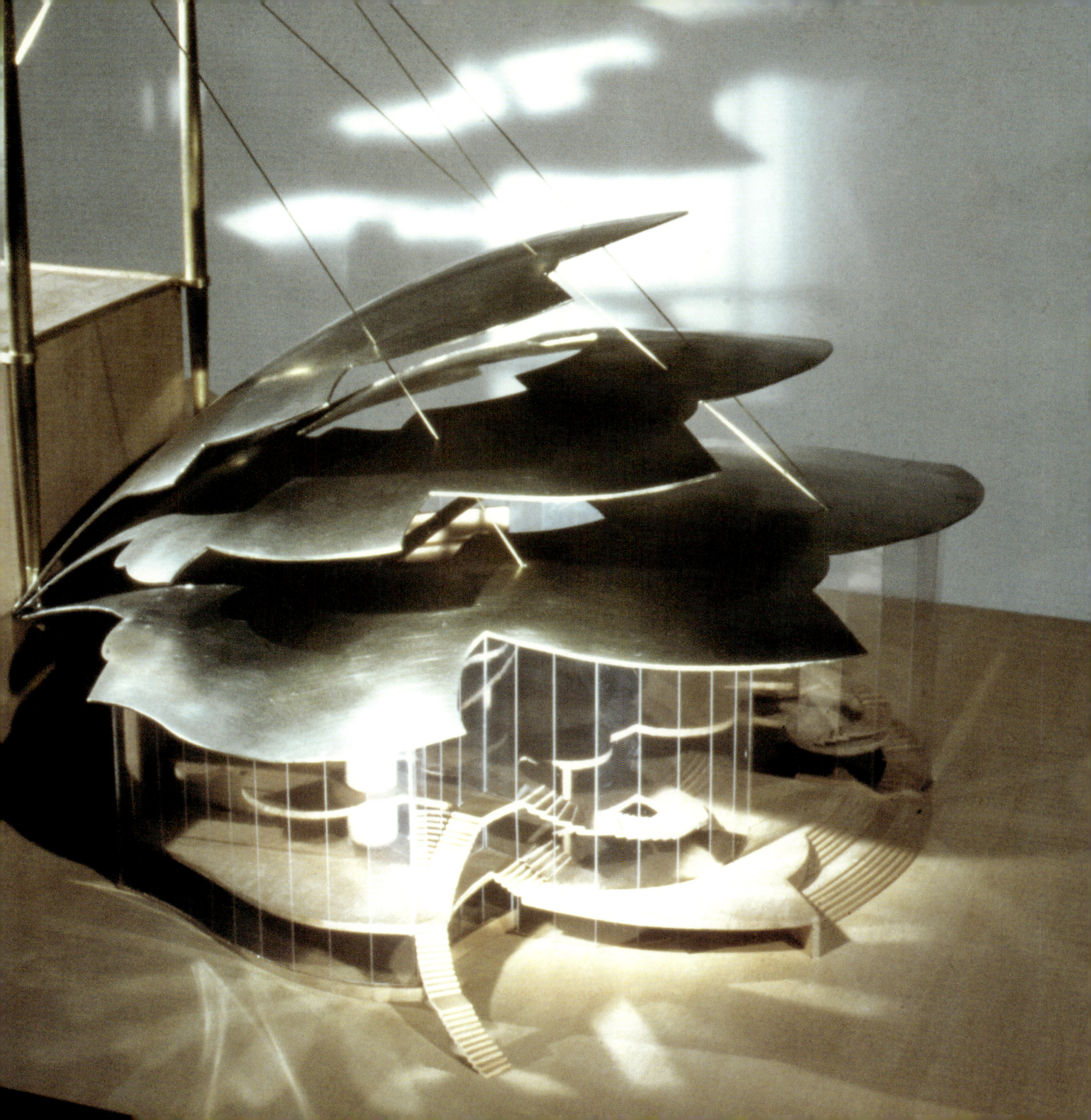

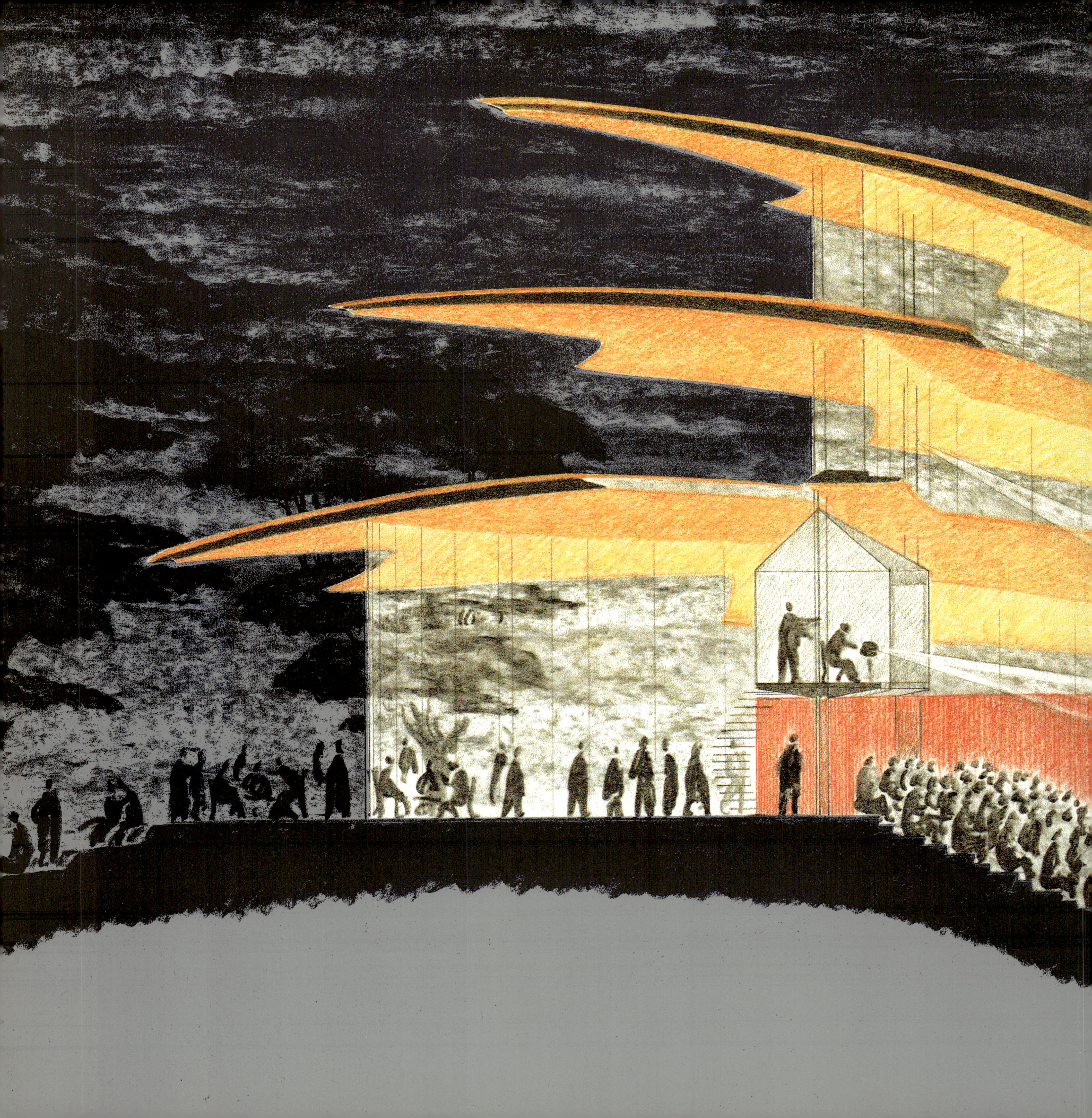

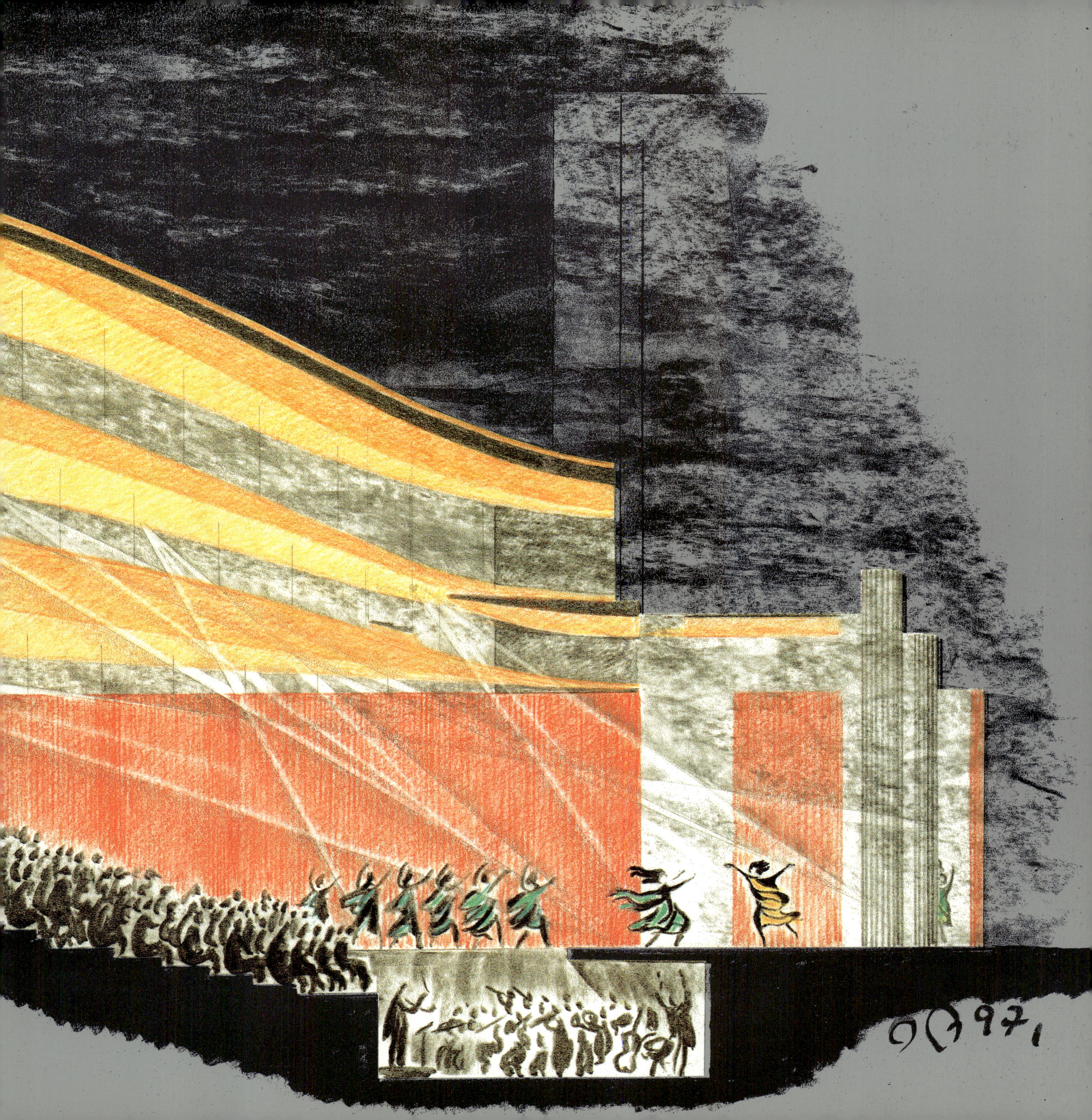

AUSZUG AUS DEM GESAMTWERK
SELECTION OF WORKS

KÖLN, MARIA IN DEN TRÜMMERN, 1949
COLOGNE, ST. MARY'S CHURCH, 1949

BENSBERG, KINDERDORF, 1965
BENSBERG, CHILDREN'S VILLAGE, 1965

SCHILDGEN, HERZ-JESU KIRCHE, 1958
SCHILDGEN, CHURCH OF THE SACRED HEART, 1958

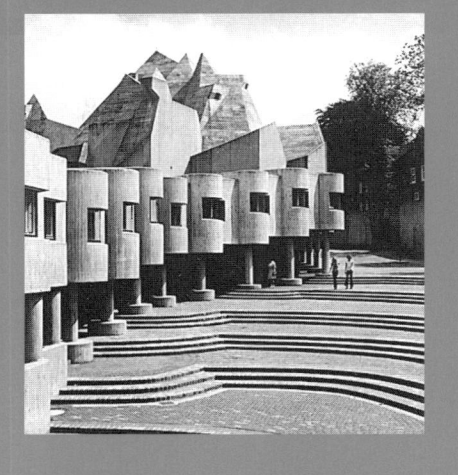

NEVIGES, MARIENDOM, 1964
NEVIGES, ST. MARY'S CATHEDRAL, 1964

BENSBERG, RATHAUS, 1964
BENSBERG, TOWN HALL, 1964

KÖLN-WEISS, WOHNHAUS, 1955
COLOGNE-WEISS, DETACHED FAMILY HOUSE, 1955

KASSEL-WILHELMSHÖHE, MARIENKIRCHE, 1978
KASSEL-WILHELMSHÖHE, ST. MARY'S CHURCH, 1978

NEVIGES, MARIENDOM
NEVIGES, ST. MARY'S CATHEDRAL

136

KÖLN-MELATEN,
AUFERSTEHUNGSKIRCHE, 1970
COLOGNE-MELATEN, CHURCH
OF THE RESURRECTION, 1970

DÜSSELDORF, STATISTISCHES
LANDESAMT, 1974
DÜSSELDORF, REGIONAL
DEPARTMENT OF STATISTICS, 1974

PADERBORN,
DIÖZESANMUSEUM, 1975
PADERBORN,
DIOCESAN MUSEUM, 1975

PADERBORN,
DIÖZESANMUSEUM
PADERBORN,
DIOCESAN MUSEUM

BERGISCH GLADBACH,
BÜRGERHAUS MIT THEATER, 1980
BERGISCH GLADBACH,
CIVIC HALL WITH THEATRE, 1980

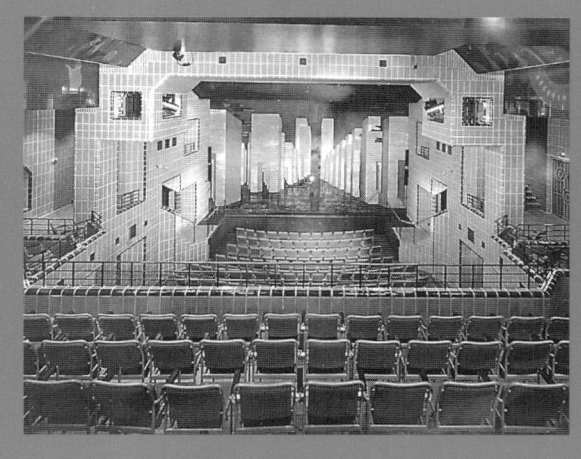

BERGISCH GLADBACH, THEATER
IM BÜRGERHAUS, 1980
BERGISCH GALDBACH, THEATRE
IN THE CIVIC HALL, 1980

KÖLN-KALK, RATHAUS, 1986
COLOGNE-KALK, TOWN HALL,
1986

KÖLN-KALK, RATHAUS
COLOGNE-KALK, TOWN HALL

137

BETEILIGTE ARCHITEKTEN / ARCHITECTS

TOKIO, OTA HALL / TOKYO, OTA HALL
MIT/WITH PA. BÖHM, S. HEIERMANN, C. SCHROEER

BERLIN, REICHSTAG
MIT/WITH PE. BÖHM, F. STEINIGEWEG, R. GOETSCH, P. JUNG, J. V. KIETZELL, E. WOLF

LOS ANGELES, PHILHARMONIE / LOS ANGELES, CONCERT HALL
MIT/WITH S. BÖHM, M. KARI, H. GROTHUES, G. KAESBACH, F. VALDA

LUXEMBURG, PHILHARMONIE / LUXEMBOURG, CONCERT HALL
MIT/WITH M. MOCANU, S. ABELEN, E. THESING, P. KLOSE, P. KREBS, M. LÜCKER, C. SCHROEER

KÖLN, WDR HAUPTVERWALTUNG / COLOGNE, ADMINISTRATIVE HEADQUARTERS OF WDR
MIT/WITH PE. BÖHM, S. ABELEN, M. BÖHM, E. BÖHM, S. HEIERMANN, F. KILIAN, P. KLOSE, E. THESING

HAMBURG, ARENA
MIT/WITH PE. BÖHM, S. HEIERMANN, A. BROCKMEIER, U. HELLER, C. SCHROEER

SAARBRÜCKEN, SCHLOSS / SAARBRÜCKEN, CASTLE
MIT/WITH N. ROSINY, H. LINDER, BÜRO KRÜGER-RIEGER, B. JOCHUM, H. BREUER, B. HELLRIEGEL, F. KILIAN

STUTTGART, ZÜBLINHAUS
MIT/WITH D. GATTERMANN, K. BECKMANNSHAGEN, J. MINKUS, F. VALDA

HAMBURG, MUSEUM FÜR MODERNE KUNST / HAMBURG, MUSEUM OF MODERN ART
MIT/WITH J. MINKUS

STUTTGART, MUSEUM FÜR MODERNE KUNST / STUTTGART, MUSEUM OF MODERN ART
MIT/WITH F. STEINIGEWEG

SEVILLA, DEUTSCHER PAVILLON FÜR DIE EXPO 1992 / SEVILLE, GERMAN PAVILION FOR EXPO 1992
MIT/WITH F. STEINIGEWEG, S. HEIERMANN, R. GOETSCH

BERLIN-TREPTOW, HOTEL AN DER SPREE / BERLIN-TREPTOW, HOTEL BY THE SPREE
MIT/WITH S. BÖHM, M. MOCANU, C. FORST

LUXEMBURG, DEUTSCHE BANK / LUXEMBOURG, DEUTSCHE BANK
MIT/WITH J. MINKUS, F. TRUMMER, E. WOLF, BÜRO KRÜGER-RIEGER, B. JOCHUM, I. DORSCHEID,
B. FOLMER, S. GROSS

LUXEMBURG-ESCH, ARBED S. A. HAUPTVERWALTUNG/ LUXEMBOURG-ESCH, HEADQUARTERS OF ARBED S. A.
MIT/WITH J. MINKUS, E. WOLF

MANNHEIM, UNIVERSITÄTSBIBLIOTHEK UND AUDITORIUM / MANNHEIM, UNIVERSITY LIBRARY AND
AUDITORIUM
MIT/WITH J. MINKUS, E. WOLF

ULM, STADTBIBLIOTHEK / ULM, CITY LIBRARY
MIT/WITH S. HEIERMANN, C. SCHROEER, I. DUELLI

BERLIN, KAUFHAUS PEEK & CLOPPENBURG / BERLIN, PEEK & CLOPPENBURG DEPARTMENT STORE
MIT/WITH J. MINKUS, J. FLOHRE, PE. BÖHM, E. THESING, K. AFHAMI, K. FISCHER, P. KOCH, E. WOLF

ITZEHOE, STADTTHEATER / ITZEHOE, MUNICIPAL THEATRE
MIT/WITH G. ADOLPHI, M. ADOLPHI, A. KLEIN, J. MINKUS, K. UNKHOFF

AACHEN, NEUGESTALTUNG DES BAHNHOFSPLATZES / AACHEN, REDEVELOPMENT OF THE STATION SQUARE
MIT/WITH PA. BÖHM, S. FORGÓ

POTSDAM, HANS-OTTO-THEATER
MIT/WITH M. MOCANU, S. BÖHM, M. AKKAD, F. KILIAN, M. LÜCKER, F. VALDA

PHOTONACHWEIS / PHOTO CREDIT

TOKIO, OTA HALL / TOKYO, OTA HALL
CHRISTOPH LEISTENSCHNEIDER

KÖLN, WDR HAUPTVERWALTUNG / COLOGNE, HEADQUARTERS OF WDR
DIETER LEISTNER, C. WILLEBRAND

SAARBRÜCKEN, SCHLOSS / SAARBRÜCKEN, CASTLE
DIETER LEISTNER

STUTTGART, ZÜBLINHAUS
HUGO SCHMÖLZ

LUXEMBURG, DEUTSCHE BANK / LUXEMBOURG, DEUTSCHE BANK
DIETER LEISTNER

LUXEMBURG-ESCH, ARBED S. A. HAUPTVERWALTUNG / LUXEMBOURG-ESCH, HEADQUARTERS OF ARBED S. A.
DIETER LEISTNER

MANNHEIM, UNIVERSITÄTSBIBLIOTHEK UND AUDITORIUM / MANNHEIM, UNIVERSITY LIBRARY AND AUDITORIUM
DIETER LEISTNER

BERLIN, KAUFHAUS PEEK & CLOPPENBURG / BERLIN, PEEK & CLOPPENBURG DEPARTMENT STORE
REINHARD GÖRNER, DIETER LEISTNER, C. WILLEBRAND

ITZEHOE, STADTTHEATER / ITZEHOE, MUNICIPAL THEATRE
DIETER LEISTNER

BERNKASTEL-KUES, KAPELLE / BERNKASTEL-KUES, CHAPEL
CHRISTOPH LEISTENSCHNEIDER

WEITERE BILDDATEN WURDEN VOM ARCHITEKTURBÜRO BÖHM ZUR VERFÜGUNG GESTELLT.
ADDITIONAL PICTORIAL MATERIAL WAS KINDLY PUT AT OUR DISPOSAL BY ARCHITECT'S OFFICE BÖHM.